Reading the Modernist Long Poem

Reading the Modernist Long Poem

John Cage, Charles Olson and the Indeterminacy of Longform Poetics

Brendan C. Gillott

BLOOMSBURY ACADEMIC
NEW YORK • LONDON • OXFORD • NEW DELHI • SYDNEY

BLOOMSBURY ACADEMIC
Bloomsbury Publishing Inc
1385 Broadway, New York, NY 10018, USA
50 Bedford Square, London, WC1B 3DP, UK

BLOOMSBURY, BLOOMSBURY ACADEMIC and the Diana logo are trademarks of Bloomsbury Publishing Plc

First published in the United States of America 2021

This paperback edition published 2022

Copyright © Brendan C. Gillott, 2021

Cover design by Eleanor Rose
Cover image © Getty Images

All rights reserved. No part of this publication may be reproduced or transmitted in any form or by any means, electronic or mechanical, including photocopying, recording, or any information storage or retrieval system, without prior permission in writing from the publishers.

Bloomsbury Publishing Inc does not have any control over, or responsibility for, any third-party websites referred to or in this book. All internet addresses given in this book were correct at the time of going to press. The author and publisher regret any inconvenience caused if addresses have changed or sites have ceased to exist, but can accept no responsibility for any such changes.

Library of Congress Cataloging-in-Publication Data
Names: Gillott, Brendan C., author.
Title: Reading the modernist long poem: John Cage, Charles Olson and the indeterminacy of longform poetics / Brendan C. Gillott.
Description: New York: Bloomsbury Academic, 2021. | Includes bibliographical references and index. | Summary: "Outlines the role of 'indeterminacy' in reading modernist long poems by way of the longform poetry of John Cage and Charles Olson"– Provided by publisher.
Identifiers: LCCN 2020022541 | ISBN 9781501363788 (hardback) | ISBN 9781501371899 (paperback) | ISBN 9781501363801 (pdf) | ISBN 9781501363795 (epub)
Subjects: LCSH: American poetry–20th century–History and criticism. | Modernism (Literature)–United States. | Cage, John–Criticism and interpretation. | Olson, Charles, 1910-1970–Criticism and interpretation.
Classification: LCC PS310.M57 G55 2021 | DDC 811/.909112–dc23
LC record available at https://lccn.loc.gov/2020022541

ISBN: HB: 978-1-5013-6378-8
PB: 978-1-5013-7189-9
ePDF: 978-1-5013-6380-1
eBook: 978-1-5013-6379-5

Typeset by Deanta Global Publishing Services, Chennai, India

To find out more about our authors and books visit www.bloomsbury.com and sign up for our newsletters.

My book experiences on board of the frigate proved an example of a fact which every book-lover must have experienced before me, namely, that though public libraries have an imposing air, and doubtless contain invaluable volumes, yet, somehow, the books that prove most agreeable, grateful, and companionable, are those we pick up by chance here and there; those which seem put into our hands by Providence; those which pretend to little, but abound in much.

Herman Melville, White-Jacket

Contents

Acknowledgements	viii
Introduction: Indeterminacy	1
1 Olson's 'Projective Verse'	21
2 Poetics of speed: Mediation in *Maximus*	41
3 Mycopoetics: Cage's *Mushroom Book*	67
4 Olson, lists and archives	93
5 Ideas in Cage's *I-VI*	121
6 Models and mereology	149
7 Typos	177
Conclusion: Nonunderstanding	205
Bibliography	209
Discography	224
Index	225

Acknowledgements

This book has been several years in the making, and the project has benefited from the suggestion, advice and commentary of too many people to recount here. However, special thanks should go to Rod Mengham, Robert Hampson and Drew Milne. Drew particularly has been instrumental in enabling me to produce what is presented here, and I am most grateful to him. I would also like to thank the anonymous readers of the manuscript for their careful and challenging suggestions. In addition, my thanks go to all those at Bloomsbury Academic who have had a hand in helping to produce this book. Any mistakes and misprisions which remain in this work are of course of my own doing.

I should also express my deep and lasting thanks to my family, whose encouragement in the long process of writing the book I could not have done without. And to Anna, with my love.

Introduction

Indeterminacy

John Cage's 'Indeterminacy' does not seem, on the surface, an especially challenging or difficult text. It does not employ unfamiliar syntax or complex rhetorical strategies. Its prose reads left-to-right and top-to-bottom. Consisting of a series of short, mostly autobiographical first-person narratives loosely strung together over a dozen double-columned pages, there seems little reason to contradict Cage's own description of the piece: he had composed '*a talk that was nothing but stories*'.[1]

'Nothing but', however, is not quite enough. As was his wont, Cage prefaces the body of the text with an explanation of the text's protocols, which can also be read as a set of instructions. Here Cage informs us that the stories are to be read aloud, according to a temporal constraint, and their presentation on the page is insecure, even arbitrary. Describing his construction and use of the text at hand, he writes,

> In oral delivery of this lecture, I tell one story a minute. If it's a short one, I have to spread it out; when I come to a long one, I have to speak as rapidly as I can. The continuity of the stories as recorded was not planned. I simply made a list of all the stories I could think of and checked them off as I wrote them. Some that I remembered I was not able to write to my satisfaction, and so they were not used. My intention in putting the stories together in an unplanned way was to suggest that all things – stories, incidental sounds from the environment, and, by extension, beings – are related, and that this complexity is more evident when it is not oversimplified by an idea of relationship in one person's mind.[2]

Despite its relatively banal presentation on the page, then, the text of 'Indeterminacy' is unusually contingent; it reflects neither the actuality of the 'realized' text in performance nor an authoritative 'source' for the work as

---

[1] John Cage, 'Indeterminacy', in *Silence: Lectures and Writings* (London and New York: Marion Boyars, 2009; first published 1961), 260–73; 260. Emphasis in original.
[2] Ibid., emphasis in original.

concrete or settled. Nor does it possess the familiar performance-contingency of a standard script or score. The limitations placed on the reading voice make of the text something quite different in performance, both difficult and absurd, whilst the happenstantial concatenation of the stories themselves suggests a myriad of other possible formulations, and so other readings and other objects of reading, without actually presenting any of them. Indeed, the compositional history of *this* 'Indeterminacy', presented in Cage's first book *Silence* (1961), points to a rather more involved and multifaceted work than the bare text suggests. Written in September 1958 to be delivered as a lecture at the Brussels World's Fair under the title 'Indeterminacy: New Aspect of Form in Instrumental and Electronic Music', the piece originally consisted of thirty stories of various lengths, each to be read in the period of one minute. This version of the text was published by Karlheinz Stockhausen in *Die Reihe 5*.[3] During the next year, Cage added another sixty stories to the set, along with David Tudor's musical accompaniment; this was recorded and released by Folkways as an LP.[4] When Cage came to publish the *Silence* text, only fifty-six stories of the ninety appeared under the title of 'Indeterminacy', and the lecture subtitle had been dropped entirely. But here again, the status of the text is more complicated than it at first appears: the other thirty-four stories have not been excised entirely, but rather distributed or scattered throughout the rest of the volume, either on their own or as integral parts of 'other' texts:

> Some of the stories have been omitted since their substance forms part of other writings in this volume. Many of those that remain are to be found below. Others are scattered through the book, playing the function that odd bits of information play at the ends of columns in a smalltown newspaper. I suggest that they be read in the manner and in the situations that one reads newspapers – even the metropolitan ones – when he does so purposelessly: that is, jumping here and there and responding at the same time to environmental events and sounds.[5]

The text of 'Indeterminacy' presented to readers of *Silence* is not, then, identical to the global sum of the textual material which makes up that work. Its superficial straightforwardness hides an array of shifting and indefinable substitutions and internal relations, as well as relations to texts which are marked as in some

---

[3] Herbert Eimert and Karlheinz Stockhausen, eds., *Die Reihe* 5 (Bryn Mawr and King of Prussia: Theodore Presser, 1961), 84–120.
[4] John Cage and David Tudor, *Indeterminacy* (Smithsonian Folkways B000001DM2, 2009). CD.
[5] Cage, 'Indeterminacy', 261. Emphasis in original.

way extrinsic to it but which it nevertheless shares parts with. This dispersal of materials, along with an intermedial division of the work between various realizations – text(s), performances, recording – was to become characteristic of Cage's work, and perhaps particularly so of his writings. Cage is today best known as an experimental composer, and indeed this was the main prism through which his contemporaries viewed his work. Yet he was also a prolific writer, poet and visual artist, an active public lecturer and teacher, and his work in all media bore the mark of these multiple commitments. As such, to treat 'Indeterminacy' merely as 'a piece of writing', exemplified by or embodied in the version presented in *Silence*, the most easily available text, is not sufficient. 'Indeterminacy' is an unevenly distributed work, in possession of moveable parts and varieties of material actualization. Though it may at first appear simple, forthright, even quotidian, this simplicity hides many uncertainties and difficulties for readers.

The significance of the title, then, can be seen in its proper light if it is read as referring not to the text itself but to a principle under the sign of which the text was constructed. 'Indeterminacy' points to the uncertain status of the text in front of readers; to the vagaries and variations it produces in performance; to the fungible, arbitrary order which structures it and to the seemingly insignificant, 'everyday' nature of the stories told.[6] Most of the stories pertain to typical Cagean concerns, and, as their distribution throughout *Silence* suggests, are frequently deployed by Cage in his other work and throughout his career. Many are structured as jokes. They flirt with triviality, leaving readers not entirely able to gauge the import of any given story, or any given aspect of a story, its vocabulary or expressions. There is a marked lack of metaphor, and the narratives are insistently literal, catalogues of events presented chronologically and with little comment. Readers can be forgiven for finding it both blank and opaque. Certainly, it is unclear to what degree any particular or close attention to the textual details will reveal anything especially interesting or remarkable – Cage's prose style is fluid and entertaining, but hardly noteworthy or masterful in the way that might attract the attention of critical connoisseurs. What is compelling about it cannot be located on a purely textual level.

What might be characterized as the 'lightness' or the seeming transparency of 'Indeterminacy' as 'writing' – understood simply as this textual stratum –

---

[6] For a lengthy account of Cage's art of the everyday, see John G. Leonard, *Into the Light of Things: The Art of the Commonplace from Wordsworth to John Cage* (Chicago and London: University of Chicago, 1994).

is belied by the shifting and unmoored nature of that stratum itself. It would in one sense be true to say that the piece is a collection of anecdotes or 'light fiction', and so belongs to a kind of writing which academic literary criticism has not historically favoured. Nonetheless, its seeming unfitness for the attentions of a critical reader is a result not only of genre but also of method – a method encapsulated in the word 'indeterminacy'. The resistance the stories present to the critical reader stems from their lack of determinate identity, position or performance within the 'work' more broadly construed. Because the piece must be conceived of as consisting in more than just *text*, and the text is presented (and presentable) in more than one concrete manner, the status of 'text' as such is repositioned so that traditional critical expectations about reading, and about the object of reading, are knocked off balance, or at least come to seem somehow unsubtle tools.

These assumptions, including affirmation of the presence of formal ingenuity and writerly virtuosity, as well as a hermeneutic conception of literary reading as the careful excavation of meaning from an intentional substratum, can be traced back to the very beginnings of literary criticism as an established academic discipline interested in vernacular poetry – though their genesis is undoubtedly older still. To take as an example the formative expression of the close-reading mode which dominated, and continues heavily to inform, criticism, we might consider the methods and values expounded by I. A. Richards in his 1929 study *Practical Criticism*, which has as good a claim as any to be the foundational text of modern criticism, seem too concerned with elucidating meaning for a reading of 'Indeterminacy'. In that book, Richards complains repeatedly of 'the widespread inability to construe meaning' which he diagnoses in his poetry-reading test-subjects.[7] They are, he claims, regularly defeated by the semantic, metaphorical and syntactic complexities of the texts with which they are confronted blind, and a major purpose of 'practical criticism' as Richards conceived of it was to produce readers capable of construing meaning from such complex objects. Yet it seems unlikely that any of Richards's students would struggle to construe Cage's stories, which, as I have stated, are semantically straightforward; they might well struggle to find any literary value in them at all. More importantly, it seems that Richards's method would offer little to a reader of Cage who was more than minimally competent *as a reader*. The virtuosic construal of meaning from text

---

[7] I. A. Richards, *Practical Criticism: A Study of Literary Judgment* (London: Routledge, 1991; first published 1929), 312.

which *Practical Criticism* prizes would do little to address the indeterminacy of 'Indeterminacy', even if such skilful local readings are entirely possible.

Other traditional critical reading protocols are similarly dulled. For example, the hermeneutic approach of William Empson's 1930 *Seven Types of Ambiguity* would struggle to gain much traction on a text (or set of texts) which, as I describe, is marked out by a sheen of literalness, even superficiality. Empson's understanding of ambiguity, in which 'a word or a grammatical structure is effective in several ways at once', is spooled out at great length through a series of readings of canonical poets.[8] The basic experience contained in *Seven Types* is that of being repeatedly reminded that you, the reader of poetry, are not in fact paying sufficient attention, that more is present in the poetic text than you bothered to notice. In the case of 'Indeterminacy', however, it seems that such a mode of attention would be inappropriate: that insisting on the multiplicity of the stories' meanings would be to pay *too much* attention, or to locate importance in the wrong place. What *Indeterminacy* might demand, then, is not *more* attention but a *different* attention. 'Odd bits of information', as Cage calls them, are not especially fecund ground for rich outgrowths of ambiguity; if, as Empson suggests, 'the reader is trained to expect [ambiguity]' in poetry, then the status and relevance of that expectation are far from obvious here.[9] Where both Richards's and Empson's critical protocols locate the first object of criticism on the micro-textual level, on the shifting meaning(s) of individual words or phrases, and then build up from these particulars, reading 'Indeterminacy' requires a reading protocol which works from the outside in, taking what I have here described as the indeterminacy principle under which the text operates as its first and central component, and as what makes its particulars of literary interest. With 'Indeterminacy', the interest is in the macropoetics. If this stratum of the text is left unaddressed, and the close-reading paradigm affirmed, then it is difficult to make any critical judgements about it at all.

The relevance of Cage's 'Indeterminacy' to my project in this book is more than just a felicity of titles. To consider the poetics of indeterminacy is to recognize both how reading itself is in some crucial ways unable to attend to that poetics, and how that poetics requires another attitude of criticism. What I want to do here, briefly, is to provide an account of how poetic indeterminacy has been conceived of and described since the shortcomings of more traditional critical

---

[8] William Empson, *Seven Types of Ambiguity* (London: Penguin, 1995; first published 1930), 21.
[9] Ibid., 50.

paradigms became evident in this regard. Whilst the word 'indeterminacy' is relatively straightforward in its dictionary sense, signifying indefiniteness, uncertainty, infixity, vagueness, undecidedness and a lack of fixed limits, its use in a literary and poetic sense gives rise to several specific problems which have their own history and legacy of articulation. Addressing these special problems, Charles Altieri has noted that

> Literary texts, after all, cannot be shown to possess the forms of determinacy exhibited by scientific propositions or even by ordinary speech acts which have specific communicative functions whose success can be measured. We might say that theories of literary meaning as indeterminate are only as good as the models of determinacy they oppose.[10]

I shall return to Altieri's essay shortly. In the meantime, it is important only to note that he insists any account of indeterminacy can only proceed in the light of a clear sense of what is determinate in literature, and that he articulates the existing question of literary indeterminacy as a question of indeterminacy in *meaning*. What follows will attempt to respond to both of these points.

* * *

A history of literary thinking about indeterminacy might well begin with the work of the Polish philosopher Roman Ingarden, whose *The Cognition of the Literary Work of Art* (1931), a phenomenological study of reading, is heavily invested in a conception of the reader as tamer of the indeterminate text.[11] Ingarden makes a central distinction between the act of reading any given text, on the one hand, and reading as an activity in itself, with characteristics not absolutely determined by any given text, on the other:

> We must distinguish between two different procedures: first, the reading of a specific literary work, or the cognition of that work which takes place during such reading, and, second, that cognitive attitude which leads to an apprehension of the essential structure and peculiar character of the literary work of art as such.[12]

---

[10] Charles Altieri, 'The Hermeneutics of Literary Indeterminacy: A Dissent from the New Orthodoxy', *New Literary History* 10, no. 1 (Autumn, 1978): 71–99; 71. For the classic account of speech acts, see J. L. Austin, *How to Do Things with Words* (Oxford: Oxford University Press, 1962).
[11] It should be observed that both Ingarden and later Iser propose a figure called 'the reader', imagined as a hypostasized character shared by all readers. In this book I will refer instead, and where possible, to 'readers', so that no such heroic figure is implied.
[12] Roman Ingarden, *The Cognition of the Literary Work of Art*, trans. Ruth Ann Crowley and Kenneth R. Olson (Evanston: Northwestern, 1973; first published 1968), 10.

What is significant here for the purposes of my argument is simply Ingarden's positing of two constitutive strata in the reading process. First, he describes the familiar conception of reading as an interaction between reader and a given – which is to say, a determined – text, at which level the various reading tactics and attentions addressed by Richards and Empson occur, and which for Ingarden always involves the production of meaning. Before this hermeneutic level, however, there exists in Ingarden's schema a foundational 'cognitive attitude' which allows readers to recognize what they are reading as a literary text, and indeed allows them to recognize it as text as such. This foundational stratum can be understood as a product of experience, education and acculturation, and it underlies the reader's ability to construe any given work. In this book I shall call this foundational level that of *readerly protocol*. Whilst Richards and Empson both discuss readerly protocol as they conceive of it – both, as educators, are implicitly engaged in shoring up this stratum and improving students' engagement with it – neither challenges its basic orientation; for both, the readerly protocols they operate according to are stable, determined. In Ingarden's account, too, the readerly protocol is taken 'as read'; all literary reading is imagined to be essentially identical, and to operate according to the same principles. Readerly protocols respond differently to texts of different types – scientific texts, for example, are imagined as calling forth different reading tactics, and these might be termed their implied *textual protocols* – but no proper reading of a scientific text can occur according to a literary protocol, and vice versa.[13]

For Ingarden, literary texts contain 'places of indeterminacy [where] it is impossible [. . .] to say whether a certain object or objective situation has a certain attribute'. These must be negotiated or 'filled-out' by the reader, who produces a more-or-less determinate reading by way of 'concretizations' which are *choices* made in the reading process.[14] The example Ingarden uses to illustrate this is taken from Thomas Mann's novel *Buddenbrooks*. Though the text may not inform the reader of the colour of Consul Buddenbrook's eyes, Ingarden believes readers implicitly imagine the character with eyes of some colour or other; they

[13] I take the phrase 'protocols of reading' from Jacques Derrida, who said in interview with Jean-Louis Houdebine and Guy Scarpetta that '[r]eading is transformational. [. . .] But this transformation cannot be executed however one wishes. It requires protocols of reading' (Derrida, 'Positions', in *Positions*, trans. Alan Bass (London: University of Chicago Press, 1981), 37–96; 63). However, in this book the sense I make of the phrase is not Derrida's. See also Robert Scholes, *Protocols of Reading* (New Haven and London: Yale University Press, 1989), in which 'protocols of reading' comes to denote 'literary theory/theories' tout court. Again, this is not quite my sense here.
[14] Ingarden, *The Cognition of the Literary Work of Art*, 13–14.

'concretize' the indeterminate eye-colour as part of their reading process.[15] The reader is thus imagined as a participant in the reading, rather than as a mere receptacle for the text's immediate meaning. Consequently, indeterminacy 'can be filled out in several different ways', such that the coherence of the work is put into peril.[16] Ingarden writes that 'This circumstance carries special dangers for the correct understanding of the literary work and for a faithful aesthetic apprehension of the literary work of art.'[17] Indeterminacy is understood as a structural instability, however necessary to the function of literary reading.

What then of texts for which such 'faithfulness' is not possible? Ingarden's study is shaped by its almost exclusive focus on prose, particularly as it operates in the novel (Conrad, Zola and Mann are the presiding spirits here). It broadly ignores the more avant-garde modernist texts with which it is contemporary, has little to say for drama, and even less for poetry. Some of these shortcomings were taken up by the German critic Wolfgang Iser in his 1976 book *The Act of Reading*, which can be usefully thought of as both a critique and a continuation of Ingarden's project. Iser notes that for Ingarden texts and readings must always finally 'come together in a polyphonic whole', in a manner that suggests the later organicist holism of the New Critics.[18] As a result, Iser argues that Ingarden's theory cannot account for the fractured textual constructions of the avant-garde, and always runs the risk of prematurely closing down interpretative complexities. Furthermore, Iser distances himself from a purely hermeneutic account of reading, writing that '[t]he search for meaning, which at first may appear so natural and so unconditioned, is in fact considerably influenced by historical norms even though this influence is quite unconscious.'[19] Nonetheless, he is of the view that 'Ingarden's incontrovertible achievement is the fact that, with the idea of concretization, he broke away from the traditional view of art as mere representation' – a rejection which I shall suggest is axiomatic to the indeterminate poetics I discuss in further chapters, and which is central to later conceptions of readers as active in texts.[20]

In place of a focus on meaning production, Iser foregrounds the pervasive indeterminacy of the literary text, with consequent attention to how readers

---

[15] Ibid., 50.
[16] Ibid., 54.
[17] Ibid., 53.
[18] Wolfgang Iser, *The Act of Reading: A Theory of Aesthetic Response* (Baltimore and London: Johns Hopkins, 1978), 172.
[19] Ibid., 3.
[20] Ibid., 178.

navigate this unsteady territory: 'Every textual model involves certain heuristic decisions; the model cannot be equated with the literary text itself, but simply opens up a means of access to it.'[21] This is something of a recapitulation of Ingarden's two stratum view of reading, though here the readerly protocol brought to a text is understood as a tactic employed to 'gain access' to what would otherwise be an impenetrable textual protocol. What this means is that indeterminacy is not understood in relation to Ingarden's determinate 'objectivities' and their concretization – Consul Buddenbrook is a human person, and so must have eyes, and so those eyes must be some colour or other, and so on – but in relation to the discovery of the proper readerly protocol to match to the textual protocol:

> Literary texts [. . .] require a resolution of indeterminacies, but, by definition, for fiction there can be no [. . .] given frames of reference. On the contrary, the reader must first discover for himself the code underlying the text, and this is tantamount to bringing out the meaning.[22]

Rather than as a search for obscure, hidden meanings or 'representations', then, Iser describes reading as shaped by a search for buried 'codes' which structure the text and the reader's response to it – for this reason, Iser's is often called a 'reader-response theory', alongside the work of critics like Stanley Fish. The 'expectation' of ambiguity which Empson invests in readers of poetry is understood by Iser as the proper ground of literary activity, and in no way given or predetermined. Indeed, amongst Iser's own preferred examples are the novels of Joyce and the works of Beckett, and in these he identifies a sustained teasing of readers with their own expectations of reading:

> It is typical of modern texts that they invoke expected functions in order to transform them into blanks. This is mostly brought about by a deliberate omission of generic features that have been firmly established by the tradition of the genre.[23]

A 'blank' is one aspect of literary indeterminacy in Iser's theory, the other being the negation. The blank is 'a vacancy in the overall system of the text, the filling of which brings about an interaction of textual patterns', so that readers must synthesize their own method of response.[24] The negation, on the other hand, is exemplified by '"minus functions" [in which] expectations are evoked

---

[21] Ibid., 53.
[22] Ibid., 60.
[23] Ibid., 208.
[24] Ibid., 182.

in the reader as a background against which the *actual* functions of the text become operative', in which case readers' frustrations become themselves a positive function of reading.[25] In both instances, Iser conceives of reading as intimately involved in questions of protocol, where that term can be understood literally as the first sheet glued to a manuscript, which presents the text's date of manufacture, any errata and *instructions* for using and/or reading it.[26] Reading is, for Iser, first a matter of knowing *how*, and learning how means making a special study of the protocols a text recommends and, often conversely, the protocols it requires. Dealing with indeterminacy does not mean finally sorting out a text's meaning to some consensual intersubjective standard, since 'a literary object never reaches the end of its multifaceted indeterminacy. In other words, a literary object can never be given final definition'.[27] What can however be determined are the reading protocols to which the text responds, both those it welcomes and those it vitiates, and indeterminacy is lodged in the hunt for them.

Here I return briefly to Altieri, who, in the same year *The Act of Reading* was published in English, wrote an essay which attempts to clarify the stakes and sense of literary indeterminacy. Like both Ingarden and Iser, Altieri objects to any theory of reading which locates its significance purely in the textual level:

> The basic units of meaning, then, are not names and predicative functions but two sets of conventions: semantic conventions allow an utterance to pick out features of a possible world or object of discourse (which may itself depend on our having learned a language rather than on empirical facts) and pragmatic or illocutionary ones which allow us to determine the use being made of the discourse and the appropriate procedures for assessing it.[28]

Again, what is presented here is an essentially two-tier model of reading which can be mapped onto a hermeneutic level and a level of protocol, the first consisting of semantic concatenation and the second of active, concrete uses that might be made of that semantic product. What has been learned or absorbed by the reader contributes to the construal of the text, but this educated construal needs to be contextualized by the reader's judgement of the situation in which the words are operative. Altieri argues that, generally speaking, the production of

---

[25] Ibid., 209.
[26] For a discussion of textual protocol in this sense, see Craig Dworkin, *Reading the Illegible* (Evanston: Northwestern, 2003), 187.
[27] Wolfgang Iser, *Prospecting: From Reader Response to Literary Anthropology* (Baltimore and London: Johns Hopkins, 1989), 9.
[28] Altieri, 'Hermeneutics of Literary Indeterminacy', 83.

meaning obliterates the physical substrate of the text in the mind of the reader – it comes to seem a transparent or frictionless medium – and so the supposedly 'natural' reading protocols which we employ when engaged in reading, say, a narrative in a newspaper often submerge the way in which they are mutually reliant on specific textual protocols with their own histories and contingencies:

> In reading it is more difficult to take letters as isolated 'objective entities' than it is to construe groups of letters as semantic units. Objectivity here depends not on the physical properties of things but on the procedures for reading which the members of a culture share by virtue simply of their education into that culture.[29]

One of the things poetry might expect or ask of us is a revaluation and reconsideration of the protocols of reading. Poetic indeterminacy breaks down the supposed objectivity of the intersubjective consensus on how reading ought to proceed by disallowing readers to relax into their 'naturalized' acculturations. Whilst, in Altieri's view, it is quite plausible that readers can and frequently do come to some kind of consensus on the question of what a text *means*, he leaves open the possibility that 'procedures for reading' between groups of people are not necessarily so stable. Where he objects to hermeneutic voluntarism in arguing that '[c]ritical thinking that gets bogged down in the hermeneutic determinability and indeterminability of statements ironically remains trapped in the last gasps of theological discourse and the theologizing of poetry those gasps produced', he nevertheless leaves open the possibility that the indeterminate can be located at the level of protocol.[30] For Altieri, what is profitably considered indeterminate is not a text's meaning or meanings, but rather the way that a text is dramatized by the protocols it is subjected to, which might be more or less successful. This, for Altieri, is the proper object of literary criticism.

Following on from Altieri's rejection of a *hermeneutics* of indeterminacy, Marjorie Perloff's extensive study *The Poetics of Indeterminacy* (1981) aims to locate indeterminate poetics in a delimited historical frame. Rejecting, with Altieri, Derrida's account of indeterminacy as 'always-already' active within texts, she outlines what she terms 'the Other Tradition', which is described as 'the "anti-Symbolist" mode of indeterminacy or "undecideability", of literalness

---

[29] Ibid, 78.
[30] Ibid., 93. Altieri explicitly distances his position from the Derridean positing of a radical disjunction between sign and signified; Perloff makes a similar disavowal.

and free play, whose first real exemplar was the Rimbaud of the *Illuminations*'.[31] As the major figures in the post-symbolist tradition she identifies T. S. Eliot, Wallace Stevens, W. H. Auden and Robert Lowell; the 'Other Tradition' includes Ezra Pound, Gertrude Stein, William Carlos Williams and Frank O'Hara, as well as Cage and Charles Olson.[32] Perloff argues that the division between these two traditions has been broadly ignored by criticism because 'readers seem bent on absorbing the unfamiliar into familiar patterns', by which she means patterns which work for reading Eliot or other poets in the post-symbolist lineage.[33] Even the experimental valences of *The Waste Land* do not avoid this domestication because, in Perloff's view, Eliot's prosodic and formal method 'assumes that there is *fixity*, a norm to be evaded gracefully'; in other words, they take certain formal operations as given or determinate, and deviate from them only so as to highlight their continual presence.[34] In some ways, then, Perloff sees Eliot's writing as in sympathy with Iser's theory of indeterminacy: *The Waste Land* asks for a reader who considers traditional metrical form as an example of a determinate protocol *against which* the poem must be read if its innovations are to 'make sense'.[35] Formal indeterminacy is always resolvable back into a determinate conception. Perloff's understanding of indeterminate poetics, on the other hand, requires a more radical model.

Perloff understands the writers of her 'Other Tradition' as undermining both the primacy of discursive interpretation in poetry in favour of a radically literal conception of form, and the primacy of formal/generic regimes which insist on divisions between prose and poetry. The text becomes the substrate which undergirds the reading process, and which cannot be easily resolved or determined into a single reading or interpretation. As such, she writes,

> William Empson's famous 'seven types of ambiguity' – that is, the multiple layers of meaning words have in poetry (and, by analogy, images in painting) – give way to what we might call an 'irreducible ambiguity' – the creation of labyrinths that have no end.[36]

---

[31] Marjorie Perloff, *The Poetics of Indeterminacy: Rimbaud to Cage* (Evanston: Northwestern, 1981), vii, 42.
[32] Though, as shall be noted in later chapters, Perloff has little time for Olson's work.
[33] Ibid., 34.
[34] Ibid., 42.
[35] For more on this, see Chapter 1.
[36] Perloff, *The Poetics of Indeterminacy*, 34. I think it is important to note here that, as already suggested, Empson *does* have a sense of the role readerly protocol and readerly expectation play in his hermeneutics of poetic ambiguity. In *Seven Types*, he merely suggests that this question of protocol is not his current focus: '"Ambiguity" itself can mean an indecision as to what you mean, an intention to mean several things, a probability that one or other or both of two things has been

In this sense, Perloff's 'poetics of indeterminacy' rests on a conception of the material text itself, the print on the page, as the only truly determinate entity in reading; all else is indeterminate in these texts, such that 'meanings' are swallowed by pure 'play', reliant more on intertextual relationships and rebarbative nonsensicality than on the critic's desire to explain or resolve.[37] For Perloff, the poetics of indeterminacy emerges where the textual protocol directly rebuffs various readerly protocols, leaving the reader to wander in its maze.

It is instructive, then, to observe how Perloff treats Cage's stories not as vectors for narrative but as profoundly physical sound- or word-art: 'Perhaps the first thing that strikes one about [Cage's] stories is their radical empiricism, their stubborn and insistent literalness.'[38] Their indeterminacy is lodged not in their meaning, which is both straightforward and nugatory, but rather in how they use their formal and verbal resources to construct a framework for reading which is untroubled by hermeneutic questions. This is '"poetry" [...] construed not as "verse" [...] but as *language art* or "word-system"'.[39] Under Perloff's interpretation Cage's work can be read as poetry even when it is laid out as prose, and this goes some way to explaining the oddity of his 'Indeterminacy'; it fits uneasily into either category. Radically indeterminate work like this responds best to reading techniques which were for Ingarden unthinkable and for Iser at best the exception to a rule into or against which readers could integrate their experience of the text. For the writers Perloff discusses, the indeterminacy of reading goes all the way down, and is indeed reading's object. In her account, this foregrounding of indeterminacy as *itself* the object of reading is a relatively modern phenomenon, growing out of the work of the French *Symbolistes* (Rimbaud, Mallarmé, Verlaine and so on) and finding its English-language expression in the works of authors such as Pound, Stein and Beckett. Only at this stage does indeterminacy become a poetics as such, rather than a mere side effect or exception which proves some determinate rule. Whilst I do not entirely concur with Perloff's delimitation or definition of indeterminate poetics, it is from this milieu that my own work will begin.

* * *

---

meant, and the fact that a statement has several meanings' (Empson, *Seven Types of Ambiguity*, 24). Empson is cognizant of the 'ambiguity of ambiguity' at the level of protocol but does not attempt to resolve this question, which he does not consider directly relevant to his study.
[37] Perloff, *The Poetics of Indeterminacy*, 34.
[38] Ibid., 312.
[39] Ibid., 43. Emphasis in original.

This study takes as its focus the poetics of John Cage and Charles Olson. My reasons for choosing these two poets as exemplars are various but hinge essentially on their position in a tradition of what I shall call 'longform' poetics. This is to say that, despite their many poetic, aesthetic, philosophical and indeed personal differences, both share in an inheritance from the modernist 'long poem', primarily via Pound, but also in a deeper American historical register which goes back at least to the nineteenth century (chiefly to Thoreau in Cage's case, and Melville in Olson's), and by way of this tradition their work can be understood as part of an even broader legacy of longform poetry with roots in the epic.[40] In keeping with the title of this study, I understand Cage and Olson both as *readers of modernism* of a peculiarly perceptive stripe, and as *modernist readers par excellence*. The novel and innovative use to which they put that reading is evident in the work they produced, which often rereads and misreads their modernist forbears in striking ways (this is as true of Cage's *Writing through the Cantos* as it is of Olson's Pound-formed and Pound-phobic *Maximus Poems*, for example). Their reading practices shaped their writing practices in a pervasive and radical manner, and to read their longform poetry is always to read them reading the longform poems of earlier modernists. The work of both exercised clear influences on later developments in the long poem in America; notable examples might include Ed Dorn's *Gunslinger*, or the collaborative project *Leningrad* (Michael Davidson, Lyn Hejinian, Ron Silliman and Barrett Watten), or the work of Susan Howe. Major currents in later writing, notably 'Language' poetry in the United States and the so-called British Poetry Revival in the United Kingdom, would not have been possible without the formative effect of their work.

I maintain that the work of Olson and Cage is both representative of a number of important innovations, which the long poem went through in the mid-to-late twentieth century, and instrumental in shaping those innovations. Equally, I think that various persistent misconceptions about each poet can be corrected by putting the one into dialogue with the other. This is not to say that the poetries of Olson and Cage are *extraordinarily* similar but rather that

---

[40] On the personal relationship, see Charles Olson, 'A Toss, for John Cage', in *Collected Poems of Charles Olson*, ed. George F. Butterick (Berkeley, Los Angeles and London: University of California, 1997), 271–3; Tom Clark, *Charles Olson: The Allegory of a Poet's Life* (Berkeley: North Atlantic, 2000), 226–7; for a brief definition of the modernist long poem, see *The Princeton Encyclopedia of Poetry and Poetics: Fourth Edition*, ed. Roland Greene (Princeton and Oxford: Princeton University Press, 2012), 813–14, particularly the comment on the long poem's genesis in a struggle with anterior forms: '*The Cantos* made the writing of such a text [the long poem] its real subject, an idea that now dominates the genre' (813).

a study of their contrast and likeness has a clarificatory function which other, seemingly more sympathetic comparisons cannot possess. I contend that the relation suggested between their writing here is useful because it offers a study of contrasts as much as of similarities; this dialogic relation is revealing precisely because it is unexpected and often frictive. I see the not-always sympathetic relation between Cage and Olson as central to the book and its argument: it looks both to highlight the features of their respective works by contrast and to discover some heretofore unremarked similarities and alliances. That this is the first study to consider the two poets together at any length or depth is not then a mark of sheer novelty or caprice – there are connections between the two poets both biographical and poetical, but also serious difference and dis-sympathy, and none of these have in my view been sufficiently remarked on, even though a large number of later writers clearly drew extensive lessons from both Cage and Olson.

The link I explore between the work of my authors is, then, only historical and biographical in the vaguest sense. Most of the writings by Cage I discuss were composed after Olson's death. Though the two met, they never really worked together, and did not see eye to eye. Underlying my argument throughout, however, there is a flavour of the attitude of experimentation and artistic iconoclasm inculcated at Black Mountain College, where the two men taught for several briefly intersecting periods, and which continued to shape their respective poetics long after its closure in 1957.[41] This attitude is handily distilled in a brief story from 'Indeterminacy', in which Cage relays an anecdote from that time:

> One day down at Black Mountain College, David Tudor was eating his lunch. A student came over to his table and began asking him questions. Finally David Tudor looked at him and said, 'If you don't know, why do you ask?'[42]

Despite their many differences, both Olson and Cage exemplified this interest in questions rather than answers, and in the potential identity of the two: in process rather than product and doing rather than meaning.

---

[41] The literature on Black Mountain College is extensive; for the major history of the college, see Martin Duberman, *Black Mountain: An Exploration in Community* (London: Northwestern, 1974; first published 1972). For two more recent books on the college, including many images and archival materials, see Eugen Blume, Matilda Felix, Gabriele Knapstein and Catherine Nichols, eds., *Black Mountain: An Interdisciplinary Experiment 1933–1957* (Leipzig: Spector, 2015), and Helen Molesworth, ed., *Leap Before You Look: Black Mountain College 1933–1957* (New Haven and London: Yale University Press, 2016).
[42] Cage, 'Indeterminacy', 266.

In part this expressed itself as an attack on the shibboleths and mores traditionally associated with 'Poetry'.[43] These works are motivated by deep scepticism about the character and status of the poetic object. In this can be seen something of the inheritance of surrealism and Dadaism, of anti-art and antibourgeois-art sentiment, but what I discuss here is not a mere outgrowth of those movements or their associated poetics. Unsatisfied with merely *liberating* the poetic subject from all previously pertaining bounds, these works *play* with bounds, proposing and rescinding several paradigms in such a way as to make reading protocols themselves indeterminate. Resultantly, what follows is not primarily concerned to provide 'readings'; rather, it discusses various *protocols for reading*, models for how to engage certain texts, thereby attempting to demonstrate how for these poems one needs to 'read through' a poetics as a sort of optic, via which such writing may, or may not, be made legible.

This implies a certain pragmatism as regards formal and generic traditions and expectations. Just as Perloff's licence to read Cage's prose as 'poetic' liberates it from one overdetermining generic categorization, reading Olson's as an *indeterminate* poetic allows an engagement with his work more capacious than the word 'poetry' usually allows to readers. Particularly, it enables a sidestepping of the label 'Black Mountain Poetry', which seems to attach itself to work which is too obviously 'Poetry' (with the almost-inevitable implication of 'lyric') to be properly in sympathy with my project here. As a result, I shall not much discuss the work of Robert Duncan, Robert Creeley, Hilda Morley, Denise Levertov or of others sometimes called 'Black Mountain Poets'. Equally, the current of interdisciplinarity and intermediality which underpins Cage's work, and which proves him an exemplary Black Mountaineer, makes his writings more appropriate to my present project than those of otherwise similar writers, Jackson Mac Low being a good example. 'Black Mountain writing' might suggest something more flexible which could accommodate both Cage and Olson (and others amongst the students and scholars of the college), but in this study the brief connection they shared at the college is let fade into the background, whilst the spirit of experimental pragmatism and formal cross-pollination remains.

Nevertheless, I treat both writers as *poets* in what follows, or at least as writers in constant dialogue with and dissent from 'Poetry'. Neither poet's work is

---

[43] I take this capitalization from Wordsworth's similarly sardonic usage, in the 'Advertisement' to the *Lyrical Ballads* of 1798: 'It is desirable that [. . .] readers, for their own sakes, should not suffer the solitary word Poetry, a word of very disputed meaning, to stand in the way of their gratification' (*The Major Works: Including the Prelude*, ed. Stephen Gill (Oxford: Oxford University Press, 2000), 591).

primarily modelled on ancient or traditional formal characteristics, and indeed much of what criticism has said about both has attempted to account for or describe the sometimes deeply idiosyncratic formal methods they employ. Yet I claim that both exist in some sort of lineage indicative of a broader and deeper critique of those ancient forms than a mere disuse of them might suggest, and I provide several potential articulations of these interventions. In this sense, this study is very much in conversation with Perloff's 'Other Tradition', with Pound, Stein, Beckett; but it is also interested in the *long poem* and in the tradition of the epic, in long forms and the 'longform', and as such it looks, however implicitly, to Homer and to Milton, to Thoreau and to Melville, all of whom, I hope to suggest, inform the work of my subjects in important, if sometimes subsumed, ways. My special interest in this book, then, is in indeterminacy as it operates in, and is generated by, long forms. Ever since Aristotle defined epic as that type of narrative poetry which both adheres to the dramatic unity of tragedy, accounting for a unified action with distinct beginning, middle and end, and which yet is distinguished from tragedy by its length and variety, longform poetics has been beset with the fear of incoherence, of creating a writing which swerves and divagates from its central purpose, heading off blithely into areas unanticipated by either reader or author.[44] There seems to be in the fact of literary length a concomitant tendency to wandering, irrelevance and dislocation, to the vitiation of textual and ideational structure. My basic contention is this: that there is something in length which creates indeterminacy, and something in indeterminacy which tends towards length. The indecision and undecidability which characterizes writing like that discussed in this book both produces and is produced by voluminousness. Length and indeterminacy belong together, and this is what I mean in claiming that the relationship between the two terms is *constitutive*.

It is generally agreed that by the end of the nineteenth century the epic, as a genre, was dead. With the advent of literary modernism came a new kind of longform poem, which became known to criticism simply as the 'modernist long poem'. Formally adventurous and discursively capacious, this 'long poem' became one of the defining products of literary modernism. Nonetheless, it has remained an object of critical contention, with many competing accounts of what constitutes the 'long poem' proposed, and subsequent serious disagreement about how best to read it. Though the 'modernist long poem' is by now universally

---

[44] Aristotle, *Poetics*, trans. Malcolm Heath (London: Penguin, 1996), 38–42.

recognized as a key feature of twentieth-century literary history – indeed, is recognized as one of that century's central poetic achievements – this has not resulted in the appearance of a broad-based consensus on how the 'modernist long poem' works or indeed what it *is*. A large number of monograph studies of the long poem have appeared in the last thirty or forty years, and recent work has advanced the field in a number of ways. Nonetheless there is as yet no account of how indeterminacy – that other characteristic feature of the twentieth-century avant-garde – figures in the development and constitution of the 'long poem'; this book looks to provide just such an account. As committed practitioners of both indeterminate and longform poetics, my contention is that this connection can be seen with exemplary clarity in the work of Cage and Olson.

Whilst I focus on a relatively constrained period, the late twentieth century, in a single country, the United States, I believe that what I discuss in the following chapters reveals a number of dynamics which are present in the longform poetries of earlier times and diffuse places. Though I concur with Perloff in the belief that an explicit efflorescence of what she terms the 'poetics of indeterminacy' can be usefully located in a particular time period, I do not follow her in drawing a strict line between the avant-garde co-option of indeterminacy and what came before, or her insistence that what she sees in Rimbaud and his descendants has 'no real precedent'.[45] Instead, I want to suggest a different lineage, one that runs not so much through France and European modernism, though this is clearly a component of both poets' work, but rather through a peculiarly American attempt to navigate the history and poetics of the long, and previously the epic, poem. There are certain kinds of excessiveness, of energetic, repetitive, collating, tangential movements both poets make which I claim connect more easily with that tradition than with anti-symbolism. Neither Cage nor Olson is so clearly indebted to the French literary modernism which Perloff highlights as are Pound, Stein, Beckett or indeed John Ashbery. This is not to object to Perloff's 'Other Tradition' but only to note that Cage and Olson share in yet another set of traditions, equally invested in and bedevilled by poetic indeterminacy, which she does not discuss. It could also be noted that Cage's *musical* inheritance is a tradition absent from Perloff's account. As such, the challenges posed to readers by Olson's *Maximus Poems* or Cage's lengthy lecture-mesostics need framing in a different manner.

---

[45] Perloff, *Poetics of Indeterminacy*, 45.

The chapters that follow are not strictly chronological, but they do broadly follow the progress of each poet's career from early to late, tracking the trajectories of their work in order to place the developments of their longform poetics within the broader architecture of their authorships – a sense of which needs to be taken into account if protocols for reading their work are to be ascertained. Indeed, knowledge of the authorial context which preceded the more mature longform poetics of both poets was an important constituent of the readerly protocols of their contemporary audiences, and this continues to be necessary for any informed reading of either today. As a result, the earlier chapters of this book attend to facets of each poet's work which prefigure rather than exemplify their mature poetics. Chapter 1, on Olson's 'Projective Verse', attempts to reread that much-read essay as anticipating his indeterminate longform poetics via its prescriptions for 'some sort of epic'. Chapter 2 describes Olson's early interest in the cinema, and how that interest feeds into his later thinking about the speed and energetics of indeterminate writing. Chapter 3, on Cage's *Mushroom Book*, considers how this early example of a longform Cage poem thinks through questions of readerly navigation and expectation in a manner which instrumentally informed the later mesostic long poems.

The latter four chapters focus on the most important longform poems of Olson's (*The Maximus Poems*) and Cage's (*I-VI, Anarchy*) careers, integrating what has been established in previous chapters as part of an attempt to characterize how indeterminacy constitutes them as long poems. Rather than being strictly linear, then, the hope is that the argument of this book accumulates as it continues, establishing certain dynamics and contexts and then using these to inform discussions of each poet's most significant works.

1

Olson's 'Projective Verse'

Since it first appeared in 1950's third issue of *Poetry New York*, Olson's essay-manifesto 'Projective Verse' has been the central object of a morass of scholarly wrangling, poetic riffing and enthusiastic Olsoniana. It has received many reprintings: the first, partial replication in 1951's *The Autobiography of William Carlos Williams*; then as a stand-alone pamphlet from Totem Press in 1959; in Donald Allen's seminal anthology *The New American Poetry 1945–1960* (1960), which volume it bookends along with Olson's poem 'The Kingfishers'; in the first collection of Olson's prose, *Human Universe and Other Essays*, from 1965; in 1966's *Selected Writings*, edited by Robert Creeley; and in a wide variety of editions which emerged after the poet's death in early 1970. There is then no reason to doubt that 'Projective Verse' was read both widely and with great interest throughout Olson's life. This situation was not changed by his untimely death, and indeed it is possible that in recent years 'Projective Verse' has come to stand in for 'Olson' as such. Certainly in the present day it is the best-read (or at least *most-read*) of Olson's writings. It has been hugely influential in the formation of a range of poetic practices on both sides of the Atlantic and beyond the English-speaking world, and belongs to a core 'postmodern' or 'avant-garde' poetics syllabus familiar no doubt to many readers of this book. And yet it is not obvious quite *why* any of this is the case. To say that the message, or thesis, or lesson of 'Projective Verse' is fundamentally *indeterminate* is, as I hope to show, perfectly true; but it is a truth which cuts both ways. Many readers are likely to find it a frustrating text, obscure and frequently obtuse. To make explicit what is really going on in 'Projective Verse', and why, is no simple task. If it is fair to say that the essay is foundational, a crucial contribution to Anglophone poetics, it is equally fair to say that its focus on the indeterminate and the processual often overwhelms its capacities as a propositional text – and many critics have said just this, sometimes in less diplomatic terms. The deep uncertainty surrounding and lodged in this most 'basic' Olsonian text goes some way towards explaining broader problematics within the history of his work's reception, but it also delineates some central tensions which carry through the next two decades of Olson's writing.

Despite an ever-increasing body of scholarly and critical work, our understanding of *how to read* Olson's writing remains much as it did at the time of his death. Notwithstanding the existence of a good dozen monographs and several essay collections dedicated to his work, a number of what might seem to be basic questions have yet to be settled, even (perhaps especially) in the cases of texts, like 'Projective Verse', which are universally read as central to Olson's thinking and writing. In the introduction to a recent and significant collection of essays entitled *Contemporary Olson* (2015), David Herd writes of the new proliferation of Olson studies that '[t]he degree to which, as a consequence of such sustained scholarship, we know how to read Olson remains a moot point.'[1] This uncertainty is hardly confined to younger or more recent commentators. Elaine Feinstein, the poet and correspondent of Olson's (his 'Letter to Elaine Feinstein' is seen as one of his key theoretical statements, and as a sequel to 'Projective Verse'), writes that '[i]n my own poems, it's easier to make out what Olson liberated me from than exactly what I learned from him.'[2] Since Olson first rose to prominence, the consensus has been that his work stages a specific, but also a paradigm-changing, set of challenges to reading, even as it provided a number of hugely permission-giving gestures to contemporary writing. One of the distinctive characteristics of Olson scholarship is the readiness with which this uncertainty is admitted.

* * *

'Projective Verse' begins with a set of sharp distinctions: 'Projective Verse / (projectile (percussive (prospective / *vs.* / The NON-Projective'; 'closed' verse against 'open' verse; Wordsworth and Milton against Pound and Williams.[3] The rhetorical force of these divisions does much more than it explicitly says – readers are pulled directly into a formal, cultural and historical polemic which is already an unanchored, floating zone of contention – already a vortex, one

---

[1] David Herd, 'Introduction: Contemporary Olson', in *Contemporary Olson*, ed. Herd (Manchester: Manchester University Press, 2015), 1–21; 11.
[2] Elaine Feinstein, 'A Fresh Look at Olson', in *Contemporary Olson*, 127–32; 127. See also Charles Bernstein, *Pitch of Poetry* (Chicago: University of Chicago, 2016), 111.
[3] Charles Olson, 'Projective Verse', in *Collected Prose*, ed. Donald Allen and Benjamin Friedlander (Berkeley, Los Angeles and London: University of California, 1997), 239–49; 239.

might say – even before any term is defined or given much context. 'Projective Verse' is divided into two sections ('I' and 'II'), which, it is claimed, will first pin down some of these terms and judgements, and then proceed to elucidate their significance and their '*essential* use'.[4] The first section is loosely technical and the second is more speculative. Olson writes,

> I want to do two things: firstly, try to show what projective or OPEN verse is, what it involves, in its act of composition, how, in distinction from the non-projective, it is accomplished; and II, suggest a few ideas about what stance toward reality brings such verse into being, what the stance does, both to poet and to his reader. (The stance involves, for example, a change beyond, and larger than, the technical, and may, the way things look, lead to a new poetics and to new concepts from which some sort of drama, say, or of epic, perhaps, may emerge.)[5]

The first section is the one more familiar to most readers and critics, containing a number of analyses, examples and suggestions which are frequently understood as a set of 'tips for poets', providing Olson's pronouncements on the primacy of breath in poetry, on poetry considered as 'high-energy transfer of perception', on the necessity of ditching received syntax, on the reclamation of the syllable against received metrics and on the utility of the typewriter pursuant to this project.[6] These have become the traditional talking points for scholars and readers of 'Projective Verse'.

The second section, briefer and more gnomic, deals with what Olson calls the 'stance toward reality', and later 'the new stance toward reality of the poem itself', which such an 'open' or 'projective' poetics would entail.[7] That this latter section has received less attention and comment is unsurprising, in part because it is unclear whether Olson's 'new stance to reality' inheres in poetry particularly or instead in some broader shift in phenomenological attitude – a tension which replicates itself across all of Olson's work, and is never really resolved – and this uncertainty makes the stakes of Olson's claims hard to assess. Primarily, however,

---

[4] Ibid., 239. Emphasis in original.
[5] Ibid. Emphasis in original.
[6] Olson's interest in Norbert Wiener's *Cybernetics*, published in 1948, is no doubt at play in his poetic-energetics; conceptions of feedback loops and entropy which persist in Olson's writing have their root at least in part in Wiener's influential work. Olson in fact directly quoted Wiener in 'The Kingfishers': 'The message is / a discrete or continuous sequence of measurable events distributed in time' (Olson, 'The Kingfishers', in *The Collected Poems of Charles Olson*, 86–93; 90; Norbert Wiener, *Cybernetics: Or, Control and Communication in the Animal and the Machine* (Cambridge: MIT, 1985; first published 1948), 8).
[7] Olson, 'Projective Verse', 246.

the statement that the stance involves 'a change beyond, and larger than, the technical' is hard to square with the avowedly 'technical' recommendations of *Projective Verse* Part I in anything but the broadest and most metaphorical terms – the 'opening' of the page as field allowing for an 'opening' of the poet's 'projective size' in some more general sense, for example. What I want to suggest here is that redescribing 'Projective Verse' according to this 'meta-technical' formula, as a text which begins to orient modernist versification in a more indeterminate fashion, provides a helpful way of thinking about the essay's significance both for Olson's own writing and for the criticism that has grown up around it. As Olson composed 'Projective Verse' he had already begun to imagine and produce what was to become *The Maximus Poems* – the work from which, as he has it, 'some sort [. . .] of epic, perhaps, might emerge' – and in this context it is not only fruitful but crucial to consider the essay operating on a level 'beyond the technical', tipping into a more ambitious and more indeterminate act of inauguration.

* * *

Most readings of 'Projective Verse' share a number of common features and concerns. These primarily coalesce around two allied issues: the *openness* of the 'field' in Olson's writing – the free use of the page and the accelerated breakdown of received poetic form he prescribes – and the *corporeality* of the future verse he imagines will populate it. This is as close as it comes to a consensus view on 'Projective Verse', a representative example of which can be found in Kaplan Harris's survey-essay on 'Black Mountain Poetry': '[Olson's] major accomplishment was to define verse according to the body rather than traditional poetic form.'[8] Questions of majority aside, this is an essentially accurate assessment of Olson's proposition in 'Projective Verse'. But it is not clear what such a statement means or indicates in practice; it risks setting up an unsustainable gulf between received and 'bodily' form in poetry of a type which seems untrue to the history of writing and theorizing poetics ranging generically from epic to lyric, and historically as far back as Homer. Nor is it obvious that 'non-traditional' poetic form is concurrent with 'the body' – notably, Olson is adamant that Eliot's (un)free versification is '*not* projective.'[9]

[8] Kaplan Harris, 'Black Mountain Poetry', in *Cambridge Companion to Modern American Poetry*, ed. Walter Kalaidjian (Cambridge and New York: Cambridge University Press, 2015), 155–66; 159.
[9] Olson, 'Projective Verse', 248. Emphasis in original.

This distinction is significant. Eliot expressed qualified opposition to the idea of a *vers libre*, writing that no verse is fully free because all verse can be described under the rules of traditional scansion, however provisionally.[10] In Eliot's view, traditional versification forms the backdrop to all English-language verse, such that in *vers libre*, so-called, the versification is not so much free as it is engaged in a game of cat and mouse with iambic pentameter and other received forms.[11] In other words, the 'freedom' of free verse only emerges in distinction from, and in dialogue with, received forms. For Eliot, traditional verse forms parallel Iser's 'minus functions' in that their absence summons their memory, and supposedly 'free' verse is only readable in contrast to them.[12] Whilst this seems a viable way of understanding the variable versification of *The Waste Land*, and even the somewhat pastiche formality of sections of *Four Quartets*, it is less clear that it is a paradigm to which Olson's adventures in non-traditional verse are easily accommodated.[13] This suggests it is not the replacement of the traditional with the bodily as line-measure which marks Olson's poetics out from those of his predecessors but rather a more 'open' liberation from the idea of a governing paradigm for versification as such. Furthermore, critical emphasis on the corporeality of Olson's poetics fails to account for the regularity with which 'traditional form' appears in his own work, with rhyme and ballad meter especially being fairly common devices. Either Olson is not following his own advice, or his own understanding of 'Projective Verse's significance was rather more complex than this skeleton account suggests. Both of these options contain some truth, and the strictures of 'Projective Verse' certainly recede as Olson's writing progresses, but it is nonetheless evident that the 'open field' and the 'bodily' require further elucidation to establish their importance both as part of 'Projective Verse' and for Olson's writing as a whole.

---

[10] T. S. Eliot, 'Reflections on *Vers Libre*', in *To Criticize the Critic and Other Writings* (London: Faber, 1965), 183–9; 185.

[11] Ibid., 186. In his recent work on poetic proceduralism, David W. Huntsperger has made a parallel argument to Eliot's, writing that '[t]oday, the desire for organic form seems to represent nostalgia for the high-bourgeois literature of the nineteenth century, a desire for a creative transcendence of the material conditions of everyday life. This desire is most manifest in free verse, the very name of which suggests the possibility of evading material, social and artistic constraints' (Huntsperger, *Procedural Form in Postmodern American Poetry: Berrigan, Antin, Silliman and Hejinian* (New York: Palgrave Macmillan, 2010), 21–2.

[12] Eliot, 'Reflections on *Vers Libre*', 184.

[13] For an account of free verse as possessed of a shaping function rather different from the one Eliot outlines here, see Andrew Crozier, *'Free Verse' as Formal Constraint*, ed. Ian Brinton (Bristol: Shearsman, 2015). Crozier studied with Olson at Buffalo, and was one of the key figures in the transmission of the poet's work and ideas over the Atlantic as part of the British Poetry Revival.

Throughout Olson criticism, some account of 'composition by field' is more or less ubiquitous, although precisely how to read the 'field' (how to 'beat a path through the field' as Peter Middleton puts it) is a matter of perennial disagreement.[14] Olson's notion of breath-composition, in which 'the line comes (I swear it) from the breath, from the breathing of the man who writes, at the moment he writes', perhaps the text's most famous single prescription, is usually taken in tandem with the idea of the 'field' to mean that lines can be as long as they 'feel' rather than as long as they are prescribed.[15] The obvious point here is that in tying the line to the variable length of a breath, Olson is explicitly demoting the importance of 'form' understood as a set of received traditions built around feet and specified metrical or syllabic line-length, and thus making the whole 'field' of the page accessible, though there is no necessary implication of the inadmissibility of received form within the field. 'Field' is also regularly taken to imply a type of geographical or 'landscape' writing, a reading which finds plenty of thematic support in Olson's Gloucester poems ('I come back to the geography of it') and is germane to the recent ecocritical turn, of which it could be argued that *Call Me Ishmael* is a forerunner.[16] Despite this enticement, variants on a space/size/landscape poetics are finally difficult to extend beyond a rhetoric of scale or excessiveness which can at any rate be taken for granted in the work of a writer so embedded within the epic/long poem tradition running through Williams and Pound, and so significantly concerned with Melville. This reading likely owes as much to the thematics of early-to-mid *Maximus* as to 'Projective Verse' in its specificity. Other readings of the piece stress the language of 'fields' as it relates to contemporaneous developments in particle physics, and of 'projection' as a proxy for a raft of masculine and phallic aspects within Olson's poetics and those of the Black Mountain grouping more generally.[17] Both these tendencies also have much to say on suppressed supposed sources

---

[14] Peter Middleton, *Physics Envy: American Poetry and Science in the Cold War and After* (Chicago and London: University of Chicago, 2015), 145.

[15] Olson, 'Projective Verse', 242; for an account of 'Projective Verse' as an attempted reconciliation between *mis-en-page* and landscape, see Harriett Tarlo, 'Open Field: Reading Field as Place and Poetics', in *Placing Poetry*, eds. Ian Davidson and Zoe Skoulding (Amsterdam and New York: Rodopi, 2013), 113–48.

[16] Charles Olson, *The Maximus Poems*, ed. George F. Butterick (Berkeley, Los Angeles and London: University of Chicago, 1983), 184.

[17] For readings of Olson's 'field' as a metaphor rooted in high-energy physics, see Don Byrd, *Charles Olson's Maximus* (Urbana, Chicago and London: University of Illinois, 1980), 38, and Middleton's *Physics Envy* throughout. For readings of Olson's poetics as essentially sexist, see Rachel Blau DuPlessis, 'Olson and His *Maximus Poems*', in *Contemporary Olson*, 135–48, and Libbie Rifkin, *Career Moves: Olson, Creeley, Zukofsky, Berrigan, and the American Avant-Garde* (Madison: University of Wisconsin, 2000), 21–6.

for 'Projective Verse', with possible candidates ranging as widely as Wallace Stevens, Marianne Moore and even I. A. Richards, though many of these assertions are self-professedly speculative. This represents only a few examples of the essentially thematic readings the essay has received. It is necessary here simply to acknowledge that whilst all these interpretations have value, they by no means exhaust the possible resonances of 'Projective Verse'. Furthermore, they are difficult to bring into coherence. Responses to 'Projective Verse' have tended to take a particular aspect of the text, extend it and run with it in order to serve some broader critical or poetic project.[18] It is more likely to be used as a highly suggestive and fungible set of cues for further work than to be treated as a complete or reconstructable theory with internal coherence, and there are good reasons for this.

Much criticism has assumed a necessary relationship between the essay and Olson's more recognizably poetic writing, especially 'The Kingfishers' and early *Maximus*, attempting to square the circle by positioning 'Projective Verse' as a basically unfinished and gestural prose-piece reliant on the poetry which accompanies and comes after it for its consummation. Stephen Fredman claims that 'Projective Verse' is the 'ground' of Olson's work, by which he means not only that it provided the basis in which his later work was received – clearly true – but furthermore that without 'Projective Verse' as a background, readers would be able to make nothing of Olson's poems.[19] This reading of 'Projective Verse' as a sort of 'background' or foundation is complemented by a recognition of what might be called its 'crowdsourced' nature; there are admissions of debt to Pound, Williams, Dahlberg, Creeley, e. e. cummings, Hart Crane and Shakespeare, and many more loans and borrowings that go unattributed. This has led some to see 'Projective Verse' as more a statement of collective achievement than as a piece which sparked anything really new; Don Byrd writes that 'Olson was not primarily an innovator. The importance of his work is its confirmation of the wild, lucky and inconsistent guesses of his immediate predecessors.'[20] As I suggested in this book's introduction, here we can read Olson reading his modernist forbears. It certainly is the case that, as Libbie Rifkin argues, a major

---

[18] See, for example, Robert Duncan's *The Opening of the Field* (London: Cape, 1969); the first poem, 'Often I am Permitted to Return to a Meadow', was highly influential in shaping readings of Olson's field as a territorial, pastoral surface. For a recent poetic interpretation of Olson's 'field' as territorial, see Tarlo's *Field* (Bristol: Shearsman, 2016).
[19] See Stephen Fredman, *The Grounding of American Poetry: Charles Olson and the Emersonian Tradition* (Cambridge and New York: Cambridge University Press, 1993), 148.
[20] Byrd, *Charles Olson's Maximus*, xiv.

part of 'Projective Verse's purpose was to set out Olson's stall as a poet at the centre of and carrying forward the avant-garde tradition of Pound and Williams, whose work was by 1950 passing from radical novelty into accepted canonicity.[21] These readings attempt to shift the weight of attention off 'Projective Verse' as such, and to share it across Olson's early work.

This is reasonable insofar as it goes, but likely leans too heavily on the presumed determinacy and definition of the prose-poetry relation on both a formal and a functional level. Olson's 'prose', I claim, is itself too indeterminate to sustain a role as the arbiter or explicator of the 'poetry', even were it strictly possible to draw such a distinction; for example, the essayistic pieces 'Ed Sanders' Language' or 'Continuing Attempt to Pull the Taffy off the Roof of the Mouth', categorized as 'prose' by Olson's editors, could easily be taken as examples of 'projective verse'.[22] Equally, it fails to account for the huge interest the essay has nonetheless accumulated, in its own right and often precisely *to the exclusion* of Olson's other work; interest in 'open poetics' and 'field composition' is not solely evinced in the context of *Maximus* or 'The Kingfishers'. These ideas have developed a life of their own, well removed from Olson's poetry. Whilst many of the particular, essentially technical prescriptions found in 'Projective Verse' are not especially original, Olson himself both forthrightly admits this and yet seems to suggest that something else, something 'beyond the technical' is going on, as here in his discussion of the typewriter:

> What I want to emphasize here, by this emphasis on the typewriter as the personal and instantaneous recorder of the poet's work, is the already projective nature of verse as the sons of Pound and Williams are practicing it. Already they are composing as though verse was to have the reading its writing involved, as though not the eye but the ear was to be the measurer, as though the intervals of its composition could be so carefully put down as to be precisely the intervals of its registration.[23]

Here is clear admission that the ideas presented are not solely Olson's; but the prepositional nature of these admissions ('as though') suggests that their realization has not yet been achieved. In its 'prospective' guise 'Projective Verse' looks forward to a poetry not yet written, and so not determined by currently

---

[21] Rifkin, *Career Moves*, 13–71.
[22] Olson, *Collected Prose*, 291, 373–4.
[23] Olson, 'Projective Verse', 246.

existing trends or practices. In what then does the originality and import of 'Projective Verse' consist?

* * *

A useful way of assessing the claim that 'Projective Verse' is incoherent, iterative and unoriginal is to compare it to a slightly earlier and longer, though less well known, text on poetics which seems to espouse many of the same ideas: Muriel Rukeyser's 1949 *The Life of Poetry*. Rukeyser's book is a significant document in its own right, putting similar arguments and resources to Olson's to use in a variety of strikingly different ways, notably as a direct cultural and political critique of the United States. Olson knew Rukeyser personally, meeting her at Kenneth Rexroth's home in San Francisco in 1947.[24] Rukeyser had read *Call Me Ishmael*, which she encouraged Olson to show to Hollywood studios as a 'shooting script'.[25] Olson read Rukeyser, though none of her works were found amongst his library upon his death, and there is no record of his having read *The Life of Poetry* either before or after the composition of 'Projective Verse'.[26] Beyond this biographical juncture, however, there are clear and at times even uncanny correspondences between aspects of Rukeyser and Olson's respective poetics, hopes expressed for the future of poetry of striking similarity, such that the one can usefully be read in the light of the other. The many similarities between Olson and Rukeyser's respective poetics provide a uniquely incisive opportunity to highlight the distinctive contribution Olson's essay made to mid-century poetics.

In this context it is instructive to speculate on why it was Olson's manifesto, and not Rukeyser's earlier and more fully fleshed book, which came to enjoy the broader currency. No doubt gendered prejudices were and are at play within this history of reception; what I want to focus on here nonetheless are the many similarities internal to these texts, in the hope of extracting some account of their subtle differences which will reveal what was felt to be new in Olson's essay, and what caused the excitement which surrounded its publication. I do not mean to allege here that Olson stole or suborned Rukeyser's ideas in order to pass them off as his own, or to engage in a debunking reading of either poet,

---

[24] Clark, *Charles Olson*, 125.
[25] See Ralph Maud, *Charles Olson at the Harbor* (Vancouver: Talon, 2008), 102–3. For more on Olson and the cinema, see the next chapter.
[26] Ralph Maud, *Charles Olson's Reading: A Biography* (Carbondale: Southern Illinois University Press, 1996), 85, 278.

but there *are* remarkable correspondences, which attest to a certain zeitgeist in mid-century American poetics of which Olson was only a part. Louise Kertesz writes that in much of her thinking, 'Rukeyser was well ahead of her time'; the obvious question, then, is why Rukeyser seems ahead of her time rather than Olson behind his.[27]

Though *The Life of Poetry* was published in New York only the year before 'Projective Verse' appeared, the ideas it contains had been long in development. In her first collection, *Theory of Flight*, from 1935, Rukeyser could already begin a poem with the line 'Breathe-in experience, breathe-out poetry': this Olson-like formulation would find several prose expressions in the work of 1949.[28] *The Life of Poetry* is a hybrid book, part a poetics, part a work of criticism, part an autobiography and part an impassioned plea for poetry as a tool of domestic and international pacifism, whereas 'Projective Verse' is manifesto-like, polemical and punchier. Despite Olson's latter-day reputation as *the* poet of breath, Rukeyser beat him to it by at least two decades: Rukeyser is insistent that 'the line in poetry – whether it be individual or traditional – is intimately bound with the poet's breathing. The line cannot go against the breathing rhythm of the poet.'[29] The assertion of an essential intimacy between poetic form and the individual poet's corporeality *as breath* is only minimally differentiated by Olson's parallel insistence on the primacy of the syllable (or 'head'), and even this is glancingly addressed by Rukeyser in her discussion of the syntactical innovations of Ernest Fenollosa, another shared source.[30]

In some degree, of course, both poets are drawing on and radicalizing the Whitmanian tradition of American poetry wherein the line is conceived of as a zone of extension. 'Projective Verse's concomitant claim that the typewriter allows for a minimally mediated correspondence between the poet's breath-as-line and *mis-en-page* – figuring 'the stave and the bar a musician has had' – was, as Olson himself notes, not an entirely new one, though his insistence on the typewriter as an instrument enabling accuracy and immediacy is characteristic.[31] Citing e. e. cummings, Rukeyser imagined 'a system of pauses which will be

---

[27] Louise Kertesz, *The Poetic Vision of Muriel Rukeyser* (Baton Rouge and London: Louisiana State University Press, 1980), 133–4. For another, British view on Rukeyser which similarly casts her as an ancestor to Olson, see Clive Bush, 'Muriel Rukeyser: The Poet as Scientific Biographer', in *Spanner Eleven* (London: Aloes, 1977), 1–22.
[28] Muriel Rukeyser, 'Poem Out of Childhood', in *A Muriel Rukeyser Reader*, ed. Jan Heller Levi (New York and London: Norton, 1994), 5.
[29] Muriel Rukeyser, *The Life of Poetry* (Ashfield: Paris Press, 1996; first published 1949), 117.
[30] Olson, 'Projective Verse', 242.
[31] Ibid., 245.

related to the time-pattern of the poem'.³² There is a shared desire here for a text which would act as a minimally mediated score for some kind of embodied and time-bound expression. The shape of the poem on the page must for both poets be considered a model for such an art of action, and not a received form governed by overdetermining convention.

This conception of form as fundamentally emergent is famously expressed in 'Projective Verse' via a phrase Olson took from Creeley, as part of their voluminous correspondence of the 1940s:

> FORM IS NEVER MORE THAN AN EXTENSION OF CONTENT. (Or so it got phrased to me by one, R. Creeley, and it makes absolute sense to me, with this possible corollary, that right form, in any given poem, is the only and exclusively possible extension of content under hand.)³³

This principle is again strongly connected with the breath-line diode: where the shape of the line is determined by the breath, by what is said (here, the 'CONTENT'), but not the other way around. This extensional model erases the putative distinction between form and content in a manner reminiscent of several statements in *The Life of Poetry*:

> The form and music of the fine poems are organic, they are not frames.³⁴

> The form and content have not yet reached their level, where one is a function of the other.³⁵

The refusal to conceive of form as a 'frame', as externally imposed delimiting determination, is a shared one; for both poets there are no formal decorations, no arabesques.³⁶ Each line, each form, is to be *completely proper* to the material at

---

[32] Rukeyser, *The Life of Poetry*, 117.
[33] Olson, 'Projective Verse', 240. The genesis of this famous passage is in Olson's letter to Creeley of 8 June 1950 (*Charles Olson & Robert Creeley: The Complete Correspondence, Volume 1*, ed. George F. Butterick (Santa Barbara: Black Sparrow, 1980, 85)); here Olson expands on a phrase from Creeley's letter of 5 June, which reads 'that form is never more than an *extension* of content' (79; emphasis in original). Creeley in turn seems to have been thinking of Wallace Stevens, who wrote in response to a questionnaire entitled 'The State of American Writing, 1948' that 'poetic form in its proper sense is a question of what appears in the poem itself' (Stevens, *Collected Poetry and Prose* (New York: Library of America, 1997), 822–5; 824).
[34] Rukeyser, *The Life of Poetry*, 30.
[35] Ibid., 39.
[36] Olson begins *Volume II* of *Maximus* 'With a leap (she said it was an arabesque / I made, off the porch, the night of the / St. Valentine's Day storm, into the snow' (171); note that 'she said' it was an arabesque, but for Olson the leap appears as a more integral and extensive gesture, one made not merely for effect. See also, for comparison, Beckett's essay 'Dante . . . Bruno . Vico . . . Joyce', in *Our Exagmination Round His Factification for Incamination of Work in Progress* (London: Faber, 1961; first published 1929), 1–22, in which it is stated that 'Here form *is* content, content *is* form' (14;

hand; form-content binaries are retired. Crucially, neither poet understands this form-content unity in terms of Cleanth Brooks's conception of the 'well-wrought urn', but rather as lively and processually inflected.[37] Form then is a matter of necessity rather than choice per se, but this is a necessity which is internally motivated rather than externally imposed. Rukeyser's assurance that 'fine poems are organic' finds subtle demurral in Olson, however, who prefers to think about organism rather than organicity – Olson's model of form is considerably more open-ended, less hypostatic, than Rukeyser's, and this is the key difference. Very broadly speaking, Olson's poems are less 'well formed', and become increasingly less so as his writing develops.

Both Rukeyser and Olson figure poiesis as constituted by the incoming of the external world ('Breathe-in experience, breathe-out poetry') such that poetry is plugged into, and effects, the shape of reality. Per their shared debt to Fenollosa, both understand this as a matter of kinetics and energy-flows. In a passage which discusses Fenollosa's *The Chinese Written Character as a Medium for Poetry*, Rukeyser writes that

> Exchange is creation.
>
> In poetry, the exchange is one of energy. Human energy is transferred, and from the poem it reaches the reader. Human energy, which is consciousness, the capacity to produce change in existing conditions.[38]

Olson's energetics propose a seemingly similar model, of the poem as kind of substation for the poet's kinetics: 'A poem is energy transferred from where the poet got it (he will have some several causations), by way of the poem itself to, all the way over to, the reader.'[39] The difference here is in the constitution of those energies. For Rukeyser, the stuff of the process is human consciousness; hers is a fundamentally humanist poetics, whereas Olson's is more diffuse, less anthropogenic. Speaking vaguely of the 'several causations' of poetic energy, Olson suggests that poems can be open to influences other than the authorial: the material and external world is not merely included in his poetics but potentially an active participant. The meaning and consequences of this claim are complex and lie at the heart of Olson's work. A distinction between Rukeyser's organicity

---

emphasis in original); interestingly, Beckett blames readers' 'decadence' and reliance on arbitrary form/content distinctions for the difficulties they find in Joyce (13).

[37] Cleanth Brooks, *The Well Wrought Urn: Studies in the Structure of Poetry* (San Diego, New York and London: Harvest, 1975; first published 1942).

[38] Rukeyser, *The Life of Poetry*, 173.

[39] Olson, 'Projective Verse', 240.

and Olson's organism is pertinent to these questions: for Rukeyser, the poem is self-contained and 'closed' insofar as its energies circulate entirely within the human realm, where energy is 'retained' within an organic propriety or closed ecosystem. Olson's energies are more dispersed and anonymous, and not only subject to but in some ways constituted by noise and loss of control. Determining-intentional authorship is abandoned, and formal energies are mediated by readers' pragmatic decisions rather than along predefined formal avenues.

This distinction can be clearly observed in the two poets' shared interest in poetic *speed*, which will be discussed in Chapter 2. 'Speed', for Rukeyser, is allied to something like 'efficiency', a well-maintained substation on a modern and comprehensive national grid, and in this her work might be more easily understood in the context of the 'clean' modernism of the Objectivists, the thirties poetry of Oppen and Zukofsky, than the considerably 'dirtier', noisier modernism (or postmodernism) of Olson (a considerable general difference can be felt in the way Olson and Rukeyser read their forbears: Rukeyser more approvingly, in many ways, than Olson). 'Projective Verse' ramifies this distinction not only conceptually but typographically, making a number of innovations in typeface, lineation and syntax which strain the category 'prose', as in the especially frenetic and impatient passage in which Olson holds forth on *his* conception of poetic speed:

> ONE PERCEPTION MUST IMMEDIATELY AND DIRECTLY LEAD TO A FURTHER PERCEPTION. [. . .] get on with it, keep moving, keep in, speed, the nerves, their speed, the perceptions, theirs, the acts, the split second acts, the whole business, keep it moving as fast as you can citizen.[40]

In stark contrast to Rukeyser's parsimony, Olson's writing has the declarative punch of the manifesto here, writing in praise of the rash and instinctual, in the radically paratactical style which became his signature essayistic mode – and which makes so much of his prose so difficult to construe. Rather than as slickness or concentration, here Olson describes poetic speed in terms of tearing and dissolution. There is little 'economy' to Olson's writing in this sense – 'Projective Verse' is in many ways remarkably spendthrift and wasteful in its rhetoric and gestures, with much that might be construed as vestigial, bombastic and nonsensical, as well as derivative. Indeed this has not infrequently been the

---

[40] Olson, 'Projective Verse', 240. Emphasis in original.

conclusion critics have come to.[41] This waste is nonetheless necessary rather than decorative in Olson's understanding, provoking a zone of indeterminacy which allows things to happen rather than simply to be expressed. In some sense poetic speed is for Olson a technique-against-technique, a radical attempt to loosen the bonds of poetic competency understood either as a New Critical mastery of organic form; as Eliot's authority of the 'Tradition' against which all else must be judged and in the context of which everything is made; or as the skilful suggestiveness of symbolism.

Olson thinks of process and objecthood as essential partners in poetry. In the second section of the essay, he describes his position as 'Objectism', a term he imagines emerging from and superseding the Objectivist tradition, having no truck with 'subjectivism' and insisting on the objecthood of everything, up to and including poets and poems. Olson is clear that 'the reality of verse' is distinct from 'that other dispersed and distributed thing' (i.e. reality at large, outside the poem), but that nonetheless poems are real objects, or acts of autonomous reality, and as such are not merely subjects to the whims of human consciousness.[42] What is being suggested here is that there is something deeply unpredictable about poetry and its production, such that the outcome of the poetic process can never be decided or predicted in advance – emergent form produces poetry with a degree of autonomy which cannot be explained-away as misidentified human agency even if it is an epiphenomenon of human action. A poem can be understood as an object distinct from either its author or its reader, with an autotelic processual capacity.

In its latter manifestations Olson's poetics tends towards burnout and dissolution, but in 1950 the primary gesture was a dismissive one, the removal of the old, making space for an as yet undefined new. Olson was deeply invested in contradiction, in poems allowed, as he writes in 'Projective Verse', to 'keep [...] their proper confusions'.[43] This matter of propriety is perhaps the major point of rupture between the poetics outlined in *The Life of Poetry* and those found in 'Projective Verse': What is the poem in itself? Rukeyser thinks in terms of organically generated determinate expression; Olson's understanding of poetry is more amorphous and open-ended.

* * *

---

[41] See Perloff's 'Charles Olson and the "Inferior Predecessors": Projective Verse Revisited', *ELH* 40 (Summer 1973): 285–306, which is critical of Olson on exactly these grounds.
[42] Olson, 'Projective Verse', 244.
[43] Ibid., 244.

'Projective Verse's innovation is located precisely in its validation of 'confusion' – a commitment to that within writing which is neither determinate nor carefully constructed and controlled. Though many of its individual prescriptions are cut of much the same cloth as those proposed by Rukeyser, the ends to which these are put are in several ways radically different. 'Confusion' is a useful term in thinking about much of Olson's writing even after 'Projective Verse' passes into the background of his work and the 'Objectism' he somewhat obscurely outlines has been dropped entirely as a rhetoric. Much of what appears obscure, wasteful, arbitrary and meaningless in *Maximus*, for example, can be better understood if it is read as part of a sustained attempt to bind what seems incoherent or nonsensical in poiesis into a fractured and contradictory whole, even where that attempt never becomes successful or finally determined. Considered in this light, the 'openness' of 'open verse' is in great degree a result of the 'proper confusion' of the poetic object as Olson understood and created it. This involved a sustained, and in a certain sense impossible, struggle to retain and communicate often incongruous impulses, impressions and actions in writing in such a way as to transfer the stuff of the poem *immediately*, where the inevitability of mediation creates a distance between the imagined formation of the poetic resources on the one hand and their actual formation on the other, allowing for an indeterminate openness: 'I take it that PROJECTIVE VERSE teaches, is, this lesson, that that verse will only do in which a poet manages to register both the acquisitions of his ear *and* the pressures of his breath.'[44] The 'input' of the poem has 'some several causations', as Olson describes them, both from internal, corporeal sources (body, breath) and from external influences (readings, landscapes, dreams), but there is no guarantee that these will be easily reconcilable, and as a result the poem's 'output' will be less than ideally formed – it will be a somewhat confused object.[45] At Black Mountain, Olson tutored his students in the 'kinetics of experience' – a technique for replicating and extending the energy of real life into real art.[46] The upshot of this in Olson's own work is that his writing is pointedly literal, often to the brink of artlessness. The change in poetics which puts writing 'beyond the technical' means abandoning 'artificial' received forms, techniques and externally licensed limits in favour of a drive towards immediacy, the notational and the everyday; even the 'techniques' Olson outlines in 'Projective Verse' are provisional insofar as they are useful only

---

[44] Ibid., 241. Emphasis in original.
[45] Olson's interest in Weiner's *Cybernetics* may have suggested this 'input-output' model.
[46] Quoted in Duberman, *Black Mountain*, 371.

until they can be overcome and replaced with even more literal, direct tactics. Along, then, with received form Olson increasingly displaces the received functions of poetry understood as reflective, symbolic or allusive.

In this context it is important to emphasize a frequently overlooked aspect of 'Projective Verse's critique of existing poetry: its opposition to reading for construal, congruence and the correlative quest for meaning of the sort I have associated with Empson and Richards. This sort of 'decoding' reading practice is the object of an underappreciated assault in the essay. The distaste for New Critical reading protocols Olson shared with Rukeyser is demonstrated not only as disregard for specific kinds of formal virtuosity but also as rejection of the hermeneutic practices common to that school of literary-critical thought. In shifting emphasis from the symbolic to the literal, Olson simultaneously engages in a search for, or a reclamation of, poetic fundamentals which he feels have been 'lost [. . .] in the sweetness of metre and rime, in a honey-head'.[47] These fundamental particles of poetry, its proper matter, are represented in 'Projective Verse' by the breath on the one hand and the syllable on the other. The foregrounding of these elements radically changes the stakes of poetic language, as Olson writes,

> It would do no harm, as an act of correction to both prose and verse as now written, if both rime and meter, and, in the quantity words, both sense and sound, were less in the forefront of the mind than the syllable, if the syllable, that fine creature, were more allowed to lead the harmony on. With this warning, to those who would try: to step back here to this place of the elements and the minims of language, is to engage speech where it is least careless – and least logical.[48]

Given that Olson's 'harmony' is almost always geared towards dissonance rather than consonance, readers might reasonably infer that the clash of sound is likely to be mirrored in the clash of sense, in contradiction, throat-clearing, paraverbal tics, meandering logics. The implication here is that even if writing with a 'projective' poetics vitiates the technical preciosity of the well-wrought urn, it is nonetheless minimally careless with regard to the operation and material of language itself – to the degree that it almost abandons imposing logic on that language in favour of unleashing its inner workings so that the syllable itself, rather than the poet's shepherding it into metre, takes the lead. This demotion

---

[47] Olson, 'Projective Verse', 241.
[48] Ibid.

of the importance of sense is a crucial part of 'Projective Verse's movement into a new zone of poetic creation. Historically it can be understood as an extension of the paratactical style of Pound and Williams, which worked in part to replace explicit connecting and causal logics and semantic precision with a more flexible and inscrutable chaining of phrases, quotations and other verbal material; what Olson's open, projective writing adds to this is an explicit focus on that material as itself the object of the poem's action, such that the poetic material is no longer overdetermined by anterior forms.

The proliferation of various incomplete thematic readings of 'Projective Verse' since its publication and subsequent absorption into the accepted canon of avant-garde poetics resulted from the text's concerted attempt not to 'make sense' at that thematic level of construal. The essay does not attempt to propose a consistent, original or delimitable set of techniques or 'types' of poetry writing, but rather to unlearn a range of techniques and tactics for reading and writing poetry which it suggests have led to a misplaced certainty regarding the question of what poetry actually *is*. In this sense it is more deeply invested in the 'input' of elements than the 'output' of themes or construable discourse, which is to say it is more concerned with beginning a writing method than in mastering it. Furthermore, Olson is clear that 'Projective Verse' is not a complete theory but rather a sally into relatively unmapped territory and a brief report back on what appear to be the major landmarks therein. He writes that

> an analysis of how far a new poet can stretch the very conventions on which communication by language rests, is too big for these notes, which are meant, I hope it is obvious, merely to get things started.
>
> Let me just throw in this. It is my impression that *all* parts of speech suddenly, in composition by field, are fresh for both sound and percussive use, spring up like unknown, unnamed vegetables in the patch, when you work it, come spring.[49]

The 'prospective' aspect of Olson's formulation for a 'projective' poetics here includes not only the writing of the future, the work to come, but also the emergent, autotelic nature of those works themselves, which bud forth with unexpected fruit, amongst which one might 'go prospecting' without prejudice or predetermining knowledge of form, genre or class. This is a vision of poetry profoundly liberated from critical, formal or discursive norms, one in which the

---

[49] Ibid., 244. The continuity between Olson's surprise vegetables and Cage's guerrilla mushrooms, described in Chapter 3, is an instructive one.

freed particles of language begin to follow their own natures under the hand of the poet. Labour is still necessary here, perhaps even more intensive because less prefigured, but the manner and matter of poetic work is changed in very many significant ways. Insofar as Olson exhorts poets to stop making sense, it is only so that their 'senses' more broadly understood, along with those of their readers, may become better attuned to what language itself is capable of doing and of being. This is the permission-giving gesture which seems to have drawn so many later poets to read and use 'Projective Verse' in such a variety of ways.

In this can be seen the fundamentally indeterminate core both of 'Projective Verse' and of Olson's later writing, which attempts to open itself to what *might* happen rather than to what 'should' or 'ought' to happen in writing labelled 'poetry'. Rather than a set of rules or 'tips for writers', the essay is best seen as a forceful smashing of poetic idols and a scavenging through the resultant pieces for what is still of use – a 'hunt among stones' as Olson writes in 'The Kingfishers'.[50] If, for Rukeyser, poetry must always be at base discursively coherent, complete in-and-of-itself, such that 'the treatment of correspondence (metaphor, analogy) is always that of a two-part equilibrium in which the parts are self-contained', then Olson's 'change beyond, and larger than, the technical' realigns the connection between part and whole, a supersession of *techne* by freedom of poiesis, the normative 'ought' embodied in received forms of expression replaced by an undecideable 'is'.[51] The various metaphorical and analogical levels of 'Projective Verse' – breath, energy, fields – do not line up as part of an 'equilibrium', and as a result correspondence and self-containment give way to free play, emergence and unbalanced formal and rhetorical structures. Poetic composition becomes, at its very root, *experimental*, reliant on the varieties of experience which can be gleaned both from language and from extra-poetic reality. If the 'new stance to reality' Olson prophesies seems vague or phantasmal it is only because such a new stance can only be brought out through the process, and cannot easily be characterized in advance of that process's use.

From this vantage, 'Projective Verse' can be seen as an errant part of the tradition which Perloff describes as 'the "anti-Symbolist" mode'.[52] Olson's work can be understood as more clearly of a piece with the interdisciplinarity of Black Mountain College, with the chance-structures of Cage or with the *matière* studies of Albers, within which emphasis is placed on the fundamentals

---

[50] Olson, *Collected Poems*, 93.
[51] Rukeyser, *The Life of Poetry*, 166.
[52] Perloff, *The Poetics of Indeterminacy*, vii.

of art, on art's materials and how to use them so that they take their native, intrinsic forms. Indeterminacy here means stepping back from formal and expressive overdetermination and reimagining poiesis as an act of discovery – a diode between world and text rather than between mind and text. Writing is then engaged in a constant process of self-revision and self-revolution, a process familiar to any reader of *The Maximus Poems* who has observed the characteristic unspooling and amendment of the textual protocols of Olson's book as it progresses through the fifties and sixties, arriving at a point at which the technical recommendations of 'Projective Verse' have passed almost entirely beyond the writing's horizon. This autotelic process of self-overcoming, which Lisa Siraganian has described as a development in which '[Olson's] poetics become almost impossibly dialectical', is in fact a vector for unbound *possibility* in poetic production.[53] The theses 'Projective Verse' proposes are only ever made meaningful by antithetical interrogation and use, by the freedom which this reflexive process provides for the development of further indeterminate poetic protocols, production equally evident in Olson's own later work and in that of others. Ultimately this means that the essay is only a stepping stone, an object for 'USE USE USE', as Olson insists repeatedly in the essay: a structure not to be believed in but to be employed as part of 'our management of daily reality as of the daily work'.[54] 'Projective Verse' is a stage of development to be absorbed and overcome, and a point of departure rather than a destination. In this sense, its fullest expression is to be found precisely in the huge diversity of writing and writing practices it has been instrumental in fostering, in its instigation of a new access to the epic, the 'unknown, unnamed' which follows after. *The Maximus Poems* may not be explicitly within the sights of 'Projective Verse', but the model of a looser, less determined longform for the poem has been prospectively established.

---

[53] Lisa Siraganian, *Modernism's Other Work: The Art Object's Political Life* (Oxford: Oxford University Press, 2012), 150.
[54] Olson, 'Projective Verse', 240. This 'USE' formulation, central to Olson's poetics, appears first in *Call Me Ishmael*; its roots can perhaps also be traced to Creeley's letter of 5 June 1950 (*Correspondence Volume I*, 78): 'Here/ of course: myth: IS in the air/ and none to do more than MAKE USE OF it in reasoning/ in apprehension of what might be around'.

2

Poetics of speed

Mediation in *Maximus*

Amongst the most unhelpful of 'Projective Verse's prescriptions is the stress it seems to place on *mis-en-page* via its organismic account of form-content unity.[1] In thereby prioritizing the *surface* of the text, as a two-dimensional plane, a reading of Olson's poetics which foregrounds *mis-en-page* risks obscuring a more significant problem for reading *Maximus* as a long work: the question of readerly speed. This is a question both of the speed of reading itself as a process in time and the speed of the thinking that practice enables and leads to.[2] This is most clearly observable when the difference between reading in the moment (the cognition or thought process that reading consists in) and thinking about the reading after the moment (reflection or criticism) is considered. Simply put, the experience of reading *The Maximus Poems* as an immersive, expansive longform text is difficult to reconcile with that more focused and precise (or precision-oriented) type of reading involving reflection and analysis, best exemplified by the practices of close reading which continue to be integral to most forms of criticism. It is my contention in this chapter that *Maximus* can best be read at fairly high speed, with a sort of restless attention, and indeed that the protocols it operates according to lend it to such a reading. Much of the critical uncertainty surrounding Olson's long poem, the way in which a given reading or interpretation never quite seems to be a finished or sufficient activity, can be put down to this difficulty of reconciliation between two speeds of reading. The relationship between the extrinsically observed parts of *Maximus* and the intrinsically experienced whole is characterized not by a settled, mappable

---

[1] For a reading of *Maximus* which attempts to find significance in 'sectors' of the page, see Paul Christensen, *Charles Olson: Call Him Ishmael* (Austin and London: University of Texas, 1979; first published 1975).
[2] On time in the reading of long poems, see Ron Silliman, '"As to Violin Music": Time in the Longpoem', *Jacket* 27 (April 2005). http://jacketmagazine.com/27/silliman.html.

structure but rather by moveable and moving sequence and the running or interruption of that sequence, the various manipulations that readers can put it through.

Olson was far from the only twentieth-century poet interested in energetic, speedy writing; such concerns can be traced back to the Futurism of F. T. Marinetti, most notably; Marinetti's manifesto-style likely filtered somewhat into the rhetoric of 'Projective Verse'. Olson's averred interest in poetic immediacy – a major concern in 'Projective Verse' which remains with his writing from thereon out – can be understood as part of a poetic tradition insistent on accelerative, kinetic models for writing. This is an impulse with many sources, but one perhaps most handily anchored in the work of Ernest Fenollosa, whose influence on American modernism in the Poundian vein is well-recognized.[3] A useful point of departure can be found in Fenollosa's much-cited belief that, under the sign of Chinese character-writing, '[t]he type of a sentence in nature is a flash of lightening. It passes between two terms, a cloud and the earth.'[4] Here literary modernism's profound interest in speed and directness, of grammar, of expression, of imagery and of perception, is succinctly expressed: the speed of light is a matter of plainly modernist concern. The particular focus in this chapter will be on speed as it concerns perception in reading. The kinetic model of poetry Olson proposes in 'Projective Verse' relies primarily on an idea of 'energy transfer' between poet and reader which describes the textual medium of the poem as a field of mutual labour in which unexpected effects can be produced. Poetry is said to transmit not so much a predetermined meaning or 'affect' as a set of dynamics which can be variously formulated so as to retain a type of energetic immediacy. As a result the question of media and of *im*mediacy is put front and centre, such that poetry is understood not as a message but as precisely a middle point which allows for certain sorts of agential action on the part of the medium *and* of the receiver-reader; speed is not merely the product of the medium itself but is cooperative. Here there is 'no medium' in Craig Dworkin's sense that media are only ever present as 'collectives', and no medium can exist as sole or isolated.[5] Poetry is always intermedial – always a gathering together of various actors who negotiate it.

---

[3] See Achilles Fang, 'Fenollosa and Pound', *Harvard Journal of Asiatic Studies* 20 (June 1957): 213–38.

[4] Ernest Fenollosa, 'The Chinese Written Character as a Medium for Poetry: An Ars Poetica', in Fenollosa and Ezra Pound, *The Chinese Written Character as a Medium for Poetry: A Critical Edition*, eds. Haun Saussy, Jonathan Stalling and Lucas Klein (New York: Fordham University Press, 2008), 41–60; 47.

[5] Craig Dworkin, *No Medium* (Cambridge and London: MIT, 2013), 28, 30.

In framing an inspection of Olson's poetics as an inspection of media, there is an opportunity to revisit a number of the central dynamics of literary modernism in a somewhat new light, insofar as traditional critical talking points about fragmentation, broken forms (and so on) fail to emphasize the way in which modernist poetics is equally interested in creating new modes of intermedial connection to replace the supposed univocity of the received formal medium ('organic form'). It is a commonplace of modernist manifestos and statements of poetics that they draw analogies between poetry and other media, to music, painting, calligraphy and so on.[6] These petitions of other arts are not simply allegorical systems – as, for example, with the 'music of the spheres' rhetoric which dominated much seventeenth-century poetics – but rather attempts to redescribe technical problems within writing – at, say, as basic a level as that of grammar and syntax – by appeals to and appropriation of the techniques of other media. Here I want to think about intermediality and its relation to poetry's speed via a thoroughgoingly modernist medium – film.[7] In this I follow David Trotter, who has argued for an understanding of the literature-film relation in modernism based not on simile or likeness but rather on 'parallel histories' between 'adjacent inscriptive media'.[8] Modernist writing did not, for the most part, attempt to create effects for readers 'like' those enjoyed by cinema audiences (e.g. to mimic camera movements or shot-sequencing), but rather looked to the technical aspects of filmic production as inspirational and instructive.[9] Olson's poetry contains no reference to particular works of cinema; rather its concern is with the technological apparata which produce film. It is these machines and their operations which appear in the discourse of *Maximus* and which provide a parallel or exemplar for the speed of Olson's poetic production. The important connection was not between poetry and cinema (the narrative medium) but between poetry and film (the technical medium). Modernist writers were not simply copying film; the intermedial relationship was both more conversational than this, and more critical. In other words, poets *read* film as critically and creatively as they did the writings of their contemporaries and forbears.

---

[6] The multimedia ethos of the Bauhaus, which filtered through into the teaching at Black Mountain, is a useful touchstone here. László Moholy-Nagy, a key Bauhaus figure, wrote in *Vision in Motion* (Chicago: Cuneo, 1947) of the relation between cinema's projection and the other arts (283).
[7] The critical literature on film and modernist poetry is extensive. Recent work relevant to my argument here includes Lawrence Goldstein, *The American Poet at the Movies: A Critical History* (Ann Arbor: University of Michigan Press, 1995); Susan McCabe, *Cinematic Modernism: Modernist Poetry and Film* (Cambridge: Cambridge University Press, 2005).
[8] David Trotter, 'T.S. Eliot and Cinema', *Modernism/Modernity* 13, no. 2 (April 2006): 237–65; 239; 241.
[9] Ibid., 238.

Plenty of poets of the early century were thinking and writing about film in precisely the terms described, as here in Rukeyser:

> If you can be flexible of mind, remember movies you have liked, and being aware of their richness and suspense and the dense texture of their realities, you are approaching what may have seemed to you the most broken of modern poetry.[10]

Movies here are not similes for unfamiliar modernist poetics. Rather they serve a fundamentally corrective function; modern poetry may seem 'broken', but it isn't. A better understanding of film helps us to better read poetic modernism, and vice versa. What can save this passage and others like it from being subsumed into banal and overdetermining accounts of 'modernist fragmentation' is reading it as an example of intermedial thinking concerned with juncture and connection. The modernist poem, Rukeyser writes, has 'dense texture', as does cinema; it is not characterized by pathologically 'broken' form but by new models of connectivity. These textures have speed because they have *velocity*, vectors which they travel, threads to follow. These are temporal and processual, as opposed to the abstracted ideality of the unified form which is theoretically removed and preserved from time.

The question of poetry's speed is then not so much one of the relation between form and content as between part and whole.[11] The denseness Rukeyser alludes to is more easily felt in the whole's process than in the isolation of the part, since, as with cinema, poetry can move through various seemingly insubstantial parts fairly quickly, thus creating a density which inheres in the depth of the book rather than the surface of any given page. It has often been said that modernist poetics is in this sense 'like' cinematic montage, creating a seeming continuity between distinct parts through the agglutinative powers of speed. Marjorie Perloff links this montage poetics to Pound's *The Cantos*, and quotes from a passage of Sergei Eisenstein's *The Film Sense* which directly links montage to part-whole relations:

> Eisenstein, who shared Pound's predilection for the ideogrammatic technique of Chinese poetry, defined *montage* as follows:
>
>> The juxtaposition of two separate shots by splicing them together resembles not so much a simple sum of one shot plus another shot – as it does a *creation*. It resembles a creation – rather than a sum of its parts – from the circumstance

---

[10] Rukeyser, *The Life of Poetry*, 19.
[11] See Chapter 6 for a fuller discussion of troublesome part-whole relations in Olson's poetics.

that in every such juxtaposition *the result is qualitatively* distinguishable from each component element viewed separately.

To put it another way, when image A is juxtaposed to image B, it loses its status as A and becomes a link in what Eisenstein calls 'a chain of representations'.[12]

Eisenstein claims that the 'creativity' of montage is a result of its derangement of part-whole relations such that montage is not merely a matter of accumulation but of emergence, where parts and wholes do not quite line up; indeed, as Susan McCabe has observed, 'montage fractures while it embodies', such that '[w]hile a painting may be seen as a whole in a moment of time, cinema cannot be reflected upon "all at once"'.[13] In other words, film's coherence is predicated on a fundamental fractiousness which confounds the organicist model of part-whole relations. Perloff discusses this as a juxtapositionary poetics, but I think here it is important to emphasize that a certain speed and velocity of representation is the mechanism which enables montage to work *as montage* rather than as simply a promenade or gallery. In cinema this mechanism is the condition of the possibility of the art, but some of the principle is exportable to poetry reading as a strategy for thinking through the question of speed. Perloff's discussion is based in a Poundian vorticist model, which is predicated not on speed but rather force. Here speed will be the model used to reinterpret modernist energetics, through an account of the parallels between Olson's poetry and film, that is, an account of what Olson saw or learnt about perceptual speed through his acquaintance with film.

***

A pronounced though under-recognized cinephilia accompanied Olson's literary career, and in fact predated it. His biographer Tom Clark notes that 'the cinema had possessed a magnetic attraction for [Olson] since even before his first inklings that he would become a writer', and his early literary career was tightly intertwined with his cinematic enthusiasms.[14] Having honed an interest in film as an undergraduate at Wesleyan, Olson was, by the time he commenced his PhD at Harvard in 1936, a keen-enough cinema-buff to merit a senior role in the university's Film Society, for which he provided introductory

---

[12] Perloff, *The Poetics of Indeterminacy*, 180. The inset quote is from Eisenstein, *The Film Sense*, trans. Jay Leyda (New York: Faber, 1975; first published 1947), 7–8.
[13] McCabe, *Cinematic Modernism*, 5, 60.
[14] Clark, *Charles Olson*, 127.

talks to each screening (these showings featured Leonard Bernstein on piano accompaniment). Despite a successful academic history and strong intellectual endorsement from F. O. Matthiessen and others, Olson was unwilling to complete his doctoral work on Herman Melville, and left Harvard in 1938, disgruntled with the methods and mores of institutional academia. For most of the next decade he laboured, with the aid of a Guggenheim Fellowship, to complete the work in isolation. The result was published in 1947 as *Call Me Ishmael*, his study of *Moby Dick*. In that same year, encouraged by Eisenstein's enthusiasm for his book, Olson travelled cross-continent to Hollywood, where he panhandled for a job writing on John Huston's ill-fated cinematic adaptation of Melville's novel. (Olson met Rukeyser during this trip.) All this, which Olson would relate to Pound at St Elizabeths hospital as 'my adventure in Hollywood, and young Huston's story of Jack Warner and the Whale', ultimately came to nothing.[15] Though Huston was impressed by Olson's knowledge of Melville, and encouraged him to seek a position on the production, the film was fast becoming impractical and overexpensive, and the studio executive Warner shut it down only a week after their meeting. Olson's career in the movies was over.

By early 1948, however, Olson was beginning his work as a poet. Material for his first collection, *Y & X*, was sent to Caresse Crosby at Black Sun Press in May; the pamphlet was published, along with illustrations by Corrado Cagli, in 1950. Olson immediately began to worry about where the next poetry was to come from, and to look for a new modus operandi. In the summer of 1950 'The Kingfishers', perhaps Olson's most famous single poem, was published in *Montevallo Review*. 'The Kingfishers' exemplified a poetic breakthrough for Olson, a new way of conceptualizing and practising poetry, a way often associated with 'Projective Verse', which appeared late in the year, and it is here that the continuing story of Olson's cinematic interests can be most easily inferred.[16] What follows is an attempted reading of 'Projective Verse' and *Maximus* as works in various ways concerned with or functioning in suggestive parallel to the operations of film. This reading will bring to light some aspects of what I am here calling the long poem's 'speed'. Olson's call for an energetic poetical

---

[15] Charles Olson, 'GrandPa, GoodBye', in *Collected Prose*, 145–51; 146. Huston would finally complete the project a decade later, with Ray Bradbury writing the adaptation.

[16] On 'The Kingfishers' and 'Projective Verse', see Guy Davenport, 'Scholia and Conjectures for Olson's "The Kingfishers"', *boundary 2* 2, nos. 1–2 (Fall 1973; Winter 1974): 250–62; especially 262: '"The Kingfishers" is a projection [. . .] of intersecting events'; and Christensen, *Charles Olson*, 17: '"The Kingfishers", [. . .] constituted a successful breakthrough to a new technique of versification. [Olson] could now with confidence begin to write his own manifesto for poetry, "Projective Verse".'

communication bears a marked rhetorical debt to the operation of cinematic representation and communication: the 'projective' is in a loose correspondence with the 'projector'. My claim is that this rhetoric points to Olson's youthful cinephilia as a source of inspiration and instruction for his own speedy, fissive acts of inscription. The point here is not to argue that *Maximus* is a 'film poem', but rather that the parallel is a useful tool in attempting to think about reading it, and other modernist long poems.[17]

***

That the poets of the early twentieth century enjoyed going to the movies is so well established a fact as now to be banal. But one thing this enthusiasm makes evident is the degree to which the tools of reading (and, by extension, the tools of writing) were brought to bear on media which had not and are not traditionally conceived of as 'literary', without any concomitant prejudice against their literary usefulness (or 'USE', as Olson might have it). In fact it was precisely the problems of mediation these differing media posed which made them useful. This was of course true of the much older relationship between writing and painting or music; but the new recording technologies popularized in the twentieth century (phonograph, radio, film and latterly television) foregrounded these complex issues just as mediation became an explicit concern of modernist writing and its inheritors.

Olson's conception of poetry makes the poem's text a *mediator* in a poetic 'field' rather than the single 'object'-location of poetry itself. The central innovative aspect of 'Projective Verse' is crucially an *innervative* one, investing poetry with a dynamic structure or nervous energy: 'A poem is energy transferred from where the poet got it [. . .] by way of the poem itself to, all the way over to, the reader.'[18] This conception of a poem as a vehicle for relay between a source – in experience or in knowledge – and a receiver – reader or auditor – is one of the characteristic tenets of 'Projective Verse', providing a foundation for Olson's kinetic poetics of process and his phenomenological concerns. Poetry has some several objects for Olson, of which text is only one. 'Projective Verse' insists that the poem operate not according to a text-mind diode but rather a text-body/

---

[17] For an example of a contemporaneous longform poem that is committedly filmic, see Lynette Roberts, *Gods with Stainless Ears* in *Collected Poems*, ed. Patrick McGuiness (Manchester: Carcanet, 2005), 43–78. In the Preface: 'The scenes and visions ran before me like a newsreel' (43).
[18] Olson, 'Projective Verse', 240.

world diode ('Because breath allows *all* the speech-force of language back in (speech is the "solid" of verse, is the secret of a poem's energy), because, now, a poem has, by speech, solidity') in which the written text serves to transfer the physical energetic state of the poet in a moment to his audience *as a physical energetic state.*[19] Text is a replicator, but a troublesome one in that it requires constant intervention and calibration on the part of readers. No one goes to the cinema to watch the equipment; the illusion of a film is in part predicated on its not acknowledging itself as a mechanical process happening *behind* the audience.[20] The cinematic equipment is a mediation we are encouraged to forget, but the textual equipment of an Olson poem is in many ways at the forefront as the zone of poetic activity, where certain expectations of reading are fulfilled or frustrated, and where decisions about readerly protocol are made, in the sense, for example, that readers might try to read his poetic 'as a projection' or 'as a projector'.

The text of the poem is more than a mechanism for Olson, though it has mechanistic aspects. Poetry as such has been located interstitially. This is initially counter-intuitive. 'Projective Verse' invests itself in 'composition by field', in painstaking and particular placement of words at any possible point on the initially blank page; Olson's poetry is typographically remarkable, if not exactly unprecedented in the context of contemporaneous writing. Why then would he theoretically denigrate the solidity of the textual in favour of a more dynamic and indeterminate arrangement?

> the *principle*, the law which presides conspicuously over such composition, and, when obeyed, is the reason why a projective poem can come into being. It is this: FORM IS NEVER MORE THAN AN EXTENSION OF CONTENT.[21]

The salient aspect of Olson's *mis-en-page* is that it has not so much an *expressive* function as a *necessary* one. The form the poem takes is imagined as constituted by the poet's perceptions; it 'extends' that source over to its audience. The more transformative aspect of its extension will be returned to.

Poetry in this formulation is a kinetic rather than a static construct, changing-through-itself as a lesson in 'how to dance / sitting down'.[22] The role of poetry as

---

[19] Ibid., 244.
[20] It has been repeatedly observed that the movie theatre is spatially organized in a manner very similar to Plato's cave, as described in the *Republic*. Olson's foregrounding of the projective mechanism can in this sense be read as an indication of his anti-Platonism.
[21] Olson, 'Projective Verse', 240. Emphasis in original.
[22] Olson, *Maximus*, 39.

embodiment of 'source' rather than its mere description dictates that it cannot simply contain a state or a passive object but must instead treat it as movement, action. Constructing form thus organically means that Olson's poetics is primarily concerned with

> the *process* of the thing, how the principle can be made so to shape the energies that the form is accomplished. And I think it can be boiled down to one statement (first pounded into my head by Edward Dahlberg): ONE PERCEPTION MUST IMMEDIATELY AND DIRECTLY LEAD TO A FURTHER PERCEPTION. It means exactly what it says, is a matter of, at *all* points (even, I should say, of our management of daily reality as of the daily work) get on with it, keep moving, keep in, speed, the nerves, their speed, the perceptions, theirs, the acts, the split second acts, the whole business, keep it moving as fast as you can, citizen. And if you also set up as a poet, USE USE USE the process at all points, in any given poem always, always one perception must must must MOVE, INSTANTER, ON ANOTHER!
>
> So there we are, fast, there's the dogma. And its excuse, its useableness, in practice.[23]

The pertinence of this passage is twofold: the injunction to speed and its subsequent insistence on the rapid continuity of perceptions ('fast' here as in both 'speedy' and 'firm', with the implication of an energy which holds things together rather than splits them apart). Rather than settling or meditating on a single perception – image, thought, surface – the poem drives down through a series of dynamic points of perception, a 'process' of energetic procession through gathering depth rather than across a plane. This procession of perceptions need not be traditionally syntactical and logical, only continuous, a case of 'USE' rather than of sense. At a fundamental level it is a matter of representing reality (however naive this effort may prove) rather than telling a story or making an argument: 'it means exactly what it says', that is, it means, for Olson, exactly what it *is*.[24] Embodiment takes precedence over explication.

The speed of perception in the poem is to resemble the speed of the 'management of daily reality as of the daily work': the mode of representation is to be analogous to the body in its everyday actions – 'the nerves, their speed, the perceptions, theirs, the acts, the split second acts, the whole business, keep it

---

[23] Olson, 'Projective Verse', 240. Emphasis in original.
[24] See Charles Olson, 'Causal Mythology', in *Muthologos: Lectures and Interviews*, 2nd ed., ed. Ralph Maud (Vancouver: Talon, 2010), 115–34; 122: 'that which exists through itself is what is called meaning.'

moving as fast as you can'. For Olson, the spasms, tics and tremors of the human perceptual apparatus provide the exemplar and limit for experience, in which the speed of electrochemical nerve impulses is the maximum, and thus desirable and necessary, pace of the poem's process; nervous activity is to the human body as parataxis is to the poem. Speed is to be involuntary, the absolute necessity, 'must must must', a flash of lightning. The perceptions will follow each other so rapidly and consecutively that they seem contiguous, not just 'instant' but with the hyperbolic illusion agitated for by Olson's 'INSTANTER, ON ANOTHER', as awarenesses blurred between and overlaid on each other. The poem is proposed as sharing in a state of perception – or an order of perceptions – analogous to what in psychology is termed the 'phi phenomenon', by which a succession of still frames of film appear to move when exposed to calculated regimes of speed and light.[25] Read in the context of Olson's cinephilia, I claim here that there are suggestive parallels between an energetic poetics of process on the one hand and the operation of a film-projector on the other, haunting Olson's thought as it is articulated in 'Projective Verse'. A kinetic poetics, one founded on (or held 'fast' by) a conceptual knot of speed, light, electricity, heat and entropy, allies itself to a *kinematic* poetics.

That alliance is an unsteady and speculative one. It is nowhere explicit, and, even where present as a tangible conceptual rhyme, any Olsonian film-poetics poses at least as many questions as it can answer. The twofold suggestiveness this poetics owes the cinema, as outlined above, leaves two serious difficulties in its wake: How is the method of a visual medium, cinema, to map onto an intellective, semantic and only secondarily imagistic art like poetry, especially if that poetry pointedly foregrounds speech over text? And how is the poem thereby to replicate, to take the correct 'stance toward reality', when the phi phenomenon is in its essence an optical trick? How, in other words, is poetry to handle the illusionary immediacy of 'INSTANTER'?

* * *

The machinic character of Olson's poetics has not gone unnoticed by previous critics. Heriberto Yépez has observed how in 'Projective Verse'

> one of the most paradigmatic essays of North American poetics takes as its fundamental concern how to pass the breath of the body (sexual) to the

---

[25] For an overview of theoretical discussion concerning cinema's realism/illusion, see Sheila Johnston, 'Film Narrative and the Structuralist Controversy', in *The Cinema Book*, ed. Pam Cook (London: BFI, 1985), 222–50.

replacement body (the textual body). 'Projective Verse' is a tract about how to make a text into a living body that breathes – assisted, says Olson, by the mechanographic machine [the typewriter] – how to make of the text, one might say, a *Frankenstein* or *spiritual cyborg*.[26]

Yépez is directly addressing Olson's poetic manifesto here, but he is thinking also of *The Maximus Poems*, and the giant body of 'Maximus' as both pseudo-persona of or sharer-of-space with Olson, and as a sprawling literary *corpus* of over 600 pages, alive and dead simultaneously. Yépez conceives of the mechanical-linguistic body Olson structures through 'Maximus' as a forerunner of postmodernity and an early sally into the realm of the posthuman; more specifically, it is a 'remix' or cathartic juxtaposition of personalities and bodies designed to homogenize and subsume the contradictions of American civilization. Yépez reads the cinematic content of *The Maximus Poems* as a hollowing out of and flight from Olson's anxieties about his own corporeal being. This interpretation occurs through a brief reading of a part of *Maximus* from the third volume, a four page passage from 1966, in which the poet considers his relationship with his father (a fraught, recurring theme). Olson is very close to his machinic manifestation here:

> I have been an ability – a machine – up to
> now. An act of 'history', my own, and my father's,
> together, a queer [Gloucester-sense] combination
> of completing something both visionary – or illusions (projection? literally
> lantern-slides, on the sheet, in the front-room Worcester,
> on the wall, and the lantern always getting too hot
> and I burning my fingers – & burning my
> nerves as in fact John says or Vincent Ferrini they too
> had to deal with their father's existence.[27]

Yépez focuses on the Freudian suggestivity of the poem, reading 'queer' into his model of Maximus as 'co-body' of Olson, at once uncanny and homoerotic.[28] In this interpretation, cinema is for Olson a felicitous metaphor enabling ahistorical

---

[26] Heriberto Yépez, *The Empire of Neomemory*, trans. Jen Hofer, Christian Nagler and Brian Whitener (Oakland and Philadelphia: Chainlinks, 2013; first publication in Spanish 2007), 15.
[27] Olson, *Maximus*, 495. Olson's square brackets. Emphasis in original.
[28] Yépez, *The Empire of Neomemory*, 217–18; for his idea of the 'co-body' in *Maximus*, see 21: 'co-bodies [are] always absent, relative to each other, one with respect to both.' For a psychoanalytic account of cinema's framerate, see Stephen Heath, 'On Suture', in *Questions of Cinema* (London: Macmillan, 1981), 76–112.

recombination and evasion of traumatic memory: a reverse-Freudian projection into the future. Despite noteworthy senses in which Yépez's critique is useful, I want to focus more explicitly and at greater length on the role that cinematic machinery plays in this poem. Particularly I want to challenge Yépez's analysis of Olson's cinematic poetics – and by extension, of his machinic poetics more generally – as a vector for the posthuman. Cinematograph, typewriter and text itself are all *tools* for poetry in Olson's work; they are not attempts to escape or fundamentally remake humanity but rather to reinstitute the human as an object in a context of other objects – anti-humanist rather than post-humanist. Certainly these tools are meant to effect a fundamental shift in *attitude* towards the reality of human capacity, but in the final analysis Olson is, by his own admission, an archaeologist rather than a futurist.[29]

In this context the tendency of the machinic in Olson's work is not so much towards the posthuman as to the 'parahuman' – writing, type and film are ancillaries to the potential of poetry. His poetry's treatment of all types of graphematic practice as technologies rather than achievements or ends in themselves can be understood as an extension and realization of capacities which are native to poetic experience. Thus in the following analysis of Olson's poetics as filmic, it is important to re-emphasize that the parallel being drawn is not perfect.

The 'machine' or 'ability' Olson writes of is a form of projecting device – a mechanism both 'visionary' and 'burning my / nerves'. Projection carries within it potential both for enlightenment and overload. As has been pointed out by Charles Stein, 'lantern-slides' are simple precursors of cinematic technology which project images onto a flat surface.[30] By the early twentieth century these were already old technology; here the magic lantern is metonymic not just for Olson's process of remembrance but for historiography, old-fashioned representation, as such.[31] It is a mode of representation that, however archaic, one must 'deal with'. I want to retain a focus on the dual valence of projective

---

[29] Charles Olson, *Archaeologist of Morning* (London: Cape Goliard, 1970); see also Matthew Corrigan, 'The Poet as Archaeologist: (Archaeologist of Morning)', *boundary 2* 2, nos. 1–2 (Fall 1973; Winter 1974): 273–8.
[30] Charles Stein, *The Secret of the Black Chrysanthemum* (Barrytown: Station Hill, 1979; first published 1987), 33. For more on the magic lantern as a precursor technology to film, particularly regarding how its projective capacities are fundamentally geared towards intelligibility and interpretability, see David Trotter, *Cinema and Modernism* (Malden and Oxford: Blackwell, 2007), 130.
[31] Eliot makes a similar connection between the magic lantern and 'nerviness' in 'The Lovesong of J. Alfred Prufrock' (Eliot, *The Poems of T.S. Eliot: The Annotated Text: Volume I*, eds. Christopher Ricks and Jim McCue (London: Faber, 2015), 5–9; 8).

technologies here as both 'visionary' and 'burning'; in this poem Olson directly addresses the problematic of 'projection' in the cinematic sense as a form of perception which traffics with illusion or even delusion. The 'act of "history"' Olson attempts in this section or part of *Maximus* – as a tribute to and redemption of his father's struggle with the historical and present iniquities of American politics – is already inflected by this problem of perception, so that it may be 'visionary – or illusions (projection? literally / lantern-slides'. The explicit confrontation with this danger links Olson's thinking here directly into another area of key concern in his poetics: the question of how to practice and write history.[32] The pressure put on this word in 'I have been an ability – a machine –' leaves 'history' held at apostrophized arm's length. If, as Yépez suggests, the primary function of Olson's cinematic poetics is recombination, 'cutting together' of various 'footage' from diverse historical periods – a reading that would find much support in this passage of *Maximus* – then 'history' is no more than a process of self-delusion, a 'vision' which destroys the historical record in an egocentric conflagration; furthermore this description of Olson's poetics would work as well for Pound's.[33] As has been suggested, Olson's putative film-poetics cannot be as easily pathologized as Yépez would like, but Olson is caught in a struggle with the delusive dynamics that the Mexican critic identifies, where the analogous cinematic quality of the poetics is both the method by which questions about illusion are negotiated and their major cause. The search for a poetics of actual, grounded perception and knowledge must engage the historical and thus entertain the 'queer' and illusionary as part of itself, and yet justify such engagement as more than mere fantasy; indeterminacy is here a fundamentally realist mode.

It is worth briefly outlining in what sense indeterminacy is realist in Olson (as in Cage). 'Realism' is one of the more contested characteristics criticism has historically appended to literary texts, particularly as poststructuralist critique came to question in what degree any writing could truly claim to contain or encapsulate 'the real'. The *locus classicus* of this argument is to be found in Roland Barthes's essay 'The Reality Effect', which identifies a 'referential illusion'

---

[32] For a lengthy consideration of Olson's historiography, see Gary Grieve-Carlson, *Poems Containing History: Twentieth-Century American Poetry's Engagement with the Past* (Lanham: Lexington, 2014), 181–202.

[33] See Lawrence Rainey, *Ezra Pound and the Monument of Culture: Text, History and the Malatesta Cantos* (Chicago: University of Chicago, 1991) for a reading of Pound which figures *The Cantos* as a sepulchre to a destroyed history.

pervading the French 'realist' writing of the nineteenth century (a close relative to the canon on which Ingarden built his own theories, as discussed in the Introduction). Barthes describes the 'referential illusion' as so:

> The truth of this illusion is this: eliminated from the realist speech-act as a signified of denotation, the 'real' returns to it as a signified of connotation: for just when these details are reputed to *denote* the real directly, all that they do – without saying so – is *signify* it; Flaubert's barometer, Michelet's little door finally say nothing but this: *we are real*; it is the category of 'the real' (and not its contingent contents) which is then signified; in other words, the very absence of the signified, to the advantage of the referent alone, becomes the very signifier of realism.[34]

The function of indeterminacy in this context, then, is that in deleting the fixity of the 'realist speech-act' the 'contingency' of the real is allowed into (or imagined to be allowed into) the writing produced. For both Olson and Cage 'details' are a central feature of their respective poetics, and ultimately it is in the proliferation of details (parts) over and against coherent organic wholes that their attention to the 'real' proceeds. Central to this is a concern for the actual operations of media and mediation.

This concern finds its way into Olson's model of history, and thus the model of record, on which his poetry will function. Again, here, film provides an instructive parallel, since, as Trotter writes, '[l]iterature is a representational medium, film a recording medium'.[35] In a crucial sense it is this recording-function which makes of film an exemplary parallel for a poetics of indeterminacy, simply because in the act of setting up a camera to film a shot or scene one runs the risk of (or welcomes the possibility of) something unscripted or unexpected *just happening* in front of the lens and being thus inscribed into the record.[36] This element of surprise is an important feature of both Cagean and Olsonian poetics, as I shall discuss in later chapters. For Olson especially, the destabilizing of the historical record thus intimated is highly conducive. Through the declaration of himself as an 'archaeologist of morning', Olson takes seriously the idea of a re-evaluative

---

[34] Roland Barthes, 'The Reality Effect', in *The Rustle of Language*, trans. Richard Howard (New York: Hill and Wang, 1986), 141–8; 148.
[35] Trotter, *Cinema and Modernism*, 3.
[36] In a discussion of D. W. Griffith's *Intolerance* (1916), Trotter notes, via Eisenstein's essay 'Dickens, Griffith and Film Today' (1944), how the 'indeterminacy' of cinema is seen in its capacity to allow the 'accident-prone' to appear in art (Ibid., 50); that is, to let unthematized actuality impinge, unbidden, on any scheme or preconception.

historical enquiry towards the future. This becomes clear when the pressurized word 'history' is investigated in its manifestations and definitions elsewhere in *The Maximus Poems*.

* * *

The poetic question of history is always in *Maximus* a question of historiography: How to use history, and for what? The relationship to historical artefacts of event and language is thus indissociably a relationship to linguistic and poetical media – a radical understanding of those artefacts as *made*. The work is explicitly archaeological, and the artefacts are discovered as broken tools, for restitution and use. Olson is insistent that history be rescued from its treatment as a mere object:

In English the poetics became meubles – furniture –
thereafter (after 1630

& Descartes was the value

until Whitehead, who cleared out the gunk
by getting the universe in (as against man alone

& that concept of history (not Herodotus's,
which was a verb, to find out for yourself:
'istorin, which makes any one's acts a finding out for him or her
self, in other words restores the traum: that we act somewhere

at least by seizure, that the objective (example Thucidides, or
the latest finest tape-recorder, or any form of record on the spot

– live television or what – is a lie

as against what we know went on, the dream: the dream being
self-action with Whitehead's important corollary: that no event

is not penetrated, in intersection or collision with, an eternal
event

The poetics of such a situation
are yet to be found out[37]

---

[37] Olson, *Maximus*, 249. Emphasis in original.

Here, in 1962, at the inception of *Maximus* book V, Olson is clear and programmatic; Whitehead and Herodotus, not Descartes and Thucydides. The distinction is fairly straightforward – history is to be understood not as an objective science ('that concept') but as an intermingling of various materials in the characteristic Olsonian mode of 'USE'.[38] There is no objective, given history because there is no uncomplicated record free from the intrusions of authorial bias or unthematized happenstance, only a number of things that have been said. History itself is to be a tool, a method, after Herodotus, and like Herodotus's it is to be a literary practice. By the same token it is not to be a solipsistic or human-centric activity in the manner of the rigid subject-object distinction espoused by Descartes; with Whitehead it recognizes the human as part of and constituted by cosmological and historical process, and grants that the universe has a life of its own, which the poetry 'lets in'. This methodology goes all the way down, as poetics itself is to be a historical process of 'finding out': a process, a *project*, rather than a product. The 'dream' of such a poetics is 'self-action', a 'transfer' of energy, as Olson would have it, 'from where the poet got it [. . .] to, the reader', but with the important admission that the universe or world intersects everything; that there is no 'man alone', no Cartesian subject parsing for an objective account. The 'self-action' of the text – the historical text, the poetical text – indicates a poetry moving beyond semantic determinacy and into a type of reading which involves negotiating dynamic and intersecting parts. This is understood as a realist poetics, 'what we know went on'.

In this case, what has been described here as a putative Olsonian film-poetics leads to a quandary: What is a film if not a *recording*, a sort of account of objects past? Olson is insistent that 'the objective (example Thucidides, or / the latest finest tape-recorder, or any form of record on the spot // – live television or what – is a lie'.[39] Discomfort with recording processes was by no means uncommon in the literary and artistic cultures of the 1960s; Cage's early antipathy to recordings of his musical performances can certainly be compared

---

[38] A similarly broad conceptualization of, and remit for, geography is present in Olson's writing; indeed, for the American poet as for Herodotus, 'history' and 'geography' are, as writing practices, barely distinguishable. The influence of Carl Ortwin Sauer can be felt in this aspect of Olson's writing. Emphasis in original.

[39] Olson's comments on television are few and rather confusing in the current context: US television ran at a significantly higher framerate than cinema (29.97 to 24 fps), so might in one sense be called a 'faster' medium, though this extra speed was not easily perceptible, as Raymond Williams notes in his 1974 study of television in Britain and America (Williams, *Television: Technology and Cultural Form* (London: Fontana, 1974), 62–3). However, Williams also comments unfavourably on 'the different light quality of the television as opposed to the film screen' (62), and it is plausibly this *unenergetic* aspect of television which makes it unattractive to Olson.

with those of his erstwhile Black Mountain colleague.[40] But Olson's thrust here is significantly, if subtly, distinguished from the lionization of the 'live' underlying the Cagean position.[41] At its bottom Olson's quarrel is with representation as it is usually understood through the relationship of the representing 'subject' to the represented 'object' (i.e. as folk-Cartesian subjectivity). Whilst Cage is as sceptical regarding Cartesianism as is Olson, his objection to recording in any capacity leans towards being a rejection of representation as such: 'I have nothing to say / and I am saying it / and that is / poetry / as I need it'.[42] For Cage no recording can ever be plausibly near recreating an event; records are inaccurate. Meanwhile for Olson recording is a 'lie' because it gives an inflexible and falsely 'objective' account of an event despite being simply one perspective amongst many, one set of actualities amongst the swarm. It is not that records are inaccurate; rather, veneration of them grants them a misleading authority. Recordings of Olson's readings, which are numerous, have a notably conversational character, such that it can be difficult to distinguish between 'poem' and surrounding 'speech' without a text to hand, or a good knowledge of the work.[43] Rukeyser writes that '[t]he history of film language is the history of essays in the colloquial'; this colloquiality, the everyday and throwaway character of recording, is closer to Olson's experience of recording as a technology than types of record-making which bear the official stamp of reliability, authority or art.[44] It is in this sense that being 'on the spot' does not matter so much for Olson as it does for Cage: Olson's project is rather less precious about the sanctity of the moment of performance. His poetry sets out its stall four-square in resistance to off-the-shelf modes of perception and representation, modes which he sees 'live television' as doing little to discourage and much to entrench. The spatialization of time already at work in Olson's thought in *Call Me Ishmael* recasts past events as distant *places* inaccessible to the poet with a less capacious and interactive definition of place.

---

[40] For more on Cage giving preference to the live over the recorded, see David Grubbs, *Records Ruin the Landscape: John Cage, the Sixties and Sound Recording* (Durham and London: Duke University Press, 2014); and Cage's work more or less in its entirety. Lytle Shaw, in his book *Narrowcast: Poetry and Audio Research* (Redwood City: Stanford University Press, 2018), provides an account of Olson's tribulations with the tape recorder (106–52). See also Philip Auslander, *Liveness: Performance in a Mediatized Culture* (London and New York: Routledge, 1999).

[41] Yasunao Tone writes, indicatively, that for Cage 'records functioned as a sort of museum'; that is, not useless, but not primary either (Tone, 'John Cage and Recording', *Leonardo Music Journal* 13 (2003): 11–15; 12).

[42] John Cage, 'Lecture on Nothing', in *Silence*, 108–27; 109.

[43] For a good example of Olson's loose, 'talk' reading, see the recording made at Goddard College: Olson, 'At Goddard College, April 12–14, 1962', PennSound, accessed 1 February 2020, https://media.sas.upenn.edu/pennsound/authors/Olson/Olson-Charles_Goddard-College_4-12-62.mp3.

[44] Rukeyser, *The Life of Poetry*, 153.

Poetry is to be an embodiment of knowledge as *active* (a Herodotean process of combination and choice: film) as opposed to *passive* (live television, in Olson's view). Historical documents as much as contemporary poetry can be read as shifting and uncertain, as texts rather than authorities.

Representation in Olson's work becomes directly an issue of perception and its possibilities. The way in which history is represented is identical with the way it is perceived. History is a practice: neither simply a subject for study nor an object for discovery. For Olson history, as poetry, is poesis.[45] If the poem is to mediate an investigative process, one concerned with uncovering and enacting a correct and useful value for experience, then it must be more than an act of mere imitation. As a result Olson's work finds itself in a peculiar and difficult position regarding mimesis: his poetry must be representational, in the limited sense that it must communicate and re-present its 'source', without being simply a rewind and replay, or a live broadcast. It must be somehow located in an active and emergent moment. Olson refuses just to describe the record; his poetry will make energetic 'USE' of it for its own ends. Furthermore this use will make the record more realistic than previously possible. These difficulties are intrinsic dynamics of a projective film-poetics; the line between illusion and delusion is thin. Film's investigative, recombinatory capacities have the potential to work change that can distort as easily as it can uncover. The writing of a film-history in a poem thus raises the spectre of ekphrasis. Originally denoting to the ancients any type of descriptive writing, ekphrasis has come to be applied primarily to literary descriptions of other arts, in particular the visual arts. Olson, as a poet of history and a poet of poiesis, that is, both a writer of history and a writer of the writing of history, preserves both the former and the latter sense as one and the same. It is, then, on this ground that the question of film's potential illusionary/delusionary effect stands. As a mode ekphrastic writing has been remarked upon for its tendency to work change whilst claiming simply to represent:

> Ekphrasis [. . .] has a Janus face; as a form of mimesis, it stages a paradoxical performance, promising to give voice to the allegedly silent image even while attempting to overcome the power of the image by transforming and inscribing it.[46]

---

[45] On the identity of poetry and poesis in Olson's work, see Shahar Bram, *Charles Olson and Alfred North Whitehead: An Essay on Poetry* (Lewisburg: Bucknell University Press, 2004), 12: '[For Olson] the poem is poiesis; the process of creation and the poem are, at most, two names or two perspectives for contemplating the same activity, the creation of a human being in the world.'

[46] Peter Wagner, 'Ekphasis, Iconotexts and Intermediality – The State(s) of the Art(s)', in Wagner (ed.), *Icons – Texts – Iconotexts: Essays on Ekphrasis and Intermediality* (Berlin and New York: De Gruyter,

Whilst the idea of 'transforming and inscribing' an image or record is in no way counter to Olson's poetical aims, indeed is a central facet of them, such an act must be a deepening of an already active dynamic rather than a mere distortion; it must focus the poetry's energetic drive rather than dissipate it. *The Maximus Poems* is a (large) book-sized rewriting of the historical record, of Gloucester and of the United States as a whole, as against a model of a classifying knowledge of inert objects personified and exemplified by Descartes (as the 'value').

'Projective Verse' is already on its guard in this particular. Any suggestion that poetry might be a nakedly imitative or simply descriptive art is strenuously resisted, and the headlong thrust of 'INSTANTER' vigorously insisted upon:

> The descriptive functions generally have to be watched, every second, in projective verse, because of their easiness, and thus their drain on the energy which composition by field allows into a poem. *Any* slackness takes off attention, that crucial thing, from the job in hand, from the *push* of the line underhand in the moment, under the reader's eye, in his moment. Observation of any kind is, like argument in prose, properly previous to the act of the poem, and, if allowed in, must be so juxtaposed, apposed, set in, that it does not, for an instant, sap the going energy of the content toward its form.[47]

Poetry which reads through history as its active pursuit does not need, then, to utterly abandon or reject description; it demands only that mimesis be, first, accurate, properly attendant to concrete specificities, and, second, that it be moving, a nexus of energy and speed. Movement is crucial because Olson understands his poetry to be an activity of the real as itself a process, a mode of attention to change. Olson's rebuttal of Platonic aesthetics is essentially Heraclitean; you cannot look at the same landscape twice. It is insistent that static imagery is an object of suspicion, not because it is knowledge-free but because, in accordance with Fenollosa, the world is made of verbs rather than nouns, of interaction and change rather than solidity.

***

The poetic usefulness of film is encapsulated in its popular appellation: the movies, moving pictures. Constituting representation via a dynamic and energetic method, film frees images for 'USE', for historical finding-out, as poetics

---

1996), 1–40; 13.
[47] Olson, 'Projective Verse', 243. Emphasis in original.

unbinds the dichotomy between dumb representation and the dead or distant represented. Knowledge is created and embodied not in the image or the imaged but in the gaps and movements between images. Historical knowledge is thus speculative in Olson's work – a concatenation of possible connections rather than a logical narrative. Here we reencounter Olson's championship of parataxis. This means that poetry cannot be merely empty imitation, static imitation being in some sense impossible anyway; it has an extending, projective, 'visionary' thrust. Olson does not thereby escape the suggestion that this 'visionary' perception is an illusion, but the conception of film as an ancillary or 'parahuman' tool at least allows such a visionary perception to exist independent of the charge that it is a mere trick.

As a result the challenge for readers is to order their own methods of perception correctly; to choose the correct vantage point, technology, protocol. A good example of Olson thinking about his work alongside film can be found in a brief poem note which he wrote on a Buffalo restaurant place mat on 14 October 1964. It was subsequently published in the *Magazine of Further Studies* 2 (October 1965), and is entitled 'The Lamp':

> you can hurry the pictures toward you but
> there is that point that the whole thing itself
> may be a passage, and that your own ability
> may be a factor in time, in fact that
> only if there is a coincidence of yourself
> & the universe is there then in fact
> an event. Otherwise – and surely here the cinema
> is large – the auditorium can be showing
> all the time. But the question is
> how you yourself are doing, if you in fact
> are equal, in the sense that as *a like power*
> you also are there when the lights
> go on. This wld seem to be a
> matter of creation, not simply
> the obvious matter, creation
> itself. Who in fact is any of us
> to be there at all? That's what
> swings the matter, also –
> the beam hanging from[48]

---

[48] Olson, *Collected Poems*, 614–15. Emphasis in original.

On the original holograph, the title of the poem is written down the side of the text, so finishing the final line ('the beam hanging from the lamp') and giving the poem a circularity as the final words link to the beginning of the poem. The 'lamp' here is the projector itself, perhaps the xenon arc lamp newly introduced to US theatres in 1963, which is in a similar spectral range to daylight. This is a poem about the necessary conditions of perception, which in the cinema are the lamp, the light itself, the shutter, which overlays one image and the next; these are the technological items which make film possible. But Olson is emphatic, even in his very first line, that this is not enough: 'but / there is that point that the whole thing itself / may be a passage', that there is a reading-choice to be made, rather than simply an objective, non-anthropogenic event. Readers are asked to deal with speed, with the 'hurry' of the 'thing itself' and the interacting, intermedial human 'ability' to catch or handle it. Film is described here as occurring at the interface between human and phenomenon; it has no singular medium: 'only if there is a coincidence of yourself / & the universe is there then in fact / an event'.[49] A film is only a film when processed through the human perceptual apparatus; otherwise it is simply a series of not-quite continuous stills. The human is a *'like power'* in this process, neither a master nor a passive receptor. Olson's model of perception is indeterminate in that neither object nor human agency has complete control or determining power over the process: rather subject and object are interlocked.

A film is not, then, an illusion for human beings occupying the kinds of bodies they do, any more than is perception of colour or line or any other mediation between body and world via the workings of the eye. To perceive is not simply to collect and collate raw data but to interpret as the eye interprets the screen in a movie theatre.[50] Cavilling over the idea that such an act of perception misrepresents what is 'really' happening is meaningless when it is considered that there could be no perception, and no memory, without the body. This commitment on Olson's part was reinforced by his reading of the French phenomenologist Maurice Merleau-Ponty, who the poet had been acquainted with since the 1962 translation of 1945's *Phenomenology of Perception*. Merleau-Ponty writes, 'The body is the vehicle of being in the world, and having a

---

[49] This sense of 'event' clearly owes much to Whitehead.
[50] This point is quite literal. Just as film's high-speed running-together of images creates the illusion of movement in the visual apparatus, so the saccades or small flickers which the eye makes over the page in reading are 'stitched' together by the brain so as to seem continuous to the reader. See Jessica Love, 'Reading Fast and Slow', *The American Scholar* 81, no. 2 (Spring 2012): 64–72; 66.

body is, for a living creature, to be intervolved in a definite environment, to identify oneself with certain projects and be continually committed to them.'[51] Perception is a *project* as well as simply a *process* because to perceive is to be 'intervolved', to be caught or rolled up in the world. What work like Olson's further suggests, however, is that not all environments are equally 'definite'; a long poem is an indefinite environment in certain ways, as when one attempts to locate the part in relation to the whole. Olson's response to his sceptical parenthesis ('illusions (projection?)') in 'I have been an ability – a machine –' is that perception is always like this at its heart, even before the addition of cinema or any other technological aid; a perception is a commitment rather than merely a value-neutral observation.[52]

An understanding of projective poetics which takes its cue from the projector gets this far; but it leaves loose ends of its own. Poetry is not cinema; Olson was not a Hollywood writer, as his abortive trip to California in the forties proved. Poetry is a visual form, but by no means exclusively so, and as has been remarked, Olson's work is focused on the oral and the aural, the visual coming in a poor second even by the normal standards of poetic production. For Olson, then, the cinematic is a staging for 'the question [of] / how you yourself are doing, if you in fact / are equal, in the sense that as *a like power* / you also are there when the lights / go on'. The equality suggested is not to cinema but to reality itself, an equality which is one of participation and use, the desire for which cultivates Olson's chase after a natural, sufficient and even Cratylic language which would make poetry a true embodiment of knowledge.[53] This equality would require a practice of perception and embodiment in language well beyond the capacity of film, as useful a jumping-off point and spur to writing as that medium is. Poetry must not just be equal to film, but it must be commensurate with the world, 'Equal, That Is, to the Real Itself'. It all starts, as so often in Olson's thought, with Melville:

> All things did come in again, in the 19th century. An idea shook loose, and energy and motion became as important a structure of thing as that they are plural, and, by matter, mass. [. . .] Quantity – the measurable and numerable –

---

[51] Maurice Merleau-Ponty, *Phenomenology of Perception*, trans. Colin Smith (London: Routledge, 2002; first published 1962), 81–2.
[52] Compare Moholy-Nagy's comment on how film presents 'the illusion of the illusion' (*Vision in Motion*, 280).
[53] For a full and useful account of Olson's Cratylism, and its context, see Carla Billiteri, *Language and the Renewal of Society in Walt Whitman, Laura (Riding) Jackson, and Charles Olson: The American Cratylus* (New York: Palgrave Macmillan, 2009).

was suddenly as shafted in, to any thing, as it was also, as had been obvious, the striking character of the external world, that all things do extend out. Nothing was now inert fact, all things were there for feeling, to promote it, and be felt; and man, in the midst of it, knowing well how he was folded in, as well as how suddenly and strikingly he could extend himself, spring or, without even moving, go, to far, the farthest – he was suddenly possessed or repossessed of a character of being, a thing among things, which I shall call his physicality. It made a re-entry of or to the universe. Reality was without interruption, and we are still in the business of finding out how all action, and thought, have to be refounded.[54]

The theorizing of 1958 becomes 1966's practice in 'I have been an ability – a machine –', where Olson's command that the poet must 'extend himself, spring or, without even moving, go, to far, the farthest' locates its enactment not just *through* projection technologies but *beyond* them. Here Olson's poetical histories turn their engines around as a projection and extension of human capacities into the future: 'I have been an ability – a machine – *up to / now*.' The projective energy, which must, according to the essay of 1950, be 'at least the equivalent of the energy which propelled' the poem, overwhelms the projection technologies its rhetoric has leant on, the techno-history which produced them and the perceptive systems it was designed for, leaving Olson 'burning my fingers – & burning my / nerves'. Cellulose nitrate film stock burns when it becomes overheated: a fitting end in a poetics predicated on such extremes of energetic writing, attention and velocity that perception is to be 'INSTANTER', faster than the speed of light and beyond the fold of visual representation. Olson's burnt nerves are not an enervation of his poetry, but rather figure such a fullness of energy that the poem becomes lightness invisible. Projective poetics can thus be understood as an extension of mimesis into the non-visual, the acceleration of representation into combustion.

***

This is the difficulty for the critic of Olson: if on the whole the history of Olson's work in the critical realm has been one of confusion and antagonism, it is in part because the projective dynamics outlined here are fundamentally unsuited to critical encapsulation or representation. There is much movement and little

---

[54] Charles Olson, 'Equal, That Is, to the Real Itself', in *Collected Prose*, 120–5; 121.

solidity in the experience of reading a book like *Maximus*, whose cogency is found in a process rather than in stasis. If reading *The Maximus Poems* is in some senses always a *fast* process, one which tends towards the reading-practices appropriate to a page-turner or even a flipbook, where the effect is located in the *blur between* the pages, then a standard textual criticism grounded in close and careful reading is difficult to deploy, and perhaps even otiose.[55] This is especially so since, if *Maximus* really *were* a flipbook, it would have to go impossibly in many directions at once, as the ever-increasing accumulation of internal reference in the work remakes it from sequence into archive or nexus – another way in which Olson's work escapes not only linear cinematic but also representation according to the normal logic of criticism. The relations of parts to parts are many and intertwined within the whole of the book, and these relations shift depending on which part is granted significance or chosen for inspection. Like the burning, overheated reel presiding over 'I have been an ability – a machine – ', Olson's work feeds on and supports itself by eating itself, by effacing its own representations. It moves too fast for traditional modes of reading, and such accounts always appear partial and imperfect.

Olson is himself cognizant of this dynamic; he always frames it as a question of perception, of how to address oneself to a set of phenomena which are forever receding or moving away, difficult to grasp. In this mode, one can understand reading Olson as akin to a certain kind of chasing or seeking, where readers can *expect* certain things to happen or appear or reveal themselves in certain ways at certain points in the reading, but never quite be certain, because the text has an emergent capacity whereby effects become apparent on one reading which were not on another. Some of this can be put down to the 'archival' nature of the work, within which readers' navigational competence can increase, but in some degree it is also a matter of what Olson terms 'USE', the sets of operational decisions readers make. What are you looking *for*, and how might you best find it? The problem of, for example, reading Olson's projective poetics as related to the cinematic projector almost immediately becomes the problem of 'how to read Olson' at the level of protocol rather than at the level of achieved literacy or readerly competence. In this Olson's process of composition and the manner in which readers respond are oddly similar. In a late passage of *Maximus*, Olson writes that he has been

---

[55] There exists, in fact, an 'Olson flipbook', entitled *Folgers from Black Mountain Groan*, made by Michael Myers, Ed Dorn and Holbrook Teter, the poet's students at the College. It depicts Olson making ridiculous baby gestures in front of a weather map.

> Bottled up for days, mostly
> in great sweat of being, seeking
> to bind in speed – <u>petere</u> –desire,
> to construct knowing back to image and
> God's face behind it turned as mine
> now is to blackness image shows
> herself, desire the light
> speed and motion alone are[56]

Much of *Maximus* is involved with this question of poetic protocol, so that the problem of how to write poetry is the major concern of much of the poetry; a lot of what seems arid or 'unpoetic' in Olson's writing results from this feedback loop. Both the writing and the reading of such poetry is intimately concerned with seeking and desire, but these desires are not necessarily fulfilled or even fulfillable – whatever it is Olson means in claiming that he wants to 'construct' an image of 'God's face behind' the poem, it seems like a task which is not eminently achievable. Most readers recognize that there are grave limitations and basic incompletenesses in Olson's thinking, that there is something short-circuited about his ideas. Whilst it is true that Olson's work is characteristically unconcerned with beauty, perfection and so on, speed is a useful concept here because it speaks to these limitations as necessary parts of a poetics which is both realist and indeterminate, which can lead both poet and readers to unexpected destinations. The speed of the projector may only be a stalking horse for or staging post towards Olson's real ambition, which was the speed of the synapse, of perception itself. But film provided a crucial avenue into conceiving how such a poetic perception might function, and what it might produce. Thinking Olson's speed highlights the poetry's resistance to comprehensive mastery, as a commitment to the shifting, processual agencies of the world the work emerges from and partakes in. The self-confuting and even self-defeating aspects of this poetics are responsive to these knots of agency and automatism. The loss of the speed of reading in reflection is part of the play of coherence and incoherence native to a type of writing which works both in two dimensions – on the page – and in four – the time of reading as a negotiation of page and depth, or 'volume' – simultaneously. Failures of readerly competence are the inevitable upshot of a poetry where mediation is precisely what needs to be discovered.

---

[56] Olson, *Maximus*, 503.

3

Mycopoetics

Cage's *Mushroom Book*

What Perloff calls the 'anti-Symbolist' mode of indeterminate writing turned its focus onto the literal, in derogation of a poetics governed by symbolic orders.[1] To say that Cage's work is in a crucial sense 'realist' is to note its fundamental orientation towards this markedly literal treatment of its own materials *as media*. Though rarely representational in any traditional sense, Cage frequently claimed his work attends to the world *as it really is*, moving beyond traditions of mimesis into active negotiation of materials in practice. Cage claimed to be embodying or revealing reality through his work, to be releasing the world of objects from mere representation. This project went hand in hand with suspicion towards, even outright rejection of, normative categories like 'art', 'music' and 'taste'. Cage presented his practice as one which let things be things. In conversation with Daniel Charles, he described his musical interest in unusual instrumentation in just these terms:

> When I was introduced to [film director Oscar Fischinger], he began to talk to me about the spirit which is inside each of the objects of this world. So, he told me, all we need to do to liberate that spirit is to brush past the object, and to draw forth its sound. [. . .] In all the many years which followed up to the war, I never stopped touching things, making them sound and resound, to discover what sounds they could produce. Wherever I went, I always listened to objects. So I gathered together a group of friends, and we began to play some pieces I had written without instrumental indications, simply to explore the instrumental possibilities not yet catalogued, the infinite number of sound sources from

---

[1] Cage criticized Allan Kaprow's symbolically inflected 'happenings' for just this reason, describing them as 'involved in a whole thing that we have been familiar with since the Renaissance and before' (quoted in Branden Wayne Joseph, *Experimentations: John Cage in Music, Art and Architecture* (New York and London: Bloomsbury, 2016), 3).

a trash heap or a junk yard, a living room or a kitchen.... We tried all the furniture we could think of.[2]

Cage justifies his practice as one which somehow *de*instrumentalizes instruments, allowing soundmaking things to be objects of open-ended, unfolding enquiry and research rather than overdetermined tools of settled musical logics. He makes this point again to Charles a couple of paragraphs later: 'What we were looking for was in a way more humble: Sounds, quite simply. Sounds, pure and simple.'[3] The secret or hidden inwardness of the object, its 'spirit', is to be sounded out and made manifest. Yet almost in the same breath he contradicts his terms. 'I never stopped touching things' admits the way in which Cage's practice is anthropogenic despite his protestations, a re-presentation of the object in the light of human action. This does not stop him, however, from attempting to access the pre-representational 'spirit' of the sound which is before and beyond even processing and interpretation by human aural systems. Cage frequently articulates a desire to escape 'relationships between noises and tonality', where 'noises' indicates the material or foundation of the world, the 'thing-in-itself', and 'tonality' the abstractions, ideas and discourses which humans employ to corral and instrumentalize those foundations (in a similar way, it might be implied from the passage above that sound is unlike language for Cage because less inherently mediate).[4] In this sense he is an anti-idealist. Cagean realism consists primarily in attempts to mitigate anthropocentric intentionality through such methods as aleatoric and chance procedures, cut-up or 'readings-through', and environmental awareness. It is underpinned by a belief that there is in fact a non-anthropomorphic real and that this real is accessible and knowable. As such Cage's work is more akin to philosophical realism than to literary realism conventionally understood, but it can perhaps be best interpreted as a pragmatic attempt to see what materials can do, and what attention can be paid to them.[5]

---

[2] John Cage, *For the Birds* (Salem and London: Boyars, 1981; first published 1976), 73–4. See another, briefer version of this story in 'An Autobiographical Statement', *Southern Review* 76, no. 1 (Winter, 1991): 59–76; 61.
[3] Cage, *For the Birds*, 74.
[4] Ibid., 76.
[5] Ron Silliman has written of how avant-garde poetics is not so much anti-realist as it is anti-*realism in the traditional literary sense*, which he describes as 'the illusion of reality in the in capitalist thought' (*The New Sentence* (New York: Roof, 1987), 10). Huntsperger extends Silliman's argumentation into territory more directly relevant to Cage's poetics, writing that '[i]n Silliman's assessment, realism – the dominant literary mode of capitalism – causes readers to stop paying attention to words in and of themselves and to pay attention instead only to the meanings behind them' (Huntsperger, *Procedural Form in Postmodern American Poetry*, 110). The development of a new and better realism is nonetheless a key component of the American experimental writing of the twentieth century.

Cage's surface resistance to mediation is then a thoroughgoing staple of his rhetoric and of the way he described his artistic practice, but is at the same time incongruent with that practice. However strong his commitment to a fantasy of immediacy – certainly less strong than Olson's – and however outspoken his distaste for the term 'art', Cage was nonetheless a multimedia artist whose ideas have had at least as much impact as his 'actual' work. Indeed there is often no clear separation between Cagean ideas and Cagean artworks (*4'33"* is only the most infamous example of this), and when Cage claims to be bad with ideas, and only able to find them in material rather than formulate them, it is hard to take him entirely seriously.[6] Cage's interest in the 'spirit [. . .]' of the objects of this world' seems like a paradoxically *conceptual* materialism, even if it is pragmatic at the practical level of its poesis. Cage's connection to the conceptual art which emerged in the 1960s and 1970s is well-attested; but what is manifested in his own work is precisely not the unconcern for the materials of art generally said to characterize conceptualism. Like many alumni of Black Mountain, Cage was primarily motivated by investigation into the materials of art, their limits and potentials. This material focus was nonetheless 'conceptual' in that it aimed at reconceiving both art and its materials, and their relation, at understanding them in a new way.

The contradictory character of Cage's realism, which reaches out to the unmediated object/world via art which is constituted *in a play of mediation*, is not unique. All art which aspires to realism must of necessity run up against its own medium, against re-presentation; against the fact that words, sounds, sensations and even thoughts are mediating and medial. Gillian Beer has identified exactly this contradiction, writing that

> [r]ealism in writing is founded on paradox. The term 'real*ism*' declares itself an approximation, or servitor: an attempt to mimic an 'other' which it must also match. The twin goals of realism are cohering and obscuring, at once. The 'other' that realism serves is assumed as prior, already *there*: out there, in there. If necessary, to be made there.[7]

Yet Cage explicitly sets his stall out against 'approximation'. His interest in nonintention, in evacuating his work of 'likes and dislikes', is integrally also an

---

[6] See Chapter 5.
[7] Gillian Beer, 'Wave Theory and the Rise of Literary Modernism', in *Realism and Representation: Essays on the Problem of Realism in Relation to Science, Literature and Culture*, ed. George Levine (Madison: University of Wisconsin, 1993), 193–213; 194. Emphasis in original.

opposition to simile, to a logic of 'likeness'. Metaphor more generally is suspect in a context where translations of whatever kind bear the compromising mark of human intentionality. In this fashion Cage's work can be understood as part of a broader late-modernist impulse towards formal and stylistic iconoclasm, as an aversion both to the heroic mastery of the Romantic artist and the visionary 'Make It New' of Poundian modernism; rather, the impulse was to 'Make It Literal'. Outside such a context Cage's hunt for the 'spirit' of things might seem to imply the achievement of a fantastically 'pure', unmediated realism, of a kind ruled impossible according to everything from Kantian epistemology to McLuhan's media theory to quantum mechanics. Cage was deeply uninterested in notions of the 'pure', a practitioner of a 'dirty' modernism characterized by interest in the decayed and the damaged, in brushing and recombining leavings from the trash heap into new forms. To attend properly to the object-world cannot then mean to somehow salvage its unmediated inward being as if it were transparent. What I want to investigate in this chapter is the way in which Cage dealt with, used and abused this contradiction.

Cage's discomfort with 'relationships between' can be read as unwillingness to reduce the non-human world to mere instrumentation, to a set of tools for wilful human production. It is in this context that I want to consider Cage's work alongside that of the French anthropologist and philosopher Bruno Latour, whose network-based theory of 'actants' could be described as a form of non-reductionist materialism. Latour's refusal to treat the things of the world as reducible to human knowledge or agency finds some parallels in Cage's theory and practice of nonintention. Though far from isomorphic thinkers, Cage and Latour share some basic concerns which make their differences mutually illuminating.

The withdrawn 'spirit which is inside each of the objects of this world' Cage described to Charles is characterized by a resistance to overdetermining human action, making its reality difficult to access. This quality of resistance is central to Latour's thought, and to his ontology specifically. The basis of his philosophy is laid out programmatically in 'Irreductions', the second half of 1984's *The Pasteurization of France*, which introduces his concept of 'actants': networks of entities which work together to undermine the model of the scientist as epistemologically masterful. Though Cage would probably seek to dispense with an over-clean, overconfidently abstracting version of scientific discourse, it is less clear that he would have welcomed Latour's anti-foundationalism with open arms. Just as Olson in 'Projective Verse' endeavoured to grapple with the question of what the fundamental stuff of poetry is or was to be, Cage was greatly concerned with identifying and attending to the fundamental materials of his practice, in assessing their potential, and indeed this is one key feature of the Black Mountain culture both men shared. As this chapter will demonstrate, Cage was predisposed to worry at the frayed edges of the seemingly inaccessible real.

* * *

Latour does not explicitly address poetry, but his work nevertheless suggests what I shall here call a *poetics of surprise*, wherein the reader navigates the text with a minimal set of expectations. In his 1999 study *Pandora's Hope: Essays on the Reality of Science Studies*, an investigation into the nature and authority of scientific knowledge-claims, Latour challenges the conception of the scientist as a subject of maximal competence who manipulates and instrumentalizes 'nature' as a tactic for gaining penetrative knowledge of it. In opposition to this view of the scientist as epistemic master of nature, he questions '[w]ho has ever mastered an action? Show me a novelist, a painter, an architect, a cook, who has not, like God, been surprised, overcome, ravished by what she was – in what *they* were – no longer doing'.[8] Though addressed to science studies, the occupations Latour chooses to illustrate his point indicate that readers are here being asked to think the practice of science analogously into the realm of aesthetic practice, of what might normally be termed the 'cultural' or 'artistic', and this move can be repurposed as a model for poiesis. The aesthetic moment shared between the scientist and the artist is located in an instance of what Cage would term nonintention, a moment in which the individual is astounded by the realization that her activity is not in fact individual but a collaborative effort between herself and 'they', the association of other entities with which she interfaces. This network of 'actants', as Latour terms them, ensures that rather than intentions and acts,

> there are events. I never *act*; I am always slightly surprised by what I do. That which acts through me is also surprised by what I do, by the chance to mutate, to change and to bifurcate, the chance that I and the other circumstances surrounding me offer to that which has been invited, recovered, welcomed.[9]

---

[8] Bruno Latour, *Pandora's Hope: Essays on the Reality of Science Studies* (Cambridge and London: Harvard University Press, 1999), 283.
[9] Ibid., 281.

Crucially, to recognize this interactivity of human agents with other entities is also to recognize the impossibility of a human agent's providing a complete description of any activity whatsoever. Just as artists open themselves to the unexpected mutations within their materials (and consider these to be an integral part of their work's being) so scientists are open to the intervention of the world of things which they study. This moment of surprise, of astonishment at what is made possible by the association of actants, is a key component of innovation in both scientific and artistic production, but one which is fundamentally impossible to relate with 'complete' sufficiency. The fact of mediation, which is also the fact of poesis, makes any human activity or experience impossible to fully describe, and this is as true of reading and writing as of anything else. The basic fact of the surprising element makes 'making' or poesis (or any activity whatsoever) more than a matter of mere *technique* in the sense of what one knows one will and/or can do; it also requires an attitude or attentiveness which is open to what might emerge from outside of expectation or technical ability.

A basic feature of Latour's thought is the undermining of subject-object dialectics, and with them the model of materialism which sees matter as merely the inert subject of force – what Timothy Morton, in a Latourian vein, has called 'clunk-causality'.[10] Instead it proposes a type of materiality in which the non-human can be a source of agency. This means that human claims to mastery, and to an intentional capacity without peer, are subject to what Jane Bennett describes, in 2010's *Vibrant Matter: A Political Ecology of Things*, as 'the strange structuralism of vital materiality, a materiality that includes the aleatory'.[11] The indeterminacy of matter in this understanding, and of the interaction between the human and the non-human, demands of any poetics that it be open both to abandonment of intention and to making space for the emergent and surprising within the textual process, where each demand is constitutive of the other.

Describing this putative 'Latourian' poetic mode provides a crop of ideas germane to Cage's own, more explicit, poetics.[12] Cage's celebrated interest in nonintention, chance procedures and ecological concerns make his work seem

---

[10] Timothy Morton, *Realist Magic: Objects, Ontology, Causality* (Ann Arbor: Open Humanities, 2013), 69.

[11] Jane Bennett, *Vibrant Matter: A Political Ecology of Things* (Durham: Duke University Press, 2010), 119.

[12] C.f. 'Projective Verse's 'unknown, unnamed vegetables'.

an ideal testing ground for what I have provisionally sketched here as a poetics of surprise – his compositions containing chance-determined environmental sound, for example, are ripe for such a theorization. However, since my focus is on Cage's practice as writer, the 'matter' I want to observe Cage collaborating with is linguistic. This presents an immediate problem: What happens when one's 'materials' are words, objects whose materiality is not easy to think in anything more than their manifestations as sound and print (i.e. for a multidisciplinary artist like Cage, in their manifestations as sonic and visual rather than strictly verbal arts, though of course the blurring of these boundaries is axiomatic for Cage's work)? Words are usually more tightly bound up with concepts than are, say, tones or colours (what sound does 'indeterminacy' make?). The critic and cyberneticist N. Katherine Hayles has expressed exactly this sort of reservation with regard to treating Cage's words as objects or materials:

> It seems to me that the analogies Cage uses are more compelling for music than for language. Whereas sounds do in fact exist in nature, written language is a purely human creation. We come to a text with the expectation that it will mean something. I am not so sure that a highly random text can continue to engage the reader's attention indefinitely, once the general point is grasped that it aims to defeat intentionality.[13]

It should be noted that no compelling reason is given here as to why readers – or writers – should 'expect' meaning from language. It is clearly an axiom of Cage's work that 'meaning' is of secondary concern in the writing process; though a less front-and-centre aspect of his work, this is also true of Olson. Nor is it immediately obvious in what sense writing is 'unnatural'. I presume that in defining writing as 'unnatural', Hayles is suggesting that it falls on the other side of a nature/art divide of the sort Cage himself would not recognize. These points aside, I want to disagree with Hayles in other ways here, and to investigate how a properly verbal art *can* possess a kind of materiality, can in some sense 'exist in nature'. I want to explore the way in which a word can be made to mean 'less than *some*thing', that is, how it can be made to be particularly '*a* thing', and how this particular thing-ness is made paradoxically possible by its participation in an ecology – a longform environment. That is, the focus here is on how words can be made indeterminate with regard to meaning across and between the

---

[13] N. Katherine Hayles, 'Chance Operations: Cagean Paradox and Contemporary Science', in *John Cage: Composed in America*, eds. Marjorie Perloff and Charles Junkerman (Chicago and London: University of Chicago, 1994), 226–41; 236.

parts of a long poetic text. Cage's writing is a particularly fruitful environment for investigating the possibilities of language as 'matter', of material language, and for considering what such a conception of language allows writers and readers to do. This is true in part because for Cage 'language' is not obviously the horizon of his practice, as it is for writers who consider language the only medium they work in, and for whom there could be a tendency to see words/language not so much as the materials worked with, but rather as the imaginable limit or horizon of practice, going beyond which is to engage in an entirely separate activity. Cage's writing is characterized by an attention to language as specifically *material* rather than simply *metier* – an insight which is one of the chief benefits of intermediality or interdisciplinarity in artistic practice (of seeing that practice as operant across rather than bounded by its materials). Here I turn to Cage's long collage poem *Mushroom Book*.

***

Cage wrote *Mushroom Book* in 1972 as part of the extensive project entitled *Diary: How to Improve the World (You Will Only Make Matters Worse)* (in instalments 1964–82). Cage describes *Mushroom Book* as an 'interlude between the sixth and seventh instalments of the diary' – a longform part of an even longer-form poetic whole.[14] The poem is made up of what Cage calls '[writing] without syntax and sometimes with it', variations on a mushroom-theme, a mosaic of mycological anecdotes and recipes interspersed with mesostics on the binomial nomenclature of mushroom species, and quotations from various favoured sources on mushrooms and mycology (on which more briefly).[15] Mushrooms are a 'theme' of the text both in the musical sense of a motif admitting of various instances or variations, and in the older, Hellenic sense of a place or region – an environment – which is administered and negotiated, though without the implication of imperial governance (the provinces of the Byzantine Empire were called *themata*). In many ways the Cagean 'theme' retains the essayistic, school-exercise sense of the word which was common in the seventeenth century and is now defunct; the mushroom-theme is an attempt at being mushroom-like, or an attempt on mushrooms, of thinking with mushrooms, which is never quite complete or successful. Olson's 'themes'

---

[14] John Cage, 'Foreword', in *M: Writings '67–'72* (Hanover: Wesleyan Univeristy Press, 1973), (unpaginated).
[15] Ibid.

are similarly distorted by their distribution across his corpus – where I use the word 'theme' in this book, I employ this modulated and less determining sense. The mushrooms of *Mushroom Book* are not merely thematic, however; they figure a structural principle, an analogy according to which the book is written. Specifically, the writing of *Mushroom Book* is to mirror the process of looking for mushrooms in the woods – a treasured pastime for Cage. The basic idea at work, the force of the analogy, is that when looking for mushrooms, one cannot be sure what one will find or even if one will find anything, fungi being unpredictable, deceptive and amorphous entities whose behaviour exhibits all manner of surprising liminalities and reversals. The peculiar characteristics of fungi, which make them of creative interest to Cage, include their great variety, their often extreme similarity *and* extreme divergence, unpredictable interbreeding and cross-breeding between 'species', and thus the great difficulty in identifying their species, edible or poisonous, even with as extensive an understanding and experience of mushroom-hunting as Cage possessed.[16] Whatever level of 'mastery', then, the hunter brings to the hunt, he can nowise be certain of even partial success. This means that expectations, and intentions, have to be lowered; as Cage writes, 'Hunting is starting from / zero, not looking for.'[17] A mushroom hunt is a collaboration with whatever the environment presents to the hunter, and not the 'object' to the hunter's 'subject' in the classic Cartesian sense; the writing and reading of *Mushroom Book* share these dynamics. Perloff notes that 'there is a big difference between the reference to indeterminacy and the creation of indeterminate forms'; in this vein, Cage's mushrooms are less the object of his writing in *Mushroom Book* than the medium.[18] The reticence of mushrooms in the face of human intention, their unwillingness to be corralled into narrateability or metaphoric control, constitutes their usefulness as analogy for Cage's process in writing *Mushroom Book*, in the sense that the analogy is necessarily self-defeating, always leaving behind an excess outside of the analogy's jurisdiction. This is what I shall call his mycopoetics.

An essential aspect of the mycopoetics is that it limits the reach of Cage's authorial intention, unpicking the heroic model of artist as master (in Latourian

---

[16] Cage was in fact deeply interested in questions of diet. Later in life, having suffered from poor health, he took up a macrobiotic diet; his interest in mushrooms was incorporated in this lifestyle change. See John Cage, 'Macrobiotic Cooking', in *Arial 6/7*, ed. Rod Smith (Washington, DC: Edge, 1991), 131–7, for a series of Cage's macrobiotic recipes, including for mushrooms.

[17] John Cage, *Mushroom Book*, in *M*, 117–83; 117.

[18] Perloff, *The Poetics of Indeterminacy*, 22.

terms 'actor') and replacing it with a negotiation between hunter/writer/ reader and a textual environment made up of extracts from books about mushrooms, the names of mushrooms, anecdotes about encounters with real mushrooms and literary forms mimicking mushroom qualities. Cage's purpose (paradoxically, the promotion of nonintention) shapes the basic orientation of the work (it decides to enter that environment) but not any specific particularity or 'encounter' within it. It is open to 'surprise' in Latour's sense; in fact it courts it, seeing in such moments of astonishment

> Freedom from likes and
> dislikes, the sudden sense of
> identification, the spirit
> of comedy.[19]

It is, of course, not exactly true that *Mushroom Book*, or indeed any of Cage's work, is entirely free of judgement or preference – he likes to quote certain texts, for example, just as he likes to pick mushrooms rather than daisies – but these are difficult to isolate and identify, hidden behind several levels of irony and evasion, and only approachable asymptotically. The 'real' of the *Mushroom Book* is obscured. Readers are asked to approach the text in a certain mode of attention rather than expectation – to be alive to things that appear, that attract notice (in a manner not dissimilar to that in which the text was composed, as I shall show). The chance procedures that produce the text for readers as for the writer are not, then, of the type employed by Cage elsewhere (dice-rolls, *I-Ching* selection processes). They are the result of a collaborative interaction between human and non-human in the reading/writing process, where chance deranges intention because the non-human refuses simply to comply with human sensibility. Another way to say this is that in Cage's *Mushroom Book* the fact of the text's intermediality, of mediation as the literal base of the text, is central to the way in which it interacts with readers' expectations of how to operate with/in the textual environment. Since the indeterminacy of the text resides not just at a hermeneutic level but moreover and more properly at the level of readerly protocol, as uncertainty about how to address oneself to the text, to read *Mushroom Book* is to risk one's competence as a reader within the work's textual environment, to be willing to surrender mastery by sharing in the text's production. Importantly this is true however readers choose to approach the

---

[19] Cage, *Mushroom Book*, 147.

text, whichever conventional or perverse textual protocols they glean from the text or develop for themselves. The solidity of the textual indeterminacy resides in its necessitating this explicit face-off with conventional reading protocol, whichever one of any number of possible protocols is finally selected in its place. Nowhere is this more evident than in the uses Cage makes of quotation from Thoreau.

* * *

Of all the sources of quotation employed by Cage in the *Mushroom Book* (including texts by Buckminster Fuller, Mao Tse-Tung, Marshall McLuhan, to name a few) the most sustained and acute attention is reserved for Henry David Thoreau's *Journal*.[20] Quotations from Thoreau's enormous text, begun in 1837 and continued sporadically until just prior to his death in 1862, are so numerous throughout *Mushroom Book* that they earn two entries in the 'recipe' or list of the book's components which Cage provides in part IV of the text:

> excerpts from Thoreau's *Journal*
>   (fungi),
> excerpts from Thoreau's *Journal*
>   (entire)[21]

The *Journal* is an important source for many of Cage's writings, but its presence is particularly strong in the *Mushroom Book*, which is itself a form of journal or daybook, forming a part of the extended *Diary* series. It contains two significant strains of excerpt from Thoreau, one of which is immediately obvious; the second requires a closer inspection and more extended reading of the *Journal* in order to be identified.

The first of these strains is, unsurprisingly, mushrooms, and more specifically their putrefaction. Almost all of the direct references to fungi in Cage's Thoreau quotations address instances in which precipitation or age has led to their decay; Thoreau is often particularly attentive to the foul smell which these fungi emit. This recurring theme is difficult to miss in reading the *Mushroom Book*, but harder to spot is the way in which decay and generative change is at work within Cage's own process of collecting and preparing quotations for his text. These are

---

[20] Cage read *On the Duty of Civil Disobedience* in college, but only became really interested in Thoreau in 1967, after being reintroduced to his work by Wendell Berry.
[21] Cage, *Mushroom Book*, 133.

always attributed to an author, but never with full citation. Resultantly, the actual providence and process of the quotation is often obscured:

> What is that now
> ancient and decayed
> fungus by the first
> mayflowers, – trumpet-shaped with a
> very broad mouth, the chief
> inner part green, the outer part brown?
> ... dirty-white fungi in nests. Each one is
> burst a little at the
> top, and is full of dust
> of a yellowish rotten stone
> color, which is perfectly dry.
> (Henry David Thoreau)[22]

Cage presents this passage on decaying mushrooms as of a piece, but it is in fact a synthesis of two proximate but separate *Journal* entries, from 24 April 1856 and 11 May 1856; the ellipsis is the only indication that these two separate pieces of text have been run or 'brushed' together. A further excision has been suppressed between 'nests' and 'each': the measurements of the mushrooms ('each about three quarters of an inch [in] diameter without any thick rind which peels off') have been omitted. Subtle, almost invisible changes like this characterize much of Cage's work. That Cage's compositional process deforms its source as well as recycling it puts a particular pressure on his 'brushing' process, figuring it as both the frictional transfer implicated in the painter's brushstroke, which leaves a transformational residue, and the sweeping up and together of litter or detritus, which enables it to be collected and reused. Texts which might seem to be quoted can in this way be seen not as replicas, either in exact or approximate form, but as emergent novelties which are not reducibly described as quotations. They are not mere examples or model instances of their source texts but the products of a set of foregrounded mediations. This dynamic enacts the suggestion of

> We imagine that
> spores that never before joined in
> reproduction on occasion in the case of

---

[22] Ibid., 127. Source from *The Journal of Henry D. Thoreau: In Fourteen Volumes, Bound as Two*, ed. Bradford Torrey and Francis H. Allen (New York: Dover, 1962), 1007; 1013. This is the edition of Thoreau's *Journal* which Cage used in composing *Mushroom Book*.

> related species sometimes do:
> >   possibility of a
> > natural invention.²³

The mushrooms' capacity to breed across 'species' and create new forms with ease is here imagined alongside (but not identified with) texts' capacities to rub off on one another. Cage's poetic preferences are ingrained in the series of meldings, substitutions and prunings that form this 'quotation' which might better be described as a mediation – preferences for the unmeasurable and uncontrollable, for things that meld or melt and thus resist stable identification, for reworking rather than repetition, for process rather than product – for what Latour describes as the actant's capacity to 'to mutate, to change and to bifurcate'. Fungal decay is the method as well as the material of these quotations from Thoreau – the matter in both senses.

Consequently Cage's materialism is one attuned to transformation, where something unaccountably extra is generated in any attempt to record a result or take a sample.²⁴ To make an image, to write a line or to sound an object is always to change it, to collaborate in its becoming something else. Latour's 'Irreductions' makes a similar point: 'We can perform, transform, deform, and thereby form and inform ourselves, but we cannot *describe* anything. In other words, there is no representation, except in the theatrical or political senses.'²⁵ Writing is a way of doing rather than a pure gnosis, and to read a text is only to add another layer of deformation to this process. No form goes unchanged in attention or study: 'We study . . . forms . . . / (Henry David Thoreau)'.²⁶

Such readerly decay is germane to the second major criterion on which Cage selects from the *Journal*, though in this second instance that decay is already at work in Thoreau's text itself. Its primary manifestation in the *Mushroom Book* is through the shorter, one-line excerpts from the text, which are the most immediately unsettling to readers because they can seem so innocuous. Part VII of the text, for example, contains a Thoreau quotation of just one word,

---

[23] Cage, *Mushroom Book*, 127.
[24] Compare the idea of the representative sample to the miniaturization logic of models, which Olson rejects (see Chapter 6); in recognizing that all samples are also mediations which act in transformative ways upon matter, it can be seen that the difficulty of reading post-Poundian 'collage' poetries engaged in these plays of part/whole relations is majorly predicated on the lack of ready reading protocols which address intermediality and mediation's generative excesses as *themselves the object of reading*.
[25] Bruno Latour, *The Pasteurization of France*, trans. Alan Sheridan and John Law (Cambridge and London: Harvard University Press, 1988), 228. Emphasis in original.
[26] Cage, *Mushroom Book*, 147.

'to-day'.²⁷ Its inclusion seems something of an anomaly; it bears limited relation to the major thematics of the *Mushroom Book*, nor does contextualization in the writing around it enable it to be easily construed. It is preceded by a statement on Cage's friends and their propensity to invite themselves to dinner, and followed by an extreme example of the 'writing without syntax' which Cage disperses through the text, a seemingly meaningless string of characters: 'ahachudegnathe e / lubuta / ne'.²⁸ In one sense, 'to-day' is fitting simply because both Thoreau's and Cage's texts are types of diaries. Even a perfunctory and incomplete reading of Thoreau's *Journal* will demonstrate that the word 'to-day' is widespread, as is to be expected in a text which is explicitly concerned with narration of the events of particular days. In fact the word, in this specific formulation, is so common as to be impossible to locate in the text, though it is tempting to think that its appearance in the very first entry in the *Journal* was the spur to its inclusion. However, it is likely that what struck Cage was not so much the word's prevalence (which might work to efface it as much as highlight it) but its antiquated spelling. Being more than a century old by the time the *Mushroom Book* was written, the *Journal* is abundant in such antiquities, but the typological oddity of 'to-day' gives it a particular perceptual kick which stops the eye in its transit across the page. In her essay 'UNCAGED WORDS: John Cage in Dialogue with Chance', Joan Retallack describes a moment of crisis in reading 'brought on by linguistic or lettristic or graphic oddments that slow the skimming glance, inviting a kind of meditative awakening in the material text. Calling attention to the arbitrary splendore of grammaticall forms & enigmaticall epithetes'.²⁹ This forms part of what Retallack calls the 'figure-ground shift' enacted in writing like Cage's, according to which the arbitrarily suppressed backgrounds or protocols of reading are foregrounded. What I want to emphasize here is not so much the arbitrariness of language as its capacity to redirect readers' attentions from the semantic level to that of readerly protocol – a revolution of attention from meaning to mediation. The residue of past forms is what makes 'to-day' remarkable, then. This seemingly innocuous piece of textual detritus thus tells readers two significant things about the *Mushroom Book*. First, that Cage is interested in variants, in things that are in one way identical – spoken, 'to-day' and 'today' are semantically and aurally indistinguishable – and yet manifest themselves with subtly and seemingly

---

[27] Ibid., 166.
[28] Ibid.
[29] Joan Retallack, *The Poethical Wager* (Berkeley, Los Angeles and London: University of California, 2003), 233.

inexplicable difference – 'today' is at least as common as 'to-day' in the *Journal*, but there is little to indicate a logic or pattern governing the two usages. Second, that this interest in variants is symptomatic of a practice of reading the *Journal* which involves being sensitive to the presence of similarities and unexpected variations in typography, spelling, expression, material and so on. This practice is closely aligned with Cage's mushroom-poetics.

Cage's mode of readerly attention is particularly attuned to the phrases in Thoreau that constitute commonplace, even formulaic expressions for 'natural' phenomena. Several examples of this can be seen in the passage from the *Journals* quoted at the beginning of section VII:

> Aug. 11. P.M. – To Assabet
> Bath.
> I have heard since the 1st of
> this month the steady creaking cricket.
> Some are digging
> early potatoes. I notice a new growth of red
> maple sprouts, small
> reddish leaves surmounting light-green
> ones, the old being
> dark-green. Green lice on
> birches.[30]

Afternoon trips to Assabet Bath are frequent features of the *Journal*, and this account of one such trip is itself host to a number of Thoreau's observational and verbal commonplaces. The combination of 'Green lice' and 'birches' is a well-established one, especially in this section of the *Journal*. An entry from about two weeks later (27 August 1854) describes 'extensive birch forests all covered with green lice'.[31] The 'steady creaking cricket' is another stock phrase; Thoreau rarely describes a cricket that is not 'creaking', and very often in a 'steady' fashion. This is in some senses unsurprising. Presumably certain times of year are more likely to engender infestations of lice or aphids, and so Thoreau is more likely to find and remark upon them at certain times and in certain habitats; crickets are more often heard than seen. In this Thoreau's writing 'environment' is more like Olson's than Cage's, insofar as it is directly responsive to external stimuli and events in and around Concord (the arrival of bugs or the placement of trees)

---

[30] Cage, *Mushroom Book*, 158; Thoreau, *Journal*, 774.
[31] Thoreau, *Journal*, 786.

just as Olson's writing is to those of Gloucester (notably, the seasonal arrival and departure of birds).[32] All three authors employ a poetics of attention, but the environment in which that attention operates varies; all are at different times responsive to both textual and worldly environments, but differences between those environments mediate the mode of their appropriate attentions. What this moment demonstrates for *Mushroom Book* at the level of a *poetics of reading* is that Cage is aware of these formulaic or 'typical' locutions in the Thoreau text and picks them out of the source text as characteristic or endemic. It is one of the peculiar features of Cage's 'writing-through' technique, developed in tandem with Jackson Mac Low, that it conveys something of the familiar 'tone' or 'atmosphere' of the texts it writes-through whilst revealing certain easily overlooked aspects of their verbal texture, leaving readers with a sense that they have learnt something of – if not, perhaps, something *about* – the source text, or that the source text has been changed for them. Here specifically, Cage's writing performs and makes legible a series of the occluded protocols of Thoreau's writing; the gestures made as much out of habit or instinct as choice.

The most remarkable such gesture is again found in one of the short, seemingly vestigial *Journal* quotations lodged in the *Mushroom Book*, following immediately the passage about Assabet Bath. The phrase quoted is 'A crescent of light'.[33] This short locution makes its appearance in the first year of the *Journal*'s existence, in the entry for 16 December 1837. This is the only time that the phrase occurs in the text; but it is far from being an isolate in the phylogenesis of Thoreau's writing. (By 'phylogenesis', I mean the process via which various species evolve; it is often opposed to 'ontogenesis', the process via which particular organisms proceed from youth to maturity. Phylogenesis is more appropriate to the development of terms in Cage's writing in the sense that it is a considerably more indeterminate process than ontogenesis, which latter instead seems appropriate to a poetics in which the semantic content of a term develops and accumulates in a manner highly determined by the author, and is interpretable according to a pre-established protocol.)

'A crescent of light' is in fact the first term in a huge array of similar locutions. On 3 March 1838 Thoreau writes of a 'crescent of night'; on 9 November 1855, there are 'crescents of dazzling white'; on 1 May 1856 he describes 'crescents of

---

[32] See Olson, *Maximus*, 418, describing Gloucester as a 'rest of / migrating birds N / a headland for migrating birds / North kr-ku her headland up above the / seashore'. *The Maximus Poems* is repeatedly concerned with the movements and dispositions of migrating seabirds.
[33] Cage, *Mushroom Book*, 158; Thoreau, *Journal*, 23.

bright brick red'; on the seventh of that month, there is a 'Crescent of white'.[34] In the seemingly unremarkable phrase 'a crescent of light' Cage uncovers a verbal tic of Thoreau's in which the figure of the crescent is thematically associated with light and luminosity, and also with an aural pattern including words which rhyme with 'light'. This is in many ways a surprising detail to notice over and across such a long text, and bespeaks an attentive openness to the emergent qualities of a text in Cage's reading practice. Here we can see Cage composing through a practice of readerly attention based around a repetitive, meditative (even obsessive) reading and rereading of Thoreau, as a result of which the text becomes a familiar landscape which is pragmatically navigable – though not comprehensively or determinately mappable – for Cage as reader-author. The sections of the *Journal* excerpted into the *Mushroom Book* are partly chosen thematically (from the index-entries for 'fungi' in the Dover edition), but others, more tellingly, are chosen via a process of gleaning whereby typographical, verbal and phonetic patterns, repetitions and variations which 'stand out' as landmarks from the texture of the writing for (Cage) the reader are treated as objects of experience and inserted into the *Mushroom Book* not as purely semantic units but as sites of recurring attention, things that keep popping up. In this way they are more like the nonsense-strings than the mushroom-mesostics or stories. It is here that Hayles's objection to Cage's writing finds its riposte: by treating Thoreau's language as an environmentally bound entity, and thus present to the 'natural' world of sense, Cage effectively turns his quotations into pieces of found-language. The distinction between the natural and the man-made does not hold in Cage's work for this reason; all things participate in networks of sensuous experience, networks which are collaborative and interactive in a fashion which circumvents the rebarbative exasperation Hayles suggests in her account.

Mushroom Book is, then, constructed not in such a fashion as to be semantically scannable, but rather to encourage and exemplify a type of readerly attention which is analogous to that of the mushroom hunter, open to what emerges from the thicket of writing 'with and without syntax', and responding to that stimulus 'as you go along', playing by ear.[35] Latour writes, 'Action is not what people do, but is instead the *"fait-faire"*, the making do, accomplished along with others in an event, with the specific opportunities provided by the circumstances.'[36] In

---

[34] Thoreau, *Journal*, 26, 934, 1010–11; 1011.
[35] Viz. Olson, 'By ear, he sd' (*Maximus*, 6).
[36] Latour, *Pasteurization of France*, 288. Emphasis in original.

his quotations from Thoreau, Cage *uses* a text (and encourages his readers to use his text) not as a semantic unit but as an environment, the surrounding set of objects and impulses capable of collaborating with and surprising readers. Finally even Latour's model of 'fait-faire' as a form of craft or practice is not sufficient to Cage's ambition; even 'making do' is finally a metaphor – an idea with an ideational history. Rather than pre-emptively foreclosing the hunt by settling with 'practice' (with 'hunting') as the putatively non-metaphoric metaphor, Cage's surprise, his 'sudden sense of / identification' is followed immediately by 'the spirit / of comedy' – a self-deprecating recognition that the real has slipped out of the hand again.

* * *

Cage's commitment to the revelation of a non-human world outside of metaphor and discourse (even discourses of practice) forces him beyond Latour's satisfaction with the always-withdrawn though interactive matter of the actant. Indeed, Latour writes that to imagine realism as built on a foundational truth is putting the cart before the horse, since 'truth' is merely how humans make sense of the real: 'A sentence does not hold together because it is true, but *because it holds together* we say that it is true.'[37] Yet as has been sketched, for Cage, the truth or 'spirit' of things inheres in their collapse and deformation, a position that could never be acceptable to Latour's vitalist perspective, wherein the withdrawn centres of things are inaccessible and destroyed, or remade, by deformation. Because Cage's optic is more focused on what is cast off as an endlessly ungraspable *product* of an ongoing *process*, rather than just a relation by which one ultimately unknowable thing becomes another, there *is* material foundation for Cage, and it is huntable if not perhaps catchable.

A clearer demonstration of this can be examined by returning to the nonsensical string of letters, and to the many others like (but of course, necessarily unlike) it in *Mushroom Book*: 'ahachudegnathe e / lubuta / ne'. In such encounters with the text, readers are nonplussed. This is a piece of writing in no identifiable language, almost entirely beyond the realm of readerly competence (though it remains in a recognizable *script*). Hayles is right that we can see it 'aims to defeat intentionality'; but what other function could such random strings of letters perform? It is here that Latour's aesthetic experience of surprise

---

[37] Ibid., 185. Emphasis in original.

('the slight surprise of action') is at its most incisive as a commentary on Cage's poetics. In part, the 'surprise' of the unreadable in the ostensibly readable (i.e. a poem) is registered as a sort of absurd comedy, and indeed Cage quotes Thoreau describing mushrooms in homophonic terms ('They impress me like humors . . . pimples on the face / of the earth').[38] The further point of the surprise is that readers recover an aesthetic experience in the non-semantic. The letters are not semantic units (they are not even standardized spellings of inarticulate sounds, say 'arggghh'), but could rather be considered the meeting point of a nexus of actants – Cage, Thoreau, mushrooms, quotation, letters, words, syntax, non-syntax and so on. Readers find the letter strings in the textual environment, and having learnt how to respond from previous adventures in that environment, treat them less as a semantic puzzle and more as a point of creative resistance – a point at which the surprise is experienced as a moment of literal contact with text as matter.

A further educative example of Cage treating words as matter can be found in his text 'Empty Words' (1974–5). 'Empty Words' is in many ways similar to *Mushroom Book*. It is made of quotations from Thoreau's *Journal* (though in this case these are chance-determined) and contains scans of the sketches Thoreau adjoined to the *Journal* entries, which are set against the words. The text itself is fed through an *I-Ching* procedure which selects excerpts by line and syllable, of which sense-making units – sentences, or even individual words – are not guaranteed outputs, so that the language of the *Journal* is thoroughly diced. As a result, 'Categories overlap. E.g., *a* is a letter, is a syllable, is a word' in a manner which hollows them out as semantic units, leading to an '*equation between letters and silence. Making language saying nothing at all*'.[39] It is not of course the case that writing can be reduced to no semantic content *at all*, but the correct linguistic mediation can reveal to readers how language is more than mere signification. Craig Dworkin writes, 'All reading, of course, involves the reader's production of signification to some degree; the point is that such production is too often routine and disciplined by pre-established and inflexible protocols.'[40] What is important here is that Cage is not claiming entirely to remove words from their structures of signification; rather, he is employing them in such a fashion that

---

[38] Cage, *Mushroom Book*, 156; Thoreau, *Journal*, 622. See Retallack on 'the reflexive humor of the figure-ground shift' (*The Poethical Wager*, 192).
[39] John Cage, 'Empty Words', in *Empty Words: Writings '73–'78* (London and Boston: Marion Boyars, 1980), 11–77, 33, 51. Emphasis in original.
[40] Dworkin, *Reading the Illegible*, 11.

they can be recognized as phenomena that are not *merely* significatory, and whose identity as word, letter or sound is not always determinate: '*What can be done with the English language? Use it as material*.'[41]

The de-semanticization of language is a function of Cage's poetic indeterminacy, where that indeterminacy is created by an abandonment of artistic mastery and a settling into a more open relationship with matter, with parliaments of texts, and where what identifies 'matter' as 'matter' is something like a quality of resistance, a refusal to be made the object of discourse. As Jane Bennett ventriloquizes Thoreau, 'I wish to speak a *word* for Nature: I will substitute words for that which is not reducible to an act of linguistic constitution.'[42] Bennett's word itself will always shift and change – it is not its semantic content but its being in the place of what is properly unnameable that 'matters'. It marks the opening in which the real can be glimpsed, outside of the overbearing intention of the author.

Hayles's uncertainty regarding the justice of the analogies on which Cage bases his writing is in fact very much the point of the analogies; that the not-quite-likeness of bad analogy – hunting mushrooms is in *some ways*, but not all, like writing a text which is in *some ways*, but not all, like reading the text which is in *some ways*, but not all, like hunting for mushrooms – gives the text and its operations a sort of real inscrutability, an intractable, unparaphraseable character it shares with matter, which can be communed with but not mastered. The analogy has in itself a resistance that is more than analogous, that is intrinsic, so that materiality is not in the mushrooms or in the words or in their analogy but in how the analogy doesn't work, as in Latour's analogy between the activities of the scientist and the artist. The dysfunctional analogy creates the opportunity for the meeting of actants, and their surprising interaction, outside of the mastery of the subject; but it also works to undo Latour's own metaphorical constructs of action, practice and strength, replacing them with a type of endemic disappointment which remains surprising and even amusing. Over the length of the longform, such unstable analogies allow for the construction of extended but undetermined texts.

* * *

---

[41] Cage, 'Empty Words', 11. Emphasis in original.
[42] Jane Bennett, *Thoreau's Nature: Ethics, Politics and the Wild* (Thousand Oaks, London and New Delhi: AltaMira, 1994), 64. Emphasis in original.

In *Darwin's Plots*, her 1983 study of evolutionary narratology, Gillian Beer explicitly links surprise with breakthroughs in scientific endeavour: 'The element of surprise, including unforeseeable reorderings of known data, new information, formal boldness, are qualities valued in scientific enquiry as in fiction. One pleasure they both offer is enfranchisement: they release us from the loop of the foreknown, they enlarge possibility.'[43] Particularly, she notes how analogy contains this ability to surprise the reader or thinker precisely because it is always on the edge of decay or overdetermination, of slipping the leash and becoming absurdity. In this way it escapes both the circuit of the already-thinkable and the necessarily unthinkable, making analogy a study of its own morphing through extension, as much as it is an extended 'likeness':

> Analogy and morphology are both concerned with discovering structures common to diverse forms. In the case of analogy this communality expresses itself by first ranging two patterns of experience alongside each other, seeking their points of identity, and then using one pattern to extend the other. There is always a sense of *story* – of sequence – in analogy, in a way that there need not be in other forms of metaphor.
>
> If allegory is narrative metaphor, analogy is predictive metaphor. Whereas in allegory the one-to-one correspondence of object and meaning is suspended, in analogy the pleasure and power of the form is felt in part because it is *precarious*. We experience a sense of trepidation as we follow the analogy through its various stages lest we arrive at the stage where the analogies disport. Disanalogy may collapse the entire sequence or vitiate it retrospectively.[44]

Beer furthermore suggests, in germane fashion, that analogy's vertiginousness provides an avenue of escape from teleological, anthropocentric thinking in terms that Cage would surely have recognized: 'The abiding problem for Darwin was how to express [natural selection] in a language which was imbued with intentionality. The lateral rather than the causal organization of analogy offered him one possibility.'[45] Beer argues that Darwin (along with Cage another principled non-believer in 'species') found in analogy a useful way of exploring things that are branching, melding, spliced and multifarious without collapsing back into categorizing or reductive language, as English is prone to do. Cage reinterprets what Beer describes as the forever-looming collapse of analogy

---

[43] Gillian Beer, *Darwin's Plots: Evolutionary Narrative in Darwin, George Eliot and Nineteenth-Century Fiction* (Cambridge: Cambridge University Press, 2009; first published 1983), 84.
[44] Ibid., 74. Emphasis in original.
[45] Ibid., 81.

as a source of comedic tension which is never quite released or dispersed entropically. Despite the many similarities between his work and Latour's, it is here that a real and substantive divide can be seen. Despite its constant change, Latour's universe of actants is stable *at the level of objects or parts* because each actant is entirely competent unto itself, oddly self-sufficient and withdrawn until it interacts. Cage's mycopoetics, meanwhile, is a poetics of incompetence, where incompleteness and inaccuracy (try to) rule.

The surprise of textual indeterminacy which Cage exploits in *Mushroom Book* is closely linked to a literal, quotidian attention to its own medium, to the nuts and bolts of text production which displace the heroic model of poet as sage or seer. When Alexander Pope coined the term bathos in 1727's 'Peri Bathous', he figured the bathetic as attention to precisely these quotidian concerns: to the low rather than the exalted or epic; to the poetic ground rather than the poetic figure, in Retallack's terms. Though the 'Scriblerian' character in which Pope writes is not without parodic intent – the most obvious target is Longinus, though Pope's more lackadaisical contemporaries are also in the firing line – the inversion of value his essay toys with and satirizes nevertheless has much to contribute to an understanding of Cage, as here:

> The sublime of nature is the Sky, the Sun, the Moon, Stars etc. The Profound of Nature is Gold, Pearls, precious Stones, and the Treasures of the Deep, which are inestimable as unknown. But all that lies between these, as Corn, Flowers, Fruits, Animals, and Things for the meer use of Man, are of mean price, and so common as not to be greatly esteemed by the curious.[46]

It is tempting, then, to add 'fungi' to Pope's list of things of 'mean price' whose revaluation he describes as the business of the bathetic mode. The destabilized humility of the object of bathos, which becomes noticeable and interesting despite being lowly esteemed in aesthetic hierarchies, is not unknowable because it exists on a sublime or cosmic scale, but because its small-scale parts, its specificities, are subject to unpredictable, morphing change, which makes the text it constitutes difficult to navigate, and moves focus onto its shifting though limited topography. Pope writes of the bathetic author that

---

[46] Alexander Pope, 'Peri Bathous: Or, Martinus Scriblerus, His Treatise on the Art of Sinking in Poetry', in *The Prose Works of Alexander Pope Volume II: The Major Works, 1725–1744*, ed. Rosemary Cowler (Oxford: Blackwell, 1986), 171–276; 191. Some of the sympathies between *Mushroom Book* and Pope's satirical prescriptions are almost uncanny: bathos 'must not always be *Grammatical*' the Scriblerian voice counsels at one point (217). Emphasis in original.

His design ought to be like a labyrinth, out of which no body can get clear but himself. And since the great Art of all Poetry is to mix the Truth with Fiction, in order to join the *Credible* with the *Surprizing*, our author shall produce the Credible, by painting nature in her lowest simplicity; and the Surprizing, by contradicting common opinion.[47]

Labyrinthine texts like Cage's articulate themselves around readers' attempts to orient themselves vis-à-vis expectations and surprises, the familiar and the subtly changed or re-presented. (Pope wrote that '*Imitation* is of two sorts; the first is when we force to our own purposes the Thoughts of others; the second consists in copying the Imperfections, or Blemishes of celebrated authors'; both iteration and deformation are central to Cage's uses of source material.[48]) What his mycopoetics shares with bathos is a constant realignment of attention, where navigation of the text, the 'hunt through' it, is surprised by or happens upon instances of textual interest which then proliferate or decay, undermining the credibility of the reading protocol in a newly generative moment of surprise. The analogy between mushroom and poetics is the type of this interaction in reading Cage; the mushroom is the figure both of its material basis and its capricious fecundity, able to produce experience beyond all expectation.

In Cage's short-circuited analogy, there is very little design and rather more hack. The analogy is set up to fail, and subsequently to exploit that failure as an object of real resistance. In this way, its own logical limitation opens up a path to escaping the paradox of representative realism. As *Mushroom Book* demonstrates, even this residual representation is deformed, found as 'raisedul'.[49] But the humorous incapacity of this blemished, anti-hierarchic moment is itself a form of achieved realism – a true account of the failure of true accounts. There has generally speaking been insufficient critical recognition of the role and importance of Cage's humour to his work, and especially his poetry, which is more often read as a grave comment on the end point of all language games. Yet greater attention to Cage's slapstick sensibility, fully evident to popular audiences – as seen in the laughter which greets the 1960 TV performance of 'Water Walk' on *I've Got A Secret* – is crucial both for Cage criticism and for an appreciation of late-modernist realism more generally.[50] This is because his

---

[47] Ibid., 192.
[48] Ibid., 204. Emphasis in original.
[49] Cage, *Mushroom Book*, 144.
[50] John Cage, 'John Cage Performs Water Walk' (1960), accessed 1 February 2020. http://exhibitions.nypl.org/johncage/node/28.

explosion of aesthetic hierarchies and expectations includes within it the failure of readers, or critics, to fully and capably account for his work's functioning, to be left with anything but a look of bemusement.

* * *

The delegitimization of aesthetic hierarchies could lead to both depths of insight and inanity. To withdraw the currency of received reading protocols proves the important point that these protocols are often speciously naturalized, but doing so also risks leaving the text a mire of failure and disarticulation. As in *Mushroom Book*, humour is a key tool in combatting the latter, one of course intrinsic to the bathetic mode, and here inflected with a mischievous Dadaist liberation from rational hierarchies and bourgeois taste. There is, however, a further valence of 'bathos' which extends and deepens the significance of Cage's poetics of surprise, and connects it to broader issues surrounding longform poetry. Harping on both the implications of bathos's depth, Pope writes, 'Thus have I (my dear Countrymen) with incredible pains and diligence, discovered the hidden sources of the *Bathos*, or, as I may say, broke open the Abysses of this Great Deep.'[51] If it is considered that a great deal of what constitutes the long or epic poem tradition, as far back as Homer, is a quest or odyssey-type narrative profoundly concerned with the ocean (as in part Pope is here), then bathos as 'depth' takes on a suggestive cast.

Here, Cage's bathos can be profitably connected to Olson's pragmatic interest in the ocean, and indeed in the 'sources' of the deep in several senses.[52] Olson considered as 'poet of the sea' is an old story, but it is worth noting that he is more specifically a poet interested in the ocean bottom, and in depth considered as instrumental in the agriculture of the sea, in hunting fish rather than mushrooms. In an early *Maximus* poem, entitled 'Letter 5', Olson berates his friend and rival, the poet Vincent Ferrini, for lacking a practical knowledge of the life of the sea as it is practised in Gloucester, and resultantly for writing poetry which fails to attend to these specificities. Ferrini's writing, Olson claims, is unable 'to read sand in the butter on the end of a lead, / and be precise about what sort of bottom your vessel's over'.[53] Here the plumbing of the oceanic floor serves a purpose

---

[51] Pope, 'Peri Bathous', 224. Emphasis in original.
[52] For a fuller exploration of Olson's depth-poetics, see Brendan C. Gillott, 'The Depth of Charles Olson's *Maximus Poems*', *English* 66, no. 255 (December 2017): 351–71.
[53] Olson, *Maximus*, 27.

analogous to the mushrooms of Cage: an exercise in navigation and applied knowledge which is highly sensitive to context (and so to mediation), and which tests the foundations of a poetic discourse both analogously and literally. Like Cage, Olson is clear that the bathyal/bathetic is a function of the literal, that it undermines poeticizing abstraction:

> on waters which are tides, Ferrini,
> are not gods
>
> on waves (and waves
> are not the same as deep water[54]

To 'discover the hidden sources' is to know the ropes, to go through the archive, to get to the bottom of things, where the glamour of the surface cannot penetrate. This is a change in writing's dimension, where the extent of the page – the 'field' of the poem, as Olson's phrase has often been interpellated – is not its only or its primary territory. Navigation of the longform poetic text is difficult in part because the map is mostly not on the page before readers at any given time; one cannot be certain of where the mushroom will pop up. Any given aspect of the text is stretched in a network across the whole of the text – beneath into the future of the text, what is left to read, and above into the past, which has already been read – and across its many and manipulated sources as well. There seems to be little to grasp onto. The surface of the page becomes unpredictable, and the orientation of the map changes depending on the conditions. The abyss of illegibility opens up in these encounters, but contact *can* be made with the bottom, surprises *can* occur, and the text can be navigated *pragmatically* even if not in a *predetermined* manner. The indeterminacy of the longform's depth, for both Cage and Olson, is structured by the three dimensions of the volume.

---

[54] Ibid., 29.

4

Olson, lists and archives

That Olson's longform poetics is deeply indebted to the work of Ezra Pound, particularly to the example set by *The Cantos*, is perhaps the single greatest commonplace in Olson criticism.[1] Nonetheless, the exact nature of that debt is hard to define. This is in no small part due to the fact that the most obvious manifestation of Poundian influence, the set of formal principles for constructing of a post-epic long poem which Olson borrows from *The Cantos*, is in fact subsidiary to a set of rather more reticent formal questions pertaining to Olson's writing and its relation to various traditions of longform poetry. The accusation that Olson was a poor man's Pound, and essentially derivative, tends to have at its centre two powerful but vague diagnoses: that, like Pound, Olson wrote poetry deeply concerned with history as theme and process; and that, again like Pound, he did so at great length. Whilst superficially true, neither of these points seems equal to the complex formal negotiations of both history and textual extent at work in Pound and reworked in Olson. The commitment of this book is to reading its authors as themselves readers, possessed of capacities for insight, criticism, enthusiasm and disappointment, and not merely as apers or influence-victims. This is especially true of Olson's relation to Pound.

A further, though equally ill-defined, genetic link between *The Cantos* and *The Maximus Poems* might be seen in their respective habits of knowing, the way in which each collates and compiles large quantities of often recondite information, reference and quotation and incorporates this material as a central component of the work. Where Cage characteristically chews through and eviscerates texts and systems of knowledge classification in aid of the liberation of the senses, both Pound and subsequently Olson seem much more interested in building up dense, vertiginous edifices of eccentric, arcane knowledge, in a poetic of accumulation rather than desiccation (Cage meanwhile wrote his way through Pound's long poem, producing a stripped back, 'anarchived' version

[1] See, for example, Christensen, *Charles Olson*, 1626; Maud, *Charles Olson at the Harbor*, 59–69.

of *The Cantos* according to the mesostic rule).[2] This is, of course, a somewhat crude sketch of both Pound's and Olson's poetics. Particularly, it leaves open the question of *accumulation* already at work in the idea of both *Maximus* and *The Cantos* as prospective 'long historical poems'. It is in the various operations and checks upon the process of poetic accumulation, in links between pieces of knowledge, in their ordering and presentation, and in their structuring via 'cantos', or individual poems as part of a sequence, or 'letters', or one long juxtapositionary whole, in which Olson's inheritances from Pound can be most usefully perceived. These are not the only possible structural models which could be used for discussing either work, and the struggle to articulate the structuration of each poem is central to their broader formal and generic negotiations. Are *The Maximus Poems* 'poems' or is 'it' a 'poem', and either way how is/are poem/poems lodged or stored within the 'work' as a whole?

Discussing his writing as part of a television series documenting the work of various contemporaneous poets, Olson promised that 'I can read you my poem – the best poem I ever wrote, "The Librarian". It's *all Frank Moore!*'[3] Addressing the National Educational Television camera, Olson here provides viewers of *USA: Poetry* with an unexpected assessment of the poem and of his work as a whole. A standard account of Olson's writing would probably not consider 'The Librarian' to be his best or most significant poem – that accolade might more likely be applied to 'The Kingfishers', or, perhaps, to *The Maximus Poems* as a whole structure. These latter are certainly the most discussed and influential items in Olson's corpus. 'The Librarian' of 1957, written in the middle of his career and read here in 1966, is an example of Olson's rather-less celebrated activity as a lyrical and a dream poet – the latter being a surprisingly common mode for Olson. That Olson, then, describes it as his 'best' poem – even if at a point before much of *Maximus* had been written – gives latter-day viewers pause.

'The Librarian' sits oddly in the catalogue of Olson's work – a marginal piece he appeared to consider his best, and a 'Maximus' poem that is not a *Maximus Poem*. This estrangement of 'The Librarian' from *Maximus* is foregrounded in the first stanzas (incidentally one of the few places in Olson's writing where the term 'stanza' can be used without much anxiety):

---

[2] John Cage, *Writing Through the Cantos* in *X: Writings '79-'82* (Hanover: Wesleyan University Press, 1983), 109–15.
[3] Olson, 'Charles Olson reads "The Librarian" (March 1966)', accessed 1 February 2020. https://www.youtube.com/watch?v=E85iFHTKrAI. Emphasis in original.

> The landscape (the landscape!) again: Gloucester,
> the shore one of me is (duplicates), and from which
> (from offshore, I, Maximus) am removed, observe.
>
> In this night I moved on the territory with combinations
> (new mixtures) of old and known personages: the leader,
> my father, in an old guise, here selling books and manuscripts.
>
> My thought was, as I looked in the window of his shop,
> there should be materials here for Maximus, when, then,
> I saw he was the young musician has been there (been before me)[4]

'Off-shore' is the word which begins *Maximus*, and Olson's return here to a position of 'remove' indicates the relation which he considers to pertain between 'The Librarian' and his longest work.[5] The amorphous dynamic which separates 'Maximus' from 'Charles Olson' in *The Maximus Poems* is here briefly resolved, as two Maximuses ('duplicates') populate the poem, one as the figure who observes and the other as the 'work' to be fed 'materials'. It is these materials that I want to explore here. Any perfunctory reading of any section of *The Maximus Poems* is enough to convince that Olson's practice as a poet was much involved with the collection, digestion and arrangement of matter from heterogeneous sources, primarily taken from outside what a New Critical poetic might consider the 'proper' realm of poetry (it being recognized that the idea of poetry as only concerned with certain types of textual material is one which would find much resistance not only in modernist writing but in many earlier poetic practices; Milton and Coleridge are two excellent examples). Under this view, 'books and manuscripts' are in *Maximus*, as in 'The Librarian', the consistency of 'Maximus', the place in which the work begins. The image is of Olson trawling the bookshops and looting the libraries of New England for inspiration and for textual materials which he then inserts into the edifice of his poems, often as relatively direct quotation (which is to say, mediated by the *idea* or *image* of a direct or immediate quotation).

Olson's poetry is not unique in developing this practice. The obvious precursor is, of course, Pound, whose *The Cantos* exemplify what he calls, in *How to Read*,

---

[4] Olson, *Collected Poems*, 412. First published in *The Distances* (New York and London: Grove; Evergreen, 1960), 90–2.
[5] Olson, *Maximus*, 5.

'logopoeia', or 'the dance of the intellect amongst words'.[6] Pound's telescoping of matter from classical Chinese, Greek, Latin and Provençal texts, lectures on history, economics and philosophy, and many other things into arrangements of poetic association is usually taken to be the genesis of what is called the 'archival poem' in the long-poem tradition of modernism. Pound had little patience for a plurality of 'books and manuscripts' as the basis for a poetic practice, stating that 'the books that a man needs to know in order to "get his bearings" [. . .] are very few', but this preference for a few exceptional works over many mediocre ones is in part a product of his vociferous autodidacticism and intellectual combativity, both clearly on display in *How to Read* (the title itself foregrounds the insolence of Pound's polemic, exemplified in his dismissal of Shakespeare).[7] These ideas and texts had a profound impact on Olson (he calls them 'the swag / of Pound', his loot and his characteristic style), and he continued to read Pound diligently even after their falling out at St Elizabeths.[8] But an account of his work, and especially of *The Maximus Poems*, as an attempt to relocate the archival aspects of *The Cantos* to seaside Massachusetts, complete with the radiant nodes and luminous vortexes of Poundian poetics, fails to address Olson's insistence that 'The Librarian' is not part of *The Maximus Poems* and its implication that his central volume is an archive without a curator. Pound's poetic is intensely curatorial; Olson's is rather more open-ended in this regard, more completely committed to a process poetics which is present but not fully developed in *The Cantos* (in this vein, George Butterick suggests that 'there was always something at bottom unsatisfying and flat about Pound's definition of an epic as "a poem including history". The form of *The Maximus Poems* is the act of history').[9] In assessing 'The Librarian' as 'the best poem I ever wrote', it is likely that Olson is tacitly removing *The Maximus Poems* from the field of candidates that might be 'the best poem' or 'my poem', and so from an inherited idea of 'the poem' metaphorized as well-wrought urn or organic whole. The 'materials' that constitute *Maximus* share much, of course, with those making up Pound's 'tale of the tribe', his archive of civilization; they continue a Poundian process which Marjorie Perloff describes as 'collapsing the boundaries' between art and

---

[6] Ezra Pound, *How to Read* (London: Harmsworth, 1931), 25. See also Olson's sceptical treatment of Pound 'as he preaches the "grrrate books"' in 'A Bibliography on America for Ed Dorn', in *Collected Prose*, 297–310; 301.
[7] Pound, *How to Read*, 28.
[8] Olson, *Maximus*, 32.
[9] George F. Butterick, *A Guide to the Maximus Poems of Charles Olson* (Berkeley, Los Angeles and London: University of California, 1978), xviii–xix.

not-art, poetry and not-poetry, resisting polysemy in favour of 'finding the appropriate phalanx of particulars'.[10] Their 'combinations / (new mixtures) of old and known personages' owe much to Pound's collagistic writing. But the particulars Olson gathers in his largest work are less susceptible to the sort of glossing Pound's archive invites.[11] They pose questions of a particular and difficult type for readers and for criticism.

* * *

'The Librarian's parting salvo is a set of questions, which brings the USA: Poetry recording of the poem finally to full circle: 'Who is // Frank Moore?'[12] This last query, rhetorical in the sense that it provides no reasonable means for an answer, or any expectation of one, has nonetheless seemingly been settled by Olson scholarship, in this particular instance by the pre-eminent Olson archivist and explicator George Butterick. In his *Guide to the Maximus Poems of Charles Olson*, Butterick glosses the long, late section entitled 'I'm going to hate to leave this Earthly Paradise', from *Volume III*, and its own brief reference to Moore:

> Cf. 'The Librarian', in which the following dream-figure appears: 'He / (not my father, / by name himself / with his face / twisted / at birth)', and which ends: 'Who is / Frank Moore?' Moore (b. 1923), a composer, was a friend of Olson's during the late 1940's and early 1950's in Washington. See also 'Olson in Gloucester', *Muthologos* I, 169–173.[13]

This entry, a small but representative part of Butterick's enormous concordance, poses many questions about his own scholarly practice and about what the

---

[10] Marjorie Perloff, *The Dance of the Intellect: Studies in the Poetry of the Pound Tradition* (Cambridge: Cambridge University Press, 1985), 78, 85.
[11] For example, in the 'Malatesta Cantos', the various references and historical voices Pound constellates have at their insistent centre Pound's admiration of Malatesta and his church; readers might add to this their knowledge that this admiration was crucially informative of Pound's enamoured attitude to Mussolini, and that the church was ruined towards the end of the war; but the variousness of historical accident is always pulled towards a centre here, determined by Pound. Concretely, this can be seen in how *The Cantos* IX–XI, structured as lists, each line beginning with 'And', deploy this 'and'-gesture as accumulative, attaching each 'and' to Malatesta as coordinating principle; as I shall show, Olson's 'plus this . . . plus this' listing is neither so coordinated nor so determinate (Pound, *The Cantos of Ezra Pound* (New York: New Directions, 1996), 34–52). For a full account of Malatesta's place in these cantos see Rainey, *Institutions of Modernism: Literary Elites and Public Culture* (New Haven: Yale University Press, 1998), 107–45. See also Lawrence Rainey, 'Introduction', in *A Poem Containing History: Textual Studies in the Cantos* (Ann Arbor: University of Michigan, 1997), 1–17; 2: '[*The Cantos*'s] massively overdetermined effort to trace a cultural genealogy of the twentieth century.'
[12] Olson, *Collected Poems*, 414.
[13] Butterick, *Guide*, 728.

correct critical stance to take towards Olson might be. The most immediate response is to say that knowing who Frank Moore 'is' is not in many ways very helpful in reading 'The Librarian', or even really to reading the (more obviously referential-and archival) *Maximus Poems*, wherein the identity of Frank Moore is too tiny a detail in the huge serial meshwork to be of much moment. 'The Librarian's question is importantly not to be answered but asked, an ending to the poem rather than a hermeneutic key to it. However, at another level, identifying Frank Moore is not meaningless or beside the point because it opens up questions about the orientation of Olson's work towards just such acts of scholarship and research, questions which need to be asked if criticism is to be able properly to respond to the challenge of Olson's writing. So, for example, there is a need to query what sort of intervention into *The Maximus Poems* Butterick's *Guide* performs and enables. What relationship does 'The Librarian', or any of Olson's non-Maximus material, bear to *The Maximus Poems*? And, expanding the circle, what relationship does material not produced by Olson have to a work which, as has been regularly observed, and as Butterick's book-hunting and bibliographical travails in producing his *Guide* attest, is deeply invested in its own reading ('He read to write,' as Olson himself wrote of Melville).[14] Is performing this sort of scholarly investigation in fact a sort of *de*formation – by elucidation, or addition – of the work? What might appear as an act of supreme critical 'faithfulness' to Olson's text could easily be interpreted as an *intervention* which in fact profoundly changes what readers of the work can and must do when reading, despite protestations of mere clarification or elucidation. In a work as autodidactically charged as *The Maximus Poems*, to be told something rather than to 'find out for oneself', in Olson's favoured phrase, is to have the dynamic of the poem short-circuited. Such deformative scholarship, which extends and distorts the work under its scrutiny, seems obviously inappropriate in the context of writing committed to process and to self-transformation through what Olson understood as history: 'finding out for oneself'.[15] It certainly bears out a disrespectful attitude to the presumed autonomous unity of the poem of the kind Olson gestures to in his introduction to 'The Librarian'. However,

---

[14] Olson, *Call Me Ishmael*, 36.
[15] Olson, 'A Bibliography on America for Ed Dorn', 308. I am taking the idea of 'deformance' from Jerome McGann and Lisa Samuels's article ('Deformance and Interpretation', in *Poetry and Pedagogy: The Challenge of the Contemporary*, eds. Joan Retallack and Juliana Spahr (New York and Basingstoke: Palgrave Macmillan, 2006), 151–80), in which they argue that '[d]eformative [reading] moves reinvestigate the terms in which critical commentary will be undertaken' (162). They take Emily Dickinson's impulse to 'read backwards' as a paradigm of deformative criticism.

Butterick suggests a number of ways in which his *Guide* – and, by extension, his kind of scholarly endeavour – should cause readers of Olson to be sceptical of this apparent congruence.

In his introduction to the *Guide*, which provides a methodological justification for the volume, its scope and aims, as well as a brief account of Olson's writing career and publication history, Butterick describes the problems faced by *Maximus*'s author as of a kind with those encountered by readers. He writes that

> The major difficulty, and it can be discouraging, is the large amount of reference needed to populate a poem that seeks to occupy and extend a world. The *Guide to the Maximus Poems* provides the scholarship useful for reading these poems which are as complex and allusive as Pound's *Cantos*.[16]

As has been observed, the equation between *The Cantos* and Olson's own project is perhaps slightly misleading, and suggests Butterick may have been modelling his own book on that of previous exegetes of *The Cantos*, notably perhaps the work of Pound's correspondent and student Achilles Fang, whose doctoral dissertation 'Materials for the Study of Pound's *Cantos*' was completed in 1958 and, though never published, remains a central source on classical allusion in Pound's poetry. The key phrase here, though, is 'the scholarship useful'; Butterick repeatedly claims that what he is doing is best described as *scholarly*. He writes that his *Guide* (itself produced as a doctoral thesis) is 'an act of scholarship of the most fundamental and traditional sort', and makes this gambit clearer in describing his method as a 'suspension of the subjective judgments and comparisons more properly called criticism than scholarship'.[17] Whilst it seems unlikely that every 'subjective' component has been purged from even so archival a project as Butterick's, the distinction he sketches out between scholarship and 'what is more properly called criticism' is nonetheless a suggestive one. Here Butterick tacitly acknowledges the first objection ascribed to the revelation of Frank Moore's identity, that is, the impulse to question how useful the *Guide* is in actually *reading Maximus* – an activity understood by Butterick as that of critic rather than scholar.[18]

---

[16] Butterick, *Guide*, ix.
[17] Ibid., ix, xv.
[18] For a lengthy consideration of the scholar-critic divide, and its place in the institutional history of literary criticism, see Joseph North, *Literary Criticism: A Concise Political History* (Cambridge and London: Harvard University Press, 2017). North's account deals extensively with several of the critics I discuss here, notably Richards, Empson and Brooks.

The distinction between scholar and critic is complicated further by the status of the poet, who, whilst in the classical account neither scholar nor critic, has always performed both functions in some degree as part of poetic practice; in Olson's case this is especially true. His work as a scholar and critic not only fed into but was in many cases the substance of his work as a poet. Blurring these lines is part of what I have described as the work's genre-defying function. A further level of complexity is added by criticism's traditional compositional mode, in a prose which is imagined as transparently informative and explicative, whereby literary criticism threatens to replicate the 'prose vs. poem' generic dichotomy which Olson's work sets its face against. The clarifying function often understood as central to critical inquiry is not only alien to Olson's own work, where, as von Hallberg has argued, the poems often throw light on the prose rather than the other way around; it is also incapable of addressing the challenge that Olson's obsessive blurring and rambling poses in its war on scholarly rigour.[19] Joan Retallack and Juliana Spahr have called this dynamic, in which a certain type of modernist poetry resists and refuses absorption into critical and pedagogical regimes, 'a kind of permanent revolution' in that the only response the academy has found in the face of such work is to allow itself to be repeatedly changed by the encounter.[20] One result of this revolution as it expresses itself in reading Olson is that the supposed antithesis between criticism and text ('prose' and 'poetry') is forced to realign and reimagine itself as a form of reading against the grain, one which is deeply disrespectful of and wilful with both its text and its own operation. Criticism must turn on the text, and in doing so turn on itself turning on the text – Olson's early interest in the weird topographies of the Moebius strip may be an interesting analogue here. In doing so, such a criticism both replicates something that was present in Olson's own practice and paradoxically does something different; that is, it both learns Olson's lesson and simultaneously deforms it.

* * *

Autodidactic learning is a central trope and method of literary modernism, common to Pound's *The Cantos*, Joyce's *Ulysses* and Zukofsky's *A*, to name a

---

[19] Robert von Hallberg, *Charles Olson: The Scholar's Art* (Cambridge and London: Harvard University Press, 1978), 49.
[20] Joan Retallack and Juliana Spahr, 'Why Teach Contemporary Poetries?', in *Poetry and Pedagogy*, 1–10; 4.

few better-known examples; the intellectual stance of *The Maximus Poems* is very much an outgrowth of this tradition. Closely allied to this autodidacticism is a deep scepticism of – and sometimes outright distaste for – traditional scholarship and its institutions. Leaving Harvard, his PhD unfinished, Olson committed to completing his work on Melville outside of the academy. With the encouragement of Edward Dahlberg, his study of *Moby Dick* became increasingly idiosyncratic and stylistically adventurous, culminating, after abandoning several full drafts, with the 1947 publication of *Call Me Ishmael*, Olson's first book. Amongst other quirks, the volume was composed in a hybrid format wherein critical and bibliographical comment on Melville's work was interspersed or juxtaposed with documentary-narrative sections which Olson titled 'FACTS'.[21] These sections focus on 'real-life' whaling tales contemporary to the purported happenings of *Moby Dick*, and demonstrate a resistance to received critical modes already well developed in Olson's earliest work. That Olson finally settled in this hybrid mode is significant in two senses: First, it provides a root and context for his patchy and peripatetic scholarly career, characterized as it was by a rocky relationship with academia and an often contemptuous account of mainstream scholars, who he lambasts as uninspired time-servers (in his 1951 poem 'Letter for Melville', as a notorious example, Olson ventriloquizes the attendees of the Melville Society's centennial conference, demurring that 'you must excuse us if we scratch each other's backs with / a dead man's hand', whilst asserting his own distinction, since 'poets move very fast, that is true / it is very wise to stay the hell out of / such traffic, of such labor / which knows no weekend').[22] Second, *Call Me Ishmael* still contains plenty of what Butterick would call 'scholarship of the most fundamental and traditional sort', most notably Olson's discovery and account of Melville's annotated copies of Shakespeare, which are discussed at length. The search for a new critical discourse, one more invested and imaginative, is not then seen as necessarily exclusive of traditional scholarly apparata – archives, book lists, annotations, bibliographies and so on – but the use to which any such apparatus must be put is to be radically different. This high-momentum, trailblazing, risk-taking spirit, visible in more developed form in 1956's 'A Bibliography on America for Ed Dorn', characterizes Olson's attitude to the academy and scholarship, and was almost certainly cemented by his years at experimentally inclined Black

---

[21] Olson, *Call Me Ishmael*, 3–7, 77–8, 109.
[22] Olson, *Collected Poems*, 234.

Mountain College. In the school of Olson's writing, detail and rigour are not abandoned so much as torqued, made to work harder (to take no weekends, as Olson has it) and traditional scholarly labour is used in more audacious and tendentious fashion:

> to make those silent vessels go-as Joseph Collins
> cldn't, with all his superior knowledge, & experience: Collins'
> 'scholarship' (work for the Federal Government) wasn't
> as <u>useful</u> as Joseph B Connolly's <u>activity</u>
> could have been, his <u>energy</u> ergon[23]

In this 1965 section of *Maximus*, Olson opposes 'scholarship' (which is not merely intellective but includes 'experience') to 'activity', 'energy', 'usefulness' and 'ergon' (work). The point to be made is that scholarship, however deep or 'superior', is to be judged against an axis of 'use', of what it does and what is done with it. Accuracy is not sufficient (or even entirely necessary – Butterick's *Guide* points out that 'Joseph B Connolly' is really called James; energy and ergon seem to have got the better of scholarship at this point).[24] Emphasis on the 'useful' rather than the merely correct had been a central feature of Olson's poetics from at least 1950, when he wrote in 'Projective Verse' that in the deployment of perceptions the poet must 'USE USE USE the process at all points'.[25] 'Usefulness' is understood as momentum, as action rather than contemplation.

That Olson's scholarship tends towards the kinetic and the processual is not to say that it is completely indifferent to accuracy. As has been frequently noted, Olson had a habit of correcting factual errors made in one section of *Maximus* in a later section, or even almost immediately:

> [just before the Indian attack, 1676, after which
> no further record* of Henry, or of Margaret his
> wife   until
>
> *not true. He died, Pemaquid, 1683.[26]

These acts of self-correction evidently constitute an important part of Olson's autodidacticism. They also demonstrate a poetics which understands itself as the process of its own making, where poetry is poesis. The role of 'FACT'

---

[23] Olson, *Maximus*, 466. Emphasis in original.
[24] Butterick, *Guide*, 598.
[25] Olson, 'Projective Verse', 240.
[26] Olson, *Maximus*, 590.

in this schema is thus one of necessity but not sufficiency, and all facts are potential placeholders. The contents of the archive are under constant threat of correction, rewriting or abandonment. As a result Olson's writing not only produces a huge ratio of waste to well-wrought urns but also destabilizes the distinction between the two, since what the poetics is interested in is interstitial, not quite a needle or a haystack. The shifting relation between parts and the whole is the central focus here – a relation which always threatens to vanish or be substituted for others. Comparing Olson to Thoreau, Stephen Fredman has written that '[a]lthough attention to the facts informs the utilitarian bent of American culture, our writers [Olson and Thoreau] take the facts beyond the realms of utility. In common usage, the term *fact* connotes something that is self-evident; for our writers, "the self-evident" is that which obscures a true apprehension of the fact: a fact is an object for investigation.'[27] The way in which 'FACT' is taken out of its 'common usage' by 'USE', making 'USE' no longer a matter of 'utility' in the functional or practical senses, is part of the paradox of Olson's process poetics, in which certain things need to be in place in order to be effaced or forgotten. Fredman's point about investigation is salient because it indicates one of the stranger implications of Olson's autodidacticism – an implication much effected by and effecting his views on scholarship. Distaste for received opinion, and the subsequent drive to 'finding out for oneself', is at the best of times difficult to balance against traditional academic endeavours that operate as long-term, even historic collaborative projects and rely on slow accumulation and judicious substitution of knowledge. This 'expert' mode of scholarly judgement which authorizes these additions and substitutions is the object under scrutiny in Olson's writing, and in Cage's too. I think that Fredman is somewhat wide of the mark in opposing 'the self-evident' to 'true apprehension', however. It is closer to the truth to say that for Olson 'the self-evident' and 'true apprehension' are potentially radically identical, and it is scholarship, or received opinion, or the state of discourse, that obscures them. Part of the work's archiving activity is not so much an accumulation of sources and authorities as a clearing-away of them in the hope of achieving a fresh mode of experience.

In Olson the insistence on first-hand, heuristic learning and idiosyncratic reading often reaches the point of mysticism or conspiracy theory. His epistemology is not only anti-institutional but deeply committed to the idea

---

[27] Fredman, *The Grounding of American Poetry*, 29. Emphasis in original.

that reality will surrender itself to the individual attention alone, unaided and unmediated:

> There are no hierarchies, no infinite, no such many as mass, there are only
> eyes in all heads,
> to be looked out of[28]

There is a suggestion of a democratic vision here, of a knowledge equally accessible to all ('Polis // is this', as '*Maximus to Gloucester, Letter 27* [withheld]' famously puts it), but it is a prospective one couched in an elitist conception of the perceiving subject as one who has transcended epistemological acculturations and mediations.[29] Not only is there nothing that cannot be known for Olson ('no infinite'), there is nothing that isn't in some way immediately apprehensible. This utopian phenomenology is an inheritance, in part, of the Objectivist tradition and William Carlos Williams's dictum that there should be 'no ideas but in things', but Olson puts a new and especial emphasis on the poetics of immediate perception through his explicit and thoroughgoing conflict with the norms of scholarly and critical endeavour.[30] Rachel Blau DuPlessis has noted that 'positing a pure (direct, untainted) source of primal data was Olson's insistent but sometimes naïve test of authenticity'.[31] The 'hierarchies' and abstract 'infinites' Olson indicted as *in*authentic and found so frustratingly endemic in the scholarly circles he moved in in the thirties were to be opposed with and replaced by a commitment to the tangible and immanent, to *things* rather than categories, to particularities rather than generalities. The archive was reconceived not as a place of preservation but of rupture.

* * *

As part of his rejection of generalities ('no such many *as mass*') Olson proposes *particularities* – a doctrine which he termed 'particularism' in an early letter to Creeley.[32] These particularities express themselves most obviously in Olson's employment of locality as a trope, in the figure and figuring of Gloucester, but his movement to larger transcontinental and cosmogenic themes in the second

---

[28] Olson, *Maximus*, 33.
[29] Ibid., 185.
[30] William Carlos Williams, *Paterson*, ed. Christopher MacGowan (New York: New Directions, 1995; first published 1946), 6; 9. Interestingly, the phrase appears twice, differently punctuated: first as '-Say it, no ideas but in things-'; second as 'Say it! No ideas but in things.'
[31] Rachel Blau DuPlessis, 'Olson and His *Maximus Poems*', in *Contemporary Olson*, 135-48; 143.
[32] Olson and Creeley, *Complete Correspondence Volume 1*, 28. Emphasis in original.

and third volumes of *Maximus* points to the way in which particularism was not conceived of as exclusively concerned with 'bits' or trivia but rather with an attempt to build such small materials into a complete image of the 'human universe', a longform poiesis: 'I am making a mappemunde. It is to include my being.'[33] The archive was to be both a universal and an idiosyncratic personal collection, and much of the difficulty in writing *Maximus* was the difficulty of making this possible. Put otherwise, the challenge was one of having particularities both as they themselves were, *as things*, particular, and as how they were particularly *for the poet*. Olson describes his solution to this problem in '*Maximus to Gloucester, Letter 27* [withheld]':

> An American
> is a complex of occasions
> themselves a geometry
> of spatial nature.[34]

The individual is described as formed by a nexus of individual facts, things or events which are also 'occasions' in the sense that they are causes, that they impel something further, in this case a 'geometry' in the literal sense, a measurement and bounding of the earth, and here even of 'spatial nature', of the entire universe. The particularities map out by their own impulsion a universal account or 'mappemunde'. There is a great deal of Whiteheadian metaphysics here (the world as a continuum of interlocking and interactive 'events'); but it is also important to note that for Olson this is true specifically of Americans, migrants to 'the New World', so confirming Fredman's point about the way in which Olson's work is both heavily informed by, and knows itself to be informed by, a particular 'bent of American culture' wherein a prioritization of the 'thing' imagines it to come before any ideas about it. A regularly cited one-page section from volume three of *Maximus* contains only the words 'tesserae / commissure', and here Olson succinctly describes his understanding of his project.[35] The tesserae, small bits of glass or stone which make up a mosaic, must come first; commissure, joining or junction, is the act of poeisis, of arranging, filing and mediating, but this must come second. An archive of facts is its prerequisite, and these facts do not break down into any smaller part.

---

[33] Olson, *Maximus*, 257.
[34] Ibid., 185.
[35] Ibid., 269.

Olson's figuring of the 'tesserae' or 'FACTS' as the basic building blocks of his work makes them oddly immune to critical reading. They have to be taken as they appear or else the writing collapses. In the section entitled '<u>Cashes</u>', from the second volume, Olson describes the near-sinking of a fishing vessel in unlikely circumstances. The passage, prose-like in its style, relates how a ship went 'stern clean over bow' in heavy seas and landed unaccountably safe on its keel.[36] This seems like a tall story of the sort associated with fictions of the sea (*Moby Dick*, perhaps), but Olson insists at the end that 'The facts in the case are as described. The man who owned the vessel was Andrew Leighton of Gloucester, and the captain who sailed her was called Bearse.'[37] In characteristically asserting the literality of the account, and collapsing the distinction between things and how they are described in the text, Olson denies that his writing is symbolic or even narrative in any simple sense. He connects the ship's misadventure laterally into a network of related but not narratively relevant details (e.g. the name of the ship's owner) both as a marker of authenticity and as a way of subverting the piece's narrative temporality. Olson was in general suspicious of narrative, and was careful to undermine and blunt it whenever it appeared in his work, as here, drawing and absorbing it into the non-narrative texture of *Maximus*'s nexal structure. In doing so he also asserts the primacy of 'facts', whose 'complex' is a geometry rather than a story. The geometrical scheme of poetry is re-envisioned not as a two-dimensional grid which is traversed left-to-right and top-to-bottom, or as a narrative which follows through time and space from beginning to end, past to future, but as a three-dimensional volume to be navigated by various vectors, putting the reading protocols which dictate that one never travels backwards, in circles, elliptically or by scattershot into question. The epic is as diligently suborned as the lyric in *The Maximus Poems*, in favour of this arrangement, and accumulating, ever-complexifying connection, of things or facts. The trajectory of *The Maximus Poems* as a whole piece is not then a narrative one but an accretive one which loops temporality back on itself as themes, facts, figures and things reappear again and again, elucidating and altering – sometimes in contradictory ways – their previous incarnations, forcing readers to shuttle inbetween various shifting points in the poem's unusual geometry. The upshot is that to question the veracity of any of Olson's factual claims is to argue past his work. A critic of Pound could, in aid

---

[36] Ibid., 189. Emphasis in original.
[37] Ibid.

of understanding *The Cantos*, take a course in classical Chinese, after which he might well find that he knew more about classical Chinese than Pound ever did. A critic who underwent similarly rigorous induction into one of Olson's pet interests, say Mayan archaeology, would find that reconstructing Olson's knowledge, likely idiosyncratic or threadbare at any rate, from its sources and situations would only reproduce the ur-archive of materials in Olson's possession which he transmuted into *The Maximus Poems* throughout the 1950s and 1960s. Work like this ends up busily ignoring the fact that the poem exists by dissolving it back into its constituent parts with no regard for the whole. This is to say that reconstructing what Olson *knew* is not a particularly useful way of looking at the writing he produced as a result.

Describing the modus operandi of *The Cantos* in *The Poetics of Indeterminacy*, Perloff notes the onus put on readers to involve themselves with the poem's comprehensibility: 'The poet [. . .] insists on our participation; it is up to us to fill in the blanks.'[38] In this judgement one can see the motivation for scholarly work such as that performed by Fang; Pound's writing requires readers to concern themselves with the 'blanks' as part of what it is to read it. However, I am less convinced that this precept holds for Olson as it does for Pound. Olson's insistence that the poet is a pedagogue ('the only pedagogue') and his enthusiastic propagation and exploration of the idea of methodology (*meta hodos* as he calls it in the *Bibliography on America*) both suggest that if *The Maximus Poems* is an archival poem in the mode of *The Cantos* then the archive is there as an exemplar rather than a research resource in and of itself.[39] 'Finding out for oneself' is to be a historian in Olson's understanding, and simply, gamely to reconstruct an author's readings or meanings, or alternatively to quibble with them, is not equal to Olson's rich suggestion, either as a teacher or as a poet. In part this focus on a methodology rather than a thematic or a form is a direct consequence of a late-modernist ambivalence towards 'Poetry' as that term was understood by the New Critics. This is as much as to say that Olson never makes any serious claims for Gloucester as of any especial poetic interest, but merely finds it as the place to hand, the soil to start the digging. It is not Gloucester, or perhaps even America, Olson is proposing to his readers but a type of practice, a way of working through the experience and knowing that one accumulates. Though figured as an idiosyncratically American epistemology, as part of the 'no

---

[38] Perloff, *The Poetics of Indeterminacy*, 183.
[39] Olson and Creeley, *Complete Correspondence, Volume 1*, 23; Olson, 'A Bibliography on America for Ed Dorn', 302.

ideas but in things' rhetoric Olson inherited from Williams, this is likely better understood as an emanation of the 'gentleman scholar' tradition of obsessive autodidacticism which preceded modern academic disciplinary divisions and labour conditions. The encyclopaedic cataloguing of bits of phenomenal data (which might only be available to the eccentric scholar himself) implied by this model is certainly congruent with Olson's lionization of the sensible over the received, and his sceptical treatment of mainstream scholarship. The identity in Olson's epistemology of what is evident to the senses with what is truly the case, independent of consensus opinion, means that a catalogue of merely quotidian occurrences can take on a certain kind of learned significance.

This ad hoc grasping of what is close to hand remembers that a part of Olson's inheritance from Pound was a transgression of the question of genre ('poetry or/vs. prose') in the sense that that question of genre had been ontologized *as a question* by Pound and other founding modernists. (Gertrude Stein's *Tender Buttons* is a good example, instructive also for reading Cage.) In this sense Olson is a faithful Poundian exactly in his wayward employment of *The Cantos*'s generic operations. So Olson is perfectly happy to include matter like 'There was a salt-works at Stage Fort' or 'Cashes', which would not sound too out of place in a historical study or guided tour, but where their prose-like style marks them out as specifically directed poetic gestures within the broader structure of the work.[40] Where for Pound 'beauty is difficult', for Olson difficulty inheres in any serious engagement with the world, and 'beauty' is more likely to be used as a term of disinterest than of recommendation.[41] Olson's 'particularism' is conceived of as *actually particular*, then, specific and distinct and cantankerous, where not only the 'blanks' but the context in which they are to be filled is determined by readers. Even though an account of reading Pound's work as a slavish process of reference-hunting and author-aping would be misleading and incomplete, Olson's poetry and his method are still markedly more heuristic than that of his mentor and rival, for whom only accurate inaccuracies can be acceptable, functioning in puns, joking phonetic spellings and mistranslations which are there to be recognized and shared in by the astute reader. Olson's

---

[40] Olson, *Maximus*, 431–2. Emphasis in original.
[41] For an account of Olson's disinterest in the idea of beauty, see Charles Boer, *Olson in Connecticut* (Rocky Mount: North Carolina Wesleyan College, 1975), 56–7: 'You talked of your work, and of yourself, as "postmodern", or "post-literary". Your purpose in writing was not in making "literature". [. . .] "Beautiful" was never the right adjective for someone to use as a description of your work. There were certain words, common enough, that rarely entered your vocabulary. "Beautiful" was one of them.' See also Pound, *The Cantos*, 466.

writing courts excess and waste in a way that Pound's does not, since for Pound mistakes are always measured against the controlled response to them, where what readers will find and what they expect to find is the same thing. In this sense Olson's writing is more indeterminate than Pound's, just insofar as Pound's archive is topographically and typologically more stable than Olson's. The point is not that Olson's poetic scholarship is more slipshod than Pound's, but rather that in being 'open' to the sensate, including thereby *reader's* sensory data as part of the poem – and so readerly uncertainty and undecidability – Olson's archive requires a more pragmatic mode of navigation, one which expects not to be able to map or describe the archive's structure with any certainty. Whilst it is imaginable that an especially assiduous and single-minded reader might become fully the master of *The Cantos* and its surrounding archival halo of texts and sources as they pertain to Pound's poem, it is less clear that such an assiduity would be possible for readers of Olson, whose object of study would include presumably un-recapturable moments and impressions in the life of the poet, material which despite being thus unrecapturable is nonetheless archived and indexed in *Maximus*, leaving thereby a mark of its absence – another way of saying this is that whilst both *The Maximus Poems* and *The Cantos* might be read as types of tangential autobiography, or at least as diaries of learning, *The Cantos* is much more directly a 'life in books' or a 'life in art' than is *Maximus*. A radical aesthetic scepticism and ambivalence towards 'The Poem' as a distinctive and validated cultural product leads Olson to include material in *The Maximus Poems* of which it is difficult to know what sort of aesthetic experience or response readers will have – if any. In a sense, the anti-modernist charge that much modernist and postmodernist work doesn't mean anything, or simply isn't poetry, parallels the feeling much of *Maximus* legitimately creates when properly understood. The point is that 'not-poetry' is understood as a useful and even a corrective value.

***

Here I want to turn briefly to Jacques Derrida, who wrote extensively on archives as structures and as forms of thought, in a way which is highly suggestive for thinking about archives as models for indeterminate poetic form. In 1995's *Archive Fever: A Freudian Impression*, Derrida suggests that thinking about archives requires, before all else, thinking about inclusion and exclusion, about insides and outsides: 'Where does the outside commence? This question is the question of the archive. There are certainly no others.'[42] As with the modernist entanglement of various generic modes with 'questions of genre' more abstractly conceived, the archive has its being only as a question in Derrida's account. To create or encounter an archive is only ever to wonder about – wander through – it in search of its principle or delimitation. This bound which determines the character of the archive is never found for Derrida; an archive must be *indeterminate* exactly as a result of its formal porousness:

> We have no concept, only an impression, a series of impressions associated with a word. To the rigor of the *concept*, I am opposing here the vagueness or open imprecision, the relative indetermination of such a *notion*. 'Archive' is only a *notion*, an impression associated with a word and for which, together with Freud, we do not have a concept. We only have an impression, an insistent impression through the unstable feeling of a shifting figure, of a schema, or of an in-finite or indefinite process.[43]

Derrida's sense of the indeterminacy of the archive is founded on *constitutive* incompleteness – an incompleteness which is always *incompleteable*, a lack which can never be filled. An archive poetics is always of necessity a process poetics, one whose sifting, cataloguing, labelling and redistributing of its material is endless. Whilst it is commonsensical to think of archival documents as 'read-only', authoritative objects for veneration and preservation, the archive requires the intervention of the archivist as a worker of a contingent poesis. Olson's archival poetics, with its illegibilities, delinquencies and excesses, is a case in point.

Intrinsic to Derrida's articulation of 'archive fever' is the conception of the 'supplement': a paradoxical addition which constitutes the gap it itself comes to fill. Though allegedly an afterthought attached to an originary substance, the supplement 'always-already' undergirds that origin. As Derrida writes in discussion of Freud elsewhere, 'The supplement, which seems to be addressed as a plenitude to a plenitude, is equally that which compensates for a lack.'[44] In other words, the excess of the supplement is found in the lack it both creates and discovers in the origin. For Derrida, writing itself is the paradigm of supplementarity in its supposedly secondary relation to speech, and the archive,

---

[42] Jacques Derrida, *Archive Fever: A Freudian Impression*, trans. Eric Prenowitz (Chicago and London: Chicago University Press, 1998; first published 1995), 8.
[43] Ibid., 29.
[44] Jacques Derrida, *Writing and Difference*, trans. Alan Bass (Abingdon: Routledge, 2009; first published 1978; 1967 in French), 266.

as a special instance of writing, is subject to this logic: its incompleteness, the fact that it forever requires addition and revision, constitutes it as the source of activity and power which demands the authorization and veneration of scholarship.[45] Extrinsically, as I shall go on to show, the logic of the supplement can be read into lists and listing as a way of accounting for the strange iterativeness of that form, its insistent gesture towards what has not yet been included – 'and this...and this...and this...'. One useful way of thinking about the list is that it has no *necessary* content, only a formal drive to self-completion which makes any given instance or piece of content substitutable or subject to effacement. The list is generated by these questions: How do we decide *what* to itemize and at what level of *granularity* (i.e. what object or part is large enough to count)? Paradoxically, the desire to collect archival material is constituted not in service of the material's own integrity but in service of the archive as an indeterminate *image* or *representation* which substitutes itself for the archive's present condition. The meaning or 'notion' of the archive is isomorphic neither with the original material nor with what could or must be added to it.

The indeterminacy of the archive is then a function of its deranging effect on the ideal of scholarship as authoritative, objective, disinterested and abstracted from its material. Archive poetics is writing and reading as annotation, comment, excision, addition and reorganization, as against the model of the authenticated 'read-only' document. Derrida writes that the archive short-circuits 'the objectivity of the historian, of the archivist, of the sociologist, of the philologist, the reference to stable themes and concepts, the relative exteriority in relation to the object, particularly in relation to an archive determined as *already given, in the past* or in any case only *incomplete*, determinable and thus terminable in a future itself determinable as future present, domination of the constative over the performative, etc.'[46] Archivists are always *in* the archive, both in the sense of being located and locatable amongst it and in leaving traceable genetic influence in it even if they are away from it. They perform the archival.

Olson's poetic archivism is explicitly concerned with this performance. As ever for Olson, this is at bottom a question of mediation and its discontents, of the tension between archaeology as objective uncovering and archaeology as creative revelation/revaluation. Derrida describes 'the nearly ecstatic instant

---

[45] In *Archive Fever* Derrida pays extended attention to the relation of the Freud scholar Yosef Hayim Yerushalmi to his subject, precisely in order to interrogate scholarship's simultaneously subordinated and suborning relation to its archival materials.
[46] Derrida, *Archive Fever*, 51. Emphasis in original.

Freud dreams of, where the very success of the dig must sign the effacement of the archivist: *the origin then speaks by itself*; it is easy to see in this a correspondence to 'no ideas but in things', to the curious desire for a poetry of unmediated access which Olson's 'objectism' seems to gesture to.[47] Yet it also indicates the iterative, indeterminately accumulative manner in which Olson's longform archive constitutes itself. Its shape is not predetermined.

* * *

The Maximus Poems consists of a vast set of multiplying and spreading references, quotations and items arranged and juxtaposed, rather than of examples of epic or lyric poetry per se. Both the simplest and the most telling locus of this tendency is in Olson's habit of listing. Lists are in no way new to longform poetry: lists of generation in the Bible, or of ships in Homer, demonstrate the technique's antiquity, but in Olson listing is particularly charged, in several senses. In part it is the simplest expression of *The Maximus Poems'* structural method, of paratactic accumulation and accretion rather than hypotactic and subordinative expression, as here:

> *The Account Book of B Ellery*
>
>   vessels
>   goods
>   voyages
>   persons
>   salaries
>   conveyances[48]

This is a list, but also, Butterick notes, an index to the contents of the book – a list of lists.[49] There is, then, some semblance of order in this list, even if it appears as a found poem. It has a generalizing rather than particularizing function. It is however indicative of the way in which Olson was deeply and continuously interested in the simultaneous activation and suspension of meaning which lists enact, especially as here when the list in question contains things that are not of the same 'type' and so whose relations and taxonomies are unclear

---

[47] Ibid., 92. Emphasis in original.
[48] Olson, *Maximus*, 204.
[49] Butterick, *Guide*, 292.

(the last page of *Maximus* is like this: 'my wife my car my color and myself').⁵⁰ Olson's suspicion of traditional syntax and its egocentric implications finds its expression in these listing structures which maintain relations between distinct things as indeterminate rather than dictated by the poet – the list maintains things in their particularities but also abstracts those particularities within a list of examples of the particular.

Perhaps the most germane example of listing in *Maximus*, however, and certainly the most extensive, can be found in *Volume I*, in the section entitled 'The Record'. As an example of a poetics of 'archive' 'The Record' is particularly apt, since it contains found-text, lists, footnotes, historical and bibliographical data – the generic traits of both archives and Butterick's 'traditional scholarship'. It also enters neatly into an Olsonian dynamic of repetition and rewriting, as its list of skins carried by the Dorchester ships *Amytie* and *Fellowship* (' fox / racons / martyns / otter / muskuatche / beaver') is replicated as part of a prose passage thirty pages later, where it is noted that some were not transported unprepared but as coats.⁵¹ The list of skins is a sublist of a larger itinerary of the ships' wares ('dry fish // corfish // train oil // quarters of oak // skins'), the first three entries of which are footnoted with contemporary comments from shore manifests or Olson's own glosses.⁵²

By far the most striking part of 'The Record', however, is the long list of requirements the men of the early 'plantation' of Gloucester needed to preserve themselves and carry out their activities to produce the items named earlier. This is a full page long and includes costs:

14 MEN STAGE HEAD WINTER 1624/5

they required

7 hundredweight biscuit bread	£ 5. 5. 0
@ 15/ per hundred	
7 hhds of beere or sider 53/4 the tun	20. 0. 0
2/3 hhd beef	3. 7. 2
6 whole sides of bacon	3. 3. 0

---

⁵⁰ Olson, *Maximus*, 635.
⁵¹ Ibid., 121, 156.
⁵² Olson's researches into the early history of Gloucester were greatly aided by his correspondent J. H. Prynne, who provided him with copies of the port books which these passages of *Maximus* rely on. For more on this, as well as the complete correspondence between Olson and Prynne in the years 1961–70, see Ryan Dobran (ed.), *The Collected Letters of Charles Olson and J.H. Prynne* (Albuquerque: University of New Mexico Press, 2017).

6 bush. pease	1.10. 0
2/3 firkin butter	1. 0. 0
2/3 cwt. cheese	2. 0
1 pecke mustard seed	6. 0
1 barrel vinegar	10. 2
15 lbs candles	1. 0. 0
3 pecks oatmeal	9. 0
2/3 hhd/ aquae vitae	3. 0. 0
2 copper kettles	3. 0. 0
1 brasse crock	1. 0. 0
1 frying pan	2. 0
1 grind stone	5. 0
2 good axes, 4 hand hatchets, 4 short wood hooks, 2 drawing irons, 2 adzes	16. 0
4 arm saws, 4 hand saws, 4 thwart saws, 3 augers, 2 crowes of iron, 2 sledges, 4 iron shovels, 2 pick axes, 4 mattocks, 4 cloe hammers	5. 0. 0
heading and splitting knives	1. 5. 0
so much hair cloth as may cost	10. 0. 0
pinnaces sails	2.10. 0
8 fishing boats iron works	2. 0. 0
10 boats' anchors, ropes	10. 0. 0
canvas to make to make boats sails and small ropes	
2 saines, a great and a less	12. 0. 0
10 good nets at 26/ a net	13. 0. 0
fitting for them at 25/ each	10. 0. 0
2000 nails to build houses at 13/4 the thousand	1. 6. 8
4000 nails at 6/8 per 1000	1. 6. 8
2000 nails at 5d per hundred	8. 0*

*Olson, *Maximus*, 122.

The provisions of the fourteen men who founded Gloucester are of historical interest, and so 'belong' in Olson's 'archive' of relevant facts; they are clearly of some importance to him, but they are disabling for readers who expect poetry to be fundamentally lyrical, who can do little with these facts except experience them as a form of *Maximus*' excessive detail, its wasteful particularity, indices of a lost world. Though there is little here of what might traditionally be considered 'poetic value', readers cannot skim or skip the list. Similarly, the critic has to quote the whole thing because the list has no possible 'etc.' moment, no 'and so on'. Each article is particular, rather than one of a predictable taxonomic group, coordinated only by abstract and historically located economic value. The unpredictability of listing sidesteps subordinating-causal syntactic structures, replacing them with an uncontrolled accumulative logic, 'plus this – plus this' as Olson has it in '*Letter 27* [withheld]'.[53] Paul Stephens has argued that where the poetries of Pound and Williams were characterized by construction of new forms of knowledge, Olson's poetics replaces knowledge with information as the field of concern.[54] Whilst I think it is true that information is a more important concept for Olson than is 'knowledge' traditionally construed, I would argue that writings like 'The Record' demonstrate a further twist to this dynamic in that they show how facts or things are often made entirely *uninformative*, otiosely literal, in the writing. Olson's notes were always well in 'excess' of what found its way into 'the poems' as such, forming a shadow archive 'behind' *The Maximus Poems*, one out of which the posthumous third volume had to be salvaged. That Olson does not include *everything* points to the way in which it is not the information itself that the writing is oriented towards but rather information driven to the point of effacement, where the movements engendered inbetween things or facts are what matter. Read as a traditional set of 'records' or accounts, *Maximus*, like 'The Record' itself, becomes a morass of barely relevant interconnection characterized only by its unwieldiness. This superplus marks the enlargement of what can be included in poetic discourse, the expansion which gave Olson the reputation he has amongst subsequent poets as the great permission-giving writer of the mid-twentieth century. Olson's 'archival poetics', then, is a paradoxically ungovernable system, one which neither keeps to its own place nor its own rules but rather attempts constantly to branch out and revolutionize itself.

All of 'The Record's material is drawn from 'Weymouth Port Book, 873', which designation Olson comments on at the beginning of the section thus:

Here we have it – the goods – from this Harbour,

1626, to Weymouth (England) consigned to

    Richard Bushrod and Company
    & Wm Derby and Company[55]

This functions as an extra piece of archival detail, locating a source, but also it *places* the material of the poem within a context and practice of reading – beyond the objectivity of the historian or archivist, as a Derridean might say.

---

[53] Ibid., 185.
[54] Paul Stephens, 'Human University: Charles Olson and the Embodiment of Information', *Paideuma* 39 (2012): 181–208; 182.
[55] Olson, *Maximus*, 121.

'Here we have it' indicates Olson as the one who 'looks in the window of [the] shop' in search of 'materials here for Maximus'. This locution adds another type of connection to 'The Record', one of methodology, but it is also what Timothy Morton calls an 'ecomimetic' gesture, one that begins writing with the gesture 'As I write ...'. In 2007's *Ecology Without Nature* Morton writes that '[e]comimesis involves a poetics of *ambience*. Ambience denotes a sense of a circumambient, or surrounding, *world*'.[56] This is what Olson performs at the beginning of 'The Record', a gesture that is intended to take what might seem an abstract extension of data and conjure a reality, a locale or 'world', around it, to integrate it into the *Maximus* project and Olson's work on that project. In other words, readers are encouraged to see 'The Record' both as a historical record in its own right *and* as Olson's act of mediation: of recording that record, of being an archivist. Yet as Morton notes, ecomimetic expressions are never entirely successful, always threatening to descend into repetitive deictic gesturing ('this – plus this – plus this', to alter Olson slightly), as ecomimesis becomes 'a list that gestures toward infinity'.[57] In Olson the list always stands on this tipping point between an assertion of material particularity (and so of authenticity), and a descent into overwhelming surplus. At this point lists become no more than declarations of their own excessiveness, of the point at which information becomes deformation, a break with accepted regimes of reading and value. Indeed the aesthetic instability of the list of supplies demonstrates the significance of listing in Olson. Morton writes that ecomimesis 'wants to go beyond the aesthetic dimension altogether. It wants to break out of the normative aesthetic frame, to go beyond art.'[58] The list's resistance to syntactical norms, found in the non-causal relations between its terms which contrive to look random, corresponds to how Olson's work wants to be radically literal, to be simply a surround, arranged to appear unarranged, to seem 'found'. Most of all it is a result of the writing's drive to escape the bounds of the poetic, literary and imaginary into something more capacious and axial – a long form around which a whole culture could revolve and be changed.

The contention that 'The Record' is difficult to read has been borne out by Olson criticism, which has generally avoided comment on it, as indeed generally it has avoided the many lists which *The Maximus Poems* includes. In one of

---

[56] Timothy Morton, *Ecology Without Nature: Rethinking Environmental Aesthetics* (Cambridge and London: Harvard University Press, 2007), 33. Emphasis in original.
[57] Ibid., 175.
[58] Ibid., 31.

the few extant critical discussions of the section, Miriam Nichols provides a summary of the contents, writing that '"The Record" and "14 MEN" suggest a skeletal history of the colonial enterprise in New England. Document [*sic*] says that the Cape Ann Settlement began with venture capital, lured by fish and fur.'[59] This is more or less the extent of Nichols's treatment of 'The Record'; though it is of course correct to note its role as part of a historical narrative which *Maximus* provides, the foregoing description promises little sense of what it is actually like to read these pages. Put another way, there is no comment here on the fact that 'The Record' might seem rubbish poetry – an assemblage of litter which is pointedly difficult to read as part of a book of 'poems' in any traditional sense. In this context it seems significant that Nichols provides not a reading of the text but rather an account or enumeration of its content which verges on being its own truncated list. It has been remarked in the past that a recurrent trend in Olson criticism has been to paraphrase the work, either by summarizing Olson's sense of his writing – usually via a reading of the prose – and then demonstrating how the poetry bears this out or by summarizing the content of certain moments of writing, as here in Nichols.[60] 'The Record' is instructive because it demonstrates the point at which this critical logic breaks down. Paraphrase is the trying temptation of Olson's lists because they both burst through the boundaries of what has been considered properly poetic discourse and so present themselves as pure archive or information available for summation and synthesis, and yet in their surfeit they are deeply resistant to critical digestion. They are ungeneralizable despite each particularity being in itself effaced, retaining a vestigial 'poetic' character in their resistance to such a reduction or digestion into *mere* information. Paradoxically, then, in being Olson's least 'poetic' or 'well-wrought' gesture, listing retains most strongly that aspect of traditional poetic function designated by a resistance to the 'heresy of paraphrase'.[61]

Ultimately, it is unhelpful to read Olson's writing as being in possession of an 'archival' poetics if that archive is understood as determined, settled and so

---

[59] Miriam Nichols, 'Myth and Document in Charles Olson's *Maximus Poems*', in *Contemporary Olson*, 25–37; 29. Nichols treats '*The Record*' (121) and '14 MEN STAGE HEAD WINTER 1624/5' (122) as distinct 'poems' or sections; following the index of my edition, I am treating them as a single entity entitled '*The Record*', but the indeterminate distinctions between poems or sections in *Maximus* is itself part of its antigeneric effect.

[60] On critical paraphrase in Olson studies, see Michael Kindellan, 'Poetic Instruction', in *Contemporary Olson*, 89–102; 93.

[61] For the classic account of the 'heresy of paraphrase', see the chapter of the same name in Brooks, *The Well-Wrought Urn*, 192–214.

dead. Thomas J. Nelson, in an article which reads 'A Bibliography on America' as a prescription for Olson's as an archive poetics, writes that '[t]he contents of the archive created the capacious form of the long poem for Olson'.[62] Nelson is right to suggest that the archival poetic of self-directed scholarship Olson inherits from Pound is a crucial baseline for his work, but this account does too little to mark out what is different about Olson's writing. It is perhaps truer to say that what may look like an archival poetics is better understood as a way of loosening the aesthetic category 'the long poem' or 'the poem', including in itself its archival materials and the indeterminacy of what readers can *imagine* might be included in or added to those materials, where the final value of both is never quite decidable. It makes the act of writing more capacious, by extending the field of what can be understood as 'form' – for example, lists, scribbles, other 'rejectamenta' as Olson calls them in 'The Kingfishers'.[63] 'The archive' here is not an attempt to build a research project so much as it is a challenge to monolithic accounts of 'the poem', pushing reading and writing into new and entropic kinesis. Olson's 'archive' is, in many ways, no such thing because it is not meant to be preserved, but rather is constituted in the process of its own redundancy and destruction, one from which it can be salvaged only by a purposeful act of readerly will. To express it otherwise: a well-ordered scholarly library has a two-dimensional structure of rows and columns under which every entry or item has a number and letter combination assigned to it – a combination which locates it within the archive's taxonomy. Even an unusually complete and well-documented archive lacks this basic ideal shape, being always extendable, its items always indeterminate in value and significance. To extend this analogue into Olson's work would require imagining not just a disorderly archive which requires the attentions of an assiduous archivist (this is perhaps appropriate to *The Cantos*), but one with an at best ill-defined field and function, which is in possession of a four-dimensional topography (at minimum) and self-generative function. If for Pound the not-quite-epic is a poem including history, then for Olson it is an archive admitting of various cultural inputs. Vice versa, this reading of Olson's poetics throws into relief the extent to which Pound's *The Cantos* contain or tacitly recommend a set of reading protocols relying on specific types of archival technologies and locales (books, libraries, art galleries, ruins) which to some

---

[62] Thomas J. Nelson, '"A Lifetime of Assiduity"': Olson's "Bibliography on America for Ed Dorn" as Program for the Archival Long Poem', in *Olson's Prose*, ed. Grieve-Carlson (Newcastle: Cambridge Scholars, 2007), 121–31; 129.
[63] Olson, *Collected Poems*, 87.

degree determine the way readers interact with the text and with its sources and referencing habits. In the age of Google, this determination has been profoundly modified for readers of Pound, and indeed for readers of Olson, in a manner which neither poet could have anticipated.

* * *

Olson's accelerating of the archive epic into something faster, more amorphous and more mobile in *The Maximus Poems* makes traditional scholarly annotation an unusually blunt reading tool. In response *critical* readers need to develop new regimes of interpretation and criticism. Doing this need not reify the distinction between scholarship and criticism as absolute or dualistic; the way in which Olson's writing takes information into a realm of *de*formation, where poetic form is in its limit case, in danger of becoming simply surfeit and excess, already demonstrates a necessary link between scholarly annotation and critical appreciation, where the latter cannot meaningfully happen without an account of the former's distortion. Finally, this will mean suspending accurate knowledge of Olsoniana as a sufficient measure of a successful reading. Olson wrote to Cid Corman that '(You cannot own a poem until you use it'.[64] What this means for Olson's own readers is that they are pushed to involve themselves in their own work on Olson, recognize that their experience of the text is part of the text's working. The stakes of scholarly objectivity are directly challenged: '[F]or to be a spectator is to assert an ownership in it which is absentee – a movie, or a painting, or a poem.'[65] In place of the absentee-ownership of the poem as an object of delimited reference and discoverable fact, the critic is invited to attend to what is noisy about the writing, a lo-fi critical response more concerned with the blur between things than the things themselves. In major part this involves a consideration of how archived materials take on newly indeterminate shape and valence within Olson's poetics, and by extension, a consideration of how readers' internalized canonical expectations are evoked and distorted by this use of the archive. It is, for example, central to the work of *The Maximus Poems* that within it Pound's *The Cantos* are refiled and resorted, such that to read Olson opens up the possibility of rereading Pound in a number of incisive ways.

---

[64] Charles Olson, *Letters for Origin: 1950–1955*, ed. Albert Glover (London: Cape Goliard, 1969), 103.
[65] Ibid.

5

Ideas in Cage's *I-VI*

Much of Cage's writing is now most easily accessible through the imprint of Wesleyan University Press, which has developed a reputation as a publisher of American avant-garde authors. The back covers of all the Wesleyan editions of Cage's work feature, in the top left corner, a small tag which locates the volumes within and between various disciplines: 'Music / Literature / Art', 'Philosophy / Music', 'Philosophy & Music'.[1] Whilst these designations are examples of a fairly common bookselling practice, they highlight the remarkably 'interdisciplinary' character of Cage's work. They also pay witness to the curious figure of 'John Cage, composer'. Though he is certainly best known – or most commonly thought of – as a musician, Cage worked in all 'the arts' and none, frequently expressing lack of interest in what is usually considered 'musical', and often employing media with at best tangential connections to 'music' under the sign of the 'classical' tradition. As such the 'Philosophy / Music' designation is in equal turns suggestive and difficult to parse. It points to the way in which Cage's 'musical' activity centrally involved putting the musical tradition in which he was educated (however haphazardly) through a trial of critique and reconceptualization, but also poses the question of what the relationship between musical and philosophical 'discourses' might be, and how appropriate *writing* is as that relationship's third term. Questions about the dynamics that pertain (and that ought to pertain) between music, writing and thought are of great antiquity and complexity, and can lead with depressing speed into a mire of confusion and interdisciplinary wrangling. Plato's *Republic* is perhaps the signal example, contribution and warning here, beginning a tradition of disciplinary policing Olson was particularly and explicitly antagonistic towards.[2] Cage's work locates itself in the middle of this vexed territory, slipping between disciplines and

---

[1] Cage, *I-VI* and *Anarchy*; *X: Writings '79-'82*; and *M: Writings '67-'72* respectively.
[2] For Olson contra Plato on the poetry-philosophy relationship, see 'Review of Eric A. Havelock's *Preface to Plato*', in *Collected Prose*, 355–8.

media without ever quite anchoring itself in, or allowing itself to be anchored to, any given one. But it is 'philosophy' that, of all his publisher's labels, seems the most ticklish, because it is the one Cage most performatively distantiates himself from. Though etymologically philosophy designates a concern with 'wisdom', it has come to connote, and indeed be practised institutionally as the study and honing of ideas, as a systematic concern with a critique and/or theory of knowledge and knowing. Yet Cage at least *performed* a certain aversion to ideas, and frequently expressed incomprehension in the face of philosophical texts and discourses, often seeming to do so in order to frustrate interlocutors searching for theoretical windows into his work.

Nowhere is this will to frustrate more evident than in Cage's last significant piece of writing, the lecture-mesostic *I-VI*, also known as 'the Norton Lectures', the 'Bolivia Mix' and most expansively as 'MethodStructureIntentionDiscipline NotationIndeterminacyInterpenetrationImitationDevotionCircumstancesVar iableStructureNonunderstandingContingencyInconsistencyPerformance', the words which constitute the mesostic line running through each of the piece's six sections. Written for Harvard's Charles Eliot Norton Lecture Series in 1988–9, and published by the university press in 1990, *I-VI* (as I shall call it here) is a masterpiece of ludic misdirection and intellectual lubriciousness.[3] In this it continues a tendency that can be traced throughout Cage's texts. The lecture is perhaps the primary mode in which Cage's writings have been received, and certainly his most famous texts (the lectures on 'Nothing' and on 'Something' being the most frequently cited) were composed and delivered in this format.[4] As such they announce themselves as in correspondence with an explicitly intellectual and educative form, since more than anything a lecture is a medium for the transmission and reinforcement of ideas, whether those of an individual or a scholarly consensus – it is, as it were, the tap from which the archive is meted. Yet this customary function is put under some degree of pressure

---

[3] The prestige of the Norton Lectures is worth noting in order to appreciate how culturally inappropriate and institutionally disruptive Cage's contribution to them was. The lectures were set up in honour of Charles Eliot Norton, one of the aristocratic 'Boston Brahmin' Eliots, who can count T. S. amongst their scions. Amongst the most distinguished art scholars of the late nineteenth-century United States, and widely considered the best-read man of his age, Norton taught as a professor of fine art at Harvard, maintaining a close association with painters such as Ruskin and Turner. The Norton Lectures were designed to be annual addresses on 'poetry in its broadest sense', and had featured both eminent poets (Eliot, Frost, Edwin Muir) and composers (Stravinsky, Hindemith) as speakers in years before Cage. Other previous speakers were senior literary critics; in perhaps symptomatic aesthetic and intellectual contrast, Harold Bloom gave the series of lectures which preceded Cage's, in the 1987–8 academic year.

[4] Cage, 'Lecture on Nothing' and 'Lecture on Something', in *Silence*, 109–45.

in Cage's repetitive, comic and seemingly inchoate pieces: 'When Reinhold Brinkmann and Christoph Wolff first visited me to discuss the project of my Norton Lectures, I told them that they would not be informative but would be as I saw it the next step in my work which, besides what else it is, is controversial.'[5] In order to frame the somewhat raw character of the material he was serving up, and on the understanding that the lectures themselves would meet with a degree of confusion – if not outrage – Cage offered to accompany each lecture with a question-and-answer session. These are printed alongside the mesostic lectures themselves, in a text that runs as a footer along the bottom of the page.

To describe the transcription of these sessions as elucidative or enlightening might be overly optimistic, but it does provide a number of intriguing and significantly evasive instances of Cage's purposeful misdirection. Following on from the introductory essay, in which he pretends to explain his choice of sources, but in fact only judiciously adds to the confusion (on Wittgenstein, for example, 'I have long been attracted to his work, reading it with enjoyment but rarely understanding'), readers can find a series of questions asked and answers given, unpunctuated and uncleaned, positioned as if to underpin or ground the display of meticulous indeterminacy above; but the presentation of the question-and-answer seminar as a kind of control case or zone of delimitation which provides a map to the lecture-poems 'proper' is itself entirely misleading.[6] Indeed, Cage seems to have employed the sessions as an extension-of-the-extension of the proper educational role of the lecture, coupling lectures in 'nonunderstanding' with offbeat and circumambulatory seminars.

The great majority of the questions Cage's audience ask are clarificatory ones, and they broadly share an interest in the intention-nonintention diode which *I-VI* claims to exemplify. Since a highly 'nonintentional' text would exist outside the bounds of what is usually thought of as 'art' or 'poetry' – as activities predicated on 'creativity', 'originality' and so on, the determinate sense of art as mastery – Cage's proclamation of 'nonintention' as *I-VI*'s primary dynamic is a source of profound curiosity tempered by scepticism. In what degree did

---

[5] Cage, *I-VI: MethodStructureIntentionDisciplineNotationIndeterminacyInterpenetrationImitation DevotionCircumstancesVariableStructureNonunderstandingContingencyInconsistencyPerformance* (Hanover and London: Wesleyan University Press, 1990), 6.

[6] *I-VI*, 3. It is worth noting that Cage's advocate and interviewer the poet and critic Joan Retallack appears to have introduced him to Wittgenstein, though the degree to which Cage really engaged with the Austrian's philosophy is uncertain. See Joan Retallack, *Musicage: Cage Muses on Words, Art, Music* (Hanover and London: Wesleyan University Press, 1996).

choice, or judgement, shape the text? And in what way is the *idea* of *I-VI* as nonintentional, noninformative lecture constitutive of those judgements?

> *in that walk through the woods one of the things that struck me was a lot of little rings of mushrooms not just single mushrooms but that little clusters of ideas that would sort of crop up and then disappear throughout the lecture and i was wondering how much the wanting or not wanting of words controlled these little rings* i notice that too of course as i write it i don't know how they come about it passed through my mind that they that there's something in the program that might bring that about *spores probably*.[7]

That favourite Cagean analogy, the mushroom hunt, is elicited here as a way of mediating the phenomenology of listening to *I-VI*. On the face of it, this seems a wise move on the part of the interlocutor, since by the time *I-VI* was composed Cage had produced a number of mushroom-centric works, and was a renowned mycophile; if a reader/auditor were to retrofit this interpretative and compositional protocol for application to the new work, then to expect it to be productive would not be unreasonable. However, Cage responds that for *I-VI*'s author this phenomenology has much in common with methodology. He expresses ignorance as to how the ideas 'come about'. In suggesting that it is 'the program' which brings forth these ideas he attempts to empty out any human decision from his process, to depict it as free from personal preference and from the traditions of his own personal canon. The very purpose of the question-and-answer seminars was of course to foreground this, to suggest that the lectures must be explained extrinsically because the texts/performances themselves form an encounter with something completely other to critical construal – and subsequently to riddle the questioners out of even this surcease from nonintention by provision of obtuse answers. But the idea that *I-VI* is intrinsically free of Cage's own ideas and intentions is clearly just that: an idea. Even to accept *I-VI* as a sort of apersonal ideation-machine would nonetheless not solve the problem of what these ideas are or how they are conceived, as the question Cage is offered here demonstrates: What does the interlocutor mean by 'ideas' when he or she says that ideas 'crop up'? Does he/she mean 'semantically construable phrases' in the text, of which there are a fair number, especially in the passages with longer strings of wing-words, or is the implication that a more meditative type of mind-wandering created by the rebarbative surface of *I-VI*

---

[7] *I-VI*, 27–8. Questioner's speech in italics.

causes the emergence of ideas not specifically tied to textual detail or semantics? Is the reception of *I-VI* propositional, in the sense that ideas can be read out of the text preformed, or conceptual, in that the meeting of audience and work conceives something intrinsic to neither party? In other words, what are the protocols of reading here? The first and most troubling casualty of nonintention is the traditional hermeneutic paradigm wherein the reader is a supplicant to the text's insight or meaning. The sort of resistance a maximally complex poetry of intention might put up – that of a precisely determinate or highly specific meaning which is obscured by various technical operations – is nothing like the resistance found in *I-VI*, which is in a certain sense frictionless and literal, with no intentional hidden meaning or key to the code. Richard Kostelanetz suggests something similar to this when he writes that 'very much like *Finnegan's Wake*, Cage's *I-VI* is at once unreadable and *re*readable'; there is repetitious, meditative encounter with the text, in which patterns are elicited, and blank, uncomprehending encounter, in which only the brutely sensible aspect of the work is engaged, but nothing just like 'a reading'.[8] Even if one committed to a standard close-reading of a selected section of the poem, which would be entirely possible if one selected judiciously, it would not be clear exactly what relation that reading had to the text 'in itself' or as a whole. It is easy to see how one could use *I-VI* as a source or set of materials but less easy to see how this would be an act of critical reading in anything like the traditional or scholarly sense.[9] This is to say that, were he to write a 'Guide to *I-VI*', Butterick would find much to go at, but the list of sources produced would bear a very limited relation to the work which it supposedly glossed. Whilst all reading is in some degree a process of 'use', as Olson has it – that is, always somewhat a 'misuse', or 'wrong' reading – this dynamic is particularly clear and privileged in *I-VI* because it decentres 'ideas' and thus shifts focus back onto reading as an activity with boundaries and potential for trespass rather than as a form of pure rational intellection possessing always-already determinate protocols.

Yet it must be admitted that there is both theory and practice in the making of *I-VI*; any theory-practice distinction would be a very unCagean one at any rate. This tension is the genesis of the questions asked of Cage in the seminars

---

[8] Richard Kostelanetz, 'John Cage's Longest and Best Poem', in *Writings About John Cage*, ed. Kostelanetz (Ann Arbor: University of Michigan, 1993), 297–300; 299–300. Emphasis in original.
[9] Even given the many possible distinctions to be drawn between 'critics' and 'scholars' of poetry, as discussed in the previous chapter, I think this point holds true in that both the critic and the scholar require a determinate object with which they may perform their differing operations. Or at least, this is what modern critical and scholarly procedures presume.

and is what makes Cage's continual profession of ignorance so amusing and so infuriating: 'something like an idea that seems to have its own presence comes to you and goes away you don't know how to catch it or you think you know what it is and then when you think further you don't know anything at all it's very mysterious'.[10] There is no doubt much simple truth to the claim that Cage does not know about *all* of the ideas the text may generate – no author could – but, on the face of it, it is ludicrous to claim that *none* of the ideas which constitute the text are Cage's.

When Cage states that the lectures are not to be 'informative', he is in one sense simply stating the obvious fact that these are not lectures in the traditional mould; but they clearly have informational effect, in that the lecture is 'informative' of *I-VI*, providing one of its essential or 'formative' principles. If information can be conceived of as an expression of organization, then *I-VI* is a poem which can seem like an excess of *meaningless* information, of egregious form. As with Olson's archival gestures, the stockpiling of *information* in no way guarantees, and is in some respects counter to, *informative* writing; the emphasis is more on accretion than knowledge production. If the poem is not read for meaning, the lecture not attended for its direct pedagogical value, then the audience return to foundational questions of reception and reading tactics. Importantly, the 'idea' of 'the Poem' or 'the Lecture' as a set of culturally defined and predictable protocols – the idea of lectures as transmitters of ideas, for example – has been subtly changed. The 'idea' of the text, the mental representation (etymologically, precisely an image) of what a text is and how it ought to behave, has been replaced by a number of possible decisions that must be made about readerly activity. A pre-modernist idea of reading is displaced, engagement with the text made a zone of contention, caught in a haze in between several possible states.

***

In a letter to the French composer Pierre Boulez, dated 17 January 1950, Cage complained of the anti-intellectualism of American cultural discourse:

> The great trouble with our life here is the absence of an intellectual life. No one has an idea. And should one by accident get one, no one would have the time to consider it. That must account for pentatonic music.[11]

---

[10] *I-VI*, 294.
[11] Jean-Jacques Nattiez, ed., *The Boulez-Cage Correspondence*, trans. Robert Samuels (Cambridge: Cambridge University Press, 1993), 50.

Cage shares an in-joke with his French friend here, referencing their shared move away from composing with traditional tonality, and into serialism, specifically via the dodecaphonic music of Arnold Schoenberg, who taught Cage in California (Oliver Messiaen, not himself a twelve-toner, introduced Boulez to the technique in Paris). Though Boulez remained an adherent of dodecaphony, extending the method into electronic music through his work at IRCAM, Cage moved away from the determinations of serialism into an exploration of composition by chance – or indeterminacy, as he preferred to call it. What is interesting about this letter is how, even at this stage in his career – as he was beginning work on his first chance compositions – Cage seems lukewarm about accident, which he figures as the idiot cousin of whatever meagre ideas American culture manages to scrounge. It seems an inauspicious arrival for a mode which has become popularly synonymous with Cage's work. Accident is present, even perhaps as a distinctly 'American' mode of ideation, but is unacknowledged and unexamined by those to whom it occurs. There is no explicit ideology of accident, Cage suggests; it just happens. It is tempting to think that this is an excoriation of America and American culture, and in some degree this is true, but it is also the seed of a more positive identification. By the end of the 1950s Cage had separated himself from the European musical scene fairly decisively. After the 1958 Darmstadt festival, at which his work and thinking were not well received, he began to present himself as a distinctly American composer.[12] A year later he wrote 'History of Experimental Music in the United States', in which he attempted to disentangle the American musical tradition from the European inheritance. If, as he complained to Boulez, accident was the specifically American form of ideation, then accident was the right place to look for a distinctly American contribution to 'the urgency of musical advance'.[13]

All of this points to the central tension of Cage's chance operations – a tension that would structure the great majority of his later work: only by explicitly and purposively examining, theorizing and dissecting accident could accident

---

[12] Conversely, Boulez is closely identified with the so-called Darmstadt School of post-war Europe, which included Stockhausen, Mauricio Kagel and Iannis Xenakis (some American composers, notably Earle Brown, are also associated with the Darmstadters). Though 'Darmstadt School' was something of a term of abuse, it does usefully describe a loose collective of twelve-tone fellow travellers. Whatever the truth of detractors' charges that Darmstadt was a sort of dodecaphonic police state, there can be no doubt that Cage was little impressed by the school's twelve-tone orthodoxy, which he distanced himself from early in his career. For a more comprehensive account of Cage's turn away from the European musical inheritance, see David Nicholls, *John Cage* (Urbana: University of Illinois, 2007), especially 73.

[13] John Cage, 'History of Experimental Music in the United States', in *Silence*, 67–75; 68.

be made into a method meet to 'intellectual life', that is, into an idea properly understood rather than merely come upon. In other words, Cage raises the seemingly paradoxical spectre of an art of controlled accident, one defined and guided by a rhetoric of nonintention and a set of cognate practices. Though the dismissive attitude to accident Cage expressed in correspondence of 1950 was soon to be reassessed, it does serve to highlight the fact that his machinations around the question of the 'idea' have deep and pervasive roots. In 1950 'accidents' are what constitute the unfortunate replacement for, or, at best, the suboptimal medium of 'ideas' in American art; but by the late 1960s, and certainly beyond, accident is a central component in a complex game of substitutions allowing the 'ideas' contained in, exhibited or espoused by any given work to slip through the fingers again and again.

Presumed opposition between American accident and European 'intellectual life' is differently thematized in Cage's 'History of Experimental Music' as a distinction between sophistication and experimentation. Writing that, in the light of recent developments 'so much of European musical studies and even so much of modern music is no longer urgently necessary', Cage argues for a new self-conception on the part of American musical practice, one which, through articulating its differences from the European tradition, comes to recognize that 'America has an intellectual climate suitable for radical experimentation'.[14] To realize this experimental character fully, American music must cast off 'sophistication', implied to be a fundamentally European characteristic, one concerned only to 'put a new wing on the academy and open no new doors to the world outside the school'.[15] As opportunistic as this justification of American exceptionalism is – the piece is as strongly motivated by a desire for redress of perceived slight as for historical clarity – it does indicate an important aspect of Cage's artistic thinking in its opposition of academy and world. The conception of education as unnecessarily abstract or formal has an extensive history in American thought and pedagogy, and can be seen in practice in institutions Cage himself taught at – notably Black Mountain and the New School in New York. This attitude to education coincides with a type of autodidacticism or intellectual self-reliance which conceives of the pioneer as outside of a learned tradition, finding expression in Thoreau, in Williams's 'no ideas but in things',

---

[14] Ibid., 70, 73.
[15] Ibid., 72. The 'sophistication' being directly discussed here is that of the composer Elliott Carter, an American, but one educated in Paris and so connected to the European musical establishment Cage is distancing himself from in this piece.

and in Cage's own similar admonition in his essay on Robert Rauschenberg: 'Not ideas but facts.'[16] It is not necessary to credit the distinctions being made here to recognize their force. If ideas are sophisticated, and ergo essentially *sophistic*, then 'facts' or 'things' are experimental, that is, based on experience rather than the strictures of a received tradition, educational lineage or receptive framework. In an odd way 'experimental art' is understood by Cage as a mode of *un*learning, with nothing like the presumption of progressive, pragmatic improvement associated with scientific experimentalism. In the introduction to *I-VI* he makes precisely this point, writing of his decades-long 'exploration of nonintention' that 'I did not know immediately what I was doing, nor, after all these years, have I found much out.'[17] The rhetoric of ignorance which runs throughout Cage's work can best be understood as a mode of negation, a resistance to institutions and traditions of thought and practice Cage considered to be constraining at best and moribund at worst. In thus resisting Cage finds himself in precisely the interdisciplinary space his publisher's tags indicate, since by criticizing, for example, the 'school' of music in 'History of Experimental Music' he criticizes 'music' as an articulable discourse or image – that is, he criticizes the *idea of music* – and so moves into a disciplinary no-man's-land where that idea is no longer the ultimate horizon of musical activity. The same could be said of Cage the poet and Cage the lecturer. To reject 'ideas' is to reject set images or 'givens', replacing them with experiment as a form of protean questioning uncommitted to improvement or accuracy, as Olson's work resists taking scholarly accuracy as the horizon of reading. Thus Cage's continuous use of analogies to 'the natural' – mushroom hunts, rivers, ambient 'environments'. These are not naive validations of an idealized organicism but a gesture towards a 'great outdoors' beyond cultural institutions and determinations.

There is something radically individualistic about this aspect of Cage's work, a something he labels anarchism, but which his less sympathetic critics have found to be a form of intellectual vapidity. Resistance to overdetermining intellectual and pedagogical practices can seem to express itself as an unusually pedantic form of obscurantism, especially as Cage employs these tactics with regard to his own work. In an illustrative passage of the Harvard seminars, the riddling style of Cage's thought performs this sort of iconoclasm in its manipulation of a questioner:

---

[16] John Cage, 'On Robert Rauschenberg, Artist, and His Work', in *Silence*, 98–108; 108.
[17] Cage, *I-VI*, 1.

can images be questions i don't know that maybe you do maybe you have an idea that i don't know do you think you do *i'm not sure i want to answer it do you feel that questions need to be answered* it's according to what you're doing i generally ask them when i want to have them answered *do you feel that questions will serve as inspiration if they're not answered* i can't deal with that very well i don't know what to think at that point it could be i think that some questions are more radical than other questions *which ones are more radical* well the ones that produce more interesting answers radical answers that often happens and you can recognise it very quickly i think if you ask uninteresting questions then your answers are uninteresting and i think that immediately sets you back to searching for more radical questions getting at the roots of the situation.[18]

This passage, in keeping with much of the seminar transcription, has something of the agon about it; Cage adeptly dodges the question by claiming to have less right to answer than his questioner, who subsequently attempts to rephrase the question several times in order to coax Cage out of his gameful recalcitrance, though to no avail. Cage succeeds in turning the question of questions round on the questioner, making the questioner's question's interest the *real* question of the question. This is a clear example of a dynamic central to Cage's work, wherein a future critical account, method or vocabulary commensurate to the experience of Cage's works – rather than, say, a bare and necessarily unnuanced *definition* of the work's constructive parameters of the type Cage provides in his slightly unhelpful introduction to *I-VI* – is the enemy to be forestalled. Indeed, one of Cage's detractors, John Hollander, wrote in a review of *Silence* that '[t]he description of one of Mr. Cage's compositional processes is often, it seems to me, more interesting than the performed result'.[19] I would here maintain that Hollander's judgement is wrong, but importantly this is because he has not found the correct framework for judging Cage's work. Descriptions of processes are what seem most interesting to a traditional critical optic because such descriptions are all that such an optic is capable of providing. Since the actual experience of a Cage work is so confusing, it is unclear how to represent it according to a critical paradigm based on creating extractable, and in some degree fungible, *images* of a form, author, genre, style and so on. These images then become identified with and themselves informative of discourse surrounding 'poetry', 'music', 'art', so that a general knowledge of what indeterminacy *is* is created by the way in

---

[18] Ibid., 73–6. Emphasis in original.
[19] John Hollander, 'Silence', in *Writings About John Cage*, 264–9; 268.

which criticism has historically characterized and described 'the indeterminate', rather than by any particular indeterminate text whatsoever. Not only is there a canon-archive of poems, there are canonical-archived idea-images of 'Poetry' which, though certainly differing between individual readers (and non-readers), are determined by broader cultural and educational context. Not everyone reads poetry, but everyone has a sense of what poetry is; this sense or idea is what Cage is reacting against when he attempts to distance himself from ideas per se. The sophisticated account of poetry thus becomes a calcified block on experiment. Counter-intuitively, ideas in this sense are for Cage marks of conservative thoughtlessness.

To construct a text which smashes the static idea/image of what a poetic or pedagogical text should 'look like' would require the building of a new set of compositional protocols from the ground up. The primary rule Cage devises as part of such a protocol is questioning: 'I gave up making choices. In their place I put the asking of questions.'[20] The purpose of this procedure is to create a firewall between Cage's compositional activity and the results thereof, such that what might be termed 'authorial intention' is at one degree of remove. The text produced would thus be 'in itself' anonymous or unsigned – a product of an inhuman process. Sophistication of discourse would be cast aside, as absurdity, non sequitur and even a form of mysticism become objects of interest.[21] Cage suggests something similar in his 'Introduction' to *I-VI*:

> In the nature of chance operations is the belief that all answers answer all questions. The non-homogeneity that characterises the source material of these lectures suggests that anything says what you have to say, that meaning is in the breath, that without thinking we can tell what is being said without understanding it.[22]

It might be thought that here Cage is attempting to elide the difference between meaning what we say and saying what we mean, allowing 'empty words' to become too much a self-fulfilling prophecy, but it is more helpful to consider how this gesture towards meaning-without-understanding both grows out of

---

[20] *I-VI*, 1.
[21] Cage sometimes refers to these priorities with regard to Buddhism. I am unconvinced that Cage's gestures towards Buddhist ideas have much more significance than is evident in this professed abandonment of logical discourse. Rather, I suspect that Cage's work is more significantly influenced by a Hindu tradition of musical thought, via Gita Sarabhai. For more on Cage and Sarabhai, see Nicholls, *John Cage*, 36.
[22] Cage, *I-VI*, 6.

Cage's musical background, where music can be considered as that art which elicits a maximum quantity of 'meaningfulness', loosely construed, from a minimum degree of semantic content, so enabling him to decentre 'poetry' as a supposedly semantic art, and allowing him to obscure the degree to which answers *are* made to line up with questions in *I-VI*, and how. In other words, the ideas that went into the creation of *I-VI* leave traces through and can be diagnosed in the judgements Cage makes.

The operation and quality of judgement is crucial for understanding *I-VI*, particularly because Cage works so hard to obscure it. A diminution of judgement is central to his rhetoric throughout his career, being the second key manoeuvre in Cage's anti-sophisticated compositional protocol, and it tends to be performed precisely where Cage feels there is a weak point in his rhetoric of nonintention. In *I-VI* a notable weak point of this kind inheres in the selection of source texts and of selection methodologies themselves, as can be seen when Cage is asked why he employed *I-Ching* procedures. He responds, 'I don't know how I came to decide upon the use of the *i ching* chance operations but they were for the purpose of freeing my mind from my likes and dislikes.'[23] That is, the *I-Ching* was chosen because Cage believed it would enable him to replace aesthetic prejudice ('sophistication') with aesthetic experiment; by using his compositional process as a form of oracle, he might be able to receive answers he didn't 'like' within his own work. The obvious rejoinder is that the *idea* of nonintention is still a privileged one here, that Cage *likes* 'freeing [his] mind from likes and dislikes', and that all Cage really achieves in his answer is to obfuscate this fact by claiming that the decision to use the *I-Ching* was somehow purely arbitrary or extrinsic to Cage's intention ('I don't know how'). Yet the idea that the process can turn out *absolutely anything* independent of Cage's preference is more thoroughly refuted by reading the text itself, which has the distinctive mark of a John Cage production, and not only because much of the source text is taken from Cage's own work. Cage presumably edited *I-VI* to the extent that if *by chance* it came to say something objectionable then he would disallow or deselect that locution – even beyond the firewall of the question-answer disjunct there is a judgemental process of *de*selection. Readers can feel this in the unerring way in which synthetic, basically happenstantial statements or 'ideas' which emerge from the text are nonetheless ideas Cage would be likely to agree with. This can be seen in this fairly arbitrary but indicative sample:

---

[23] Ibid, 243–4.

> the Dance
> the magIc
> in Some way
> the Contours
> 'I was standing quite close to
> Process'
> mind to worLd around'[24]

Though these words come from several sources (McLuhan, Wittgenstein, Cage himself), they nonetheless possess a definite coherence and even thematic felicity. To 'stand quite close to process' could be to pay close attention in order to understand; to be close to an ongoing process of the sort *I-VI* enacts and Cage is more generally interested in; to work on or through the various media mentioned. All of these fall in various ways under the rubric of 'discipline'. Behind the complexities of Cagean indeterminacy there remains a more familiar kind of literary *ambiguity*. There are several ways in which Cage could have disarticulated this rather Cagean passage, for example, by reducing or increasing the number of wing-words, or by placing the pauses differently; that he has not done so indicates a process of positive decision which includes preference, and consequently a readability not completely vitiated by the text's indeterminate construction.

One of the pleasures inherent in reading Cage comes with his carefully constructed sleight of hand, which points towards a process of judgemental filtration, of composition-as-reading, in which ideas of the well formed or the sophisticated are pragmatically let into the text whilst the audience is looking the other way. The degree to which the writing of *I-VI* proceeded through a type of judgemental reading can be seen in Cage's selection of texts, where he admits to the operation of personal preference (the presumption being that this input preference is negated in the output by the compositional process), and in selection of extracts from those texts (or at least, which centre-word to use in any given situation and how many if any wing-words), for which Cage admits the use of 'common sense', which he opposes to chance.

Again counter-intuitively, 'common sense' takes the part of 'sophistication' here:

> *i'd like you to talk about how you came about deciding on things like the 49 quotes from thoreau maybe the 93 quotes from wittgenstein and how you put the pauses in because in your introduction you said that breath is important and pauses had*

---

[24] Ibid., 220.

> to come from somewhere tell us why you don't like emerson and why i like thoreau it's easy to tell you that i chose the wittgenstein ones after having received a page and then i read the whole page and i took one rather than another one paragraph rather than another and i at that point did something connected with what i liked [...] i'm not working with chance now i'm working with my common sense i'm looking for ideas now.[25]

Though Cage's rhetoric again encourages us to think that the process of decision is fairly arbitrary ('i took one rather than another'), there is something both suggestive and obfuscatory in the phrase 'looking for ideas'. Metaphorically it has much in common with the mushroom analogy provided by the previous questioner as a call back to Cage's mycopoetics, and the sense that in reading *I-VI* ideas are fortuitously 'come upon' like fungi in a forest rather than being mappable or 'followed through'. Indeed, Cage's process of compositional judgement here unusually reflects the process of reading the completed text.

Cage's response to a request for a clarification of his preference for Thoreau over Emerson, another long-standing Cagean judgement, goes in this direction too: 'emerson tends to get one idea and develop it thoreau doesn't do that there's an unexpectedness from sentence to sentence and paragraph to paragraph in thoreau one's constantly surprised and refreshed'.[26] Emerson is sophisticated, Thoreau experimental. More to the point, however, Thoreau is preferred in the sense that the experience of reading his writing is the same as the experience of reading Cage – 'surprise' being a central principle of Cagean poetics. In making this judgement, Cage links his work to a particular type of nonconformist American tradition, but also makes the nature of that link pointedly unreadable. By painting the compositional process employed as uncannily like the process of reading the text, where ideas can be scanned for and found or not found in a relatively opaque way, Cage undermines any attempt to gain critical traction on *I-VI* by forming an initial, stable image of its compositional process against which to measure the resulting text. Mirroring the composed indeterminacy of the textual output in his account of the process of production, Cage makes whatever ideas surely subtend *I-VI* difficult to expound systematically. In response to the central question of judgement, Cage states tautologically that sections of text were chosen for *I-VI* because selecting them was like the experience of reading *I-VI*. Because the lectures themselves are so protean and

---

[25] Ibid., 90–2; 94. Emphasis in original.
[26] Ibid., 95–6.

contingent, this response leaves it unclear where any criticism engaged in its traditional function of explication and subsequent evaluation would begin. The presentation of *I-VI* is specifically designed to frustrate critical assessment focused on questions of meaning, thematics and value. Such an idea of criticism will find itself sorely challenged by *I-VI*'s textual dynamics. On this basis I shall attempt to demonstrate the problems a prospective Cage criticism will encounter, by looking more closely, though with necessarily limited success, at the *I-VI* mesostics themselves.

* * *

A compositional emphasis on nonintention and indeterminacy validates the making of mistakes on the part of the author. Accident as 'surprise', it has been noted, is an important conceptual tool for Cage, one he associates with a peculiarly American cultural outlook and with the experimental in art. Mistake is perhaps a particularly powerful instance of accident in this experimental sense because rather than simply being a type of aesthetic – an openness to chance, of the sort the mushroom-hunt analogy gestures to – to make a mistake is to demonstrate concretely how one could be other to one's own intentions. Cage makes this point when he describes how he read the lectures: 'i feel best when something happens to my voice that is not normal that perks up my ears like a loss of breath or a loss of tone in other words some deviation from the expected.'[27] Again, Cage refers to the breath of the lecturer as a key component of *I-VI*'s function ('meaning is in the breath'), where rather than the identity implied by 'voice' – an identity that could be that of 'poetry' itself – breath is pragmatically instrument(al) and impersonal, even to the point of dysfunction, as shall be seen. That is, breath is an instrument in the sense discussed with regard to *Mushroom Book*; not a dead 'tool' so much as a usable, and unpredictable, found process. This appeal to breath is again a marker of Cage's mixed-media approach, of the fact that if *I-VI* is not exactly a piece of music it remains a Cage production and so an instance of 'musicage', to employ Retallack's evocative pun. Generic, formal and disciplinary markers are unbalanced in contact with *I-VI*; their failure is a major component of its aesthetic effect. When Richard Kostelanetz describes *I-VI* as 'Cage's Longest and Best Poem', then, it is tempting both to agree and to dismiss his judgement as a category error, precisely because we do not yet possess the

[27] Ibid., 216.

critical vocabulary for discussing what *I-VI* is, or how successful it might be as an example of its type or genre.

The first and plainest reason one might have for worrying at *I-VI*'s place in the category 'Poetry' – a term Wesleyan University Press do not use, preferring the more non-commital 'literature' – is the indeterminate nature of the relationship between text and performance, or text and realization, where it is not clear which is to take priority. Is the text only a set of notes or suggestions which enables the giving of the lecture – or, put another way, a score enabling a performance – or is it itself the main event, which the performance exists only to dramatize? It should be noted here that the dichotomy of primacy between text and performance is closely related to more general generic issues inherent in longform poetics: a tradition of the long poem, and particularly the epic, as a monolithic, authoritative archival document whose achievement is *civilizational* and so creates for itself the capacity to legislate for other works (becoming the *arkhe* in Derrida's sense) is always haunted by an aural/oral archeopoetics – a memory of the voice which it can never quite suppress.[28] That this question of primacy is undecidable here without severely curtailing *I-VI*'s potential can be seen clearly enough in paying close attention to how the recordings of the Harvard lectures differ from the published text.[29] No doubt, due to the difficulty of anticipating the 'correct' word in such a semantically diffuse textual environment, Cage several times mispronounces or replaces particular words with different ones, as in this passage, from the 'Method' string of part IV:

> To
> Hundreds
> **Of**
> haD

---

[28] Derrida, *Archive Fever*, 1–5. It is suggestive here to think that Milton's *dictation* of *Paradise Lost* to his daughter represents more than a wrinkle of biographical happenstance; rather, it at least part-constituted that poem's superlative success by literalizing the leaky suppression of the oral which epic has always enacted, and which Olson's *Maximus* inverts as one of its most formally and generically radical gestures.

[29] All of the examples I use in this part of the chapter will be from section IV, for the simple reason that it is the section accompanied by most easily accessible recording, one supplied on CD (tape in the first editions) alongside the Wesleyan edition. These recordings can be found online at http://ubuweb.com/sound/cage_norton.html. However, I think it is worth noting that it may not really matter that a good five-sixths of the text is ignored in this discussion, since to object that such a delimited focus lacks comprehensiveness or is misrepresentative is to miss the particular character of a text with little or no representative or argumentative function. It is hard to imagine how a scrupulously 'complete' approach would produce different results, or to understand what it might mean to say that *I-VI* has 'proper' or 'necessary' parts which *must* be taken into account if a successful 'critical reading' is to be carried out.

> Making
> **thE**
> iTself
> wHen **they**
> it **is**[30]

which is performed as,

> To
> Hundreds
> **Of**
> haD
> *[Taking]*
> **thE**
> iTself
> wHen **they**
> it **is**

where the replacement of one word by another, with a slip of the tongue, in fact makes very little semantic difference at all. Because the replacement of 'Making' with 'Taking' turns the term in the mesostic string into 'Tethod' not 'Method', there is an amusing sense in which Cage's slip of the tongue undermines the formal operation of the text, and yet this makes little difference to the performance – there is no reasonable way for the audience to know, absent members in possession of superhuman aural attentiveness. If a poet giving a 'standard' reading were to read the wrong word she might well restart or return to correct her mistake, but with *I-VI* it is less clear that such a gesture would be worthwhile, since the degree to which the text has semantic 'content' is limited – or at least, the semantic level is generated by a number of rather singular textual protocols. Similarly, Cage on occasion adds words which one might normally anticipate as part of a sense-bearing statement, as here in lecture IV's 'interpenetration' string:

> thEy burst to disappear '
> souNds '
> citiEs '
> wiTh *[what]*
> is the diffeRence '[31]

---

[30] Cage, *I-VI*, 215–16. Cage's 'mistakes' in square-brackets and italics. Emphasis in original.
[31] Ibid., 229.

Again, this accidental supplement makes no especially notable difference to the *experience* of the performance, only being noticeable when the text is followed alongside the recording, but it peels the performance away from the text it is supposedly based on in a way which puts into question the meticulousness of that text's construction. The idea of the text, or the ideas which produced the text, are reduced to waste here, or used wastefully, depending on whether the text or the speaking of it is figured as primary.

In the seminars, via a comparison to electronic music and to Thoreau, Cage suggests that this is fine, since the ideational structure which assigns the judgements 'correct' or 'mistaken' to any given action or sound is an overweening victory of sophistication over experiment: 'this is what composers of electronic music do now they listen they don't listen to sounds theoretically they don't have notions about what sounds are good and what sounds are bad and that's how they should be treated they just listen and that's what thoreau did'.[32] Even taking into account Cage's condemnation of the prejudice and preconception such tags imply, I want to claim here that the judgements 'correct' and 'mistaken' are vital for reading *I-VI*, and that what is accidental in the delivery of the lectures must be retained as precisely an accident to have any particular use in an account of the lectures and their poetics. This is to say that for all their bluntness in the face of Cagean indeterminacy, the tools of traditional criticism cannot just be cast aside as soon as their utility comes into question. Indeed, at the very moments in which Cage declares the collapse of traditional regimens of reception and judgement these tools are at their most relevant. So, for example, when Cage claims that after Rauschenberg, '[b]eauty is now underfoot wherever we take the trouble to look. (This is an American discovery.)', the temporality of this claim ('now') indicates how it only makes sense *after* something.[33] Only after the collapse of traditional regimes of value would such a democracy of beauty seem radical; only in this context is it a 'discovery'. But readers need to retain the traditional critical categories, at least in part, to notice this.

Cage's 'post-poetic' poetics is evident in as superficially simple a thing as the title of the work under discussion. It has a variety: *I-VI*, 'The Charles Eliot Norton Lectures', 'Bolivia Mix', 'MethodStructureIntentionDisciplineNotationIn determinacyInterpenetrationImitationDevotionCircum   stancesVariableStruc tureNonunderstandingContingencyInconsistencyPerformance'. In part the usefulness of noting this variety pertains in how several media are elicited

[32] Ibid., 191–2.
[33] Cage, 'On Robert Rauschenberg', 98.

through these titles; 'I-VI' and 'Bolivia Mix' are musical titles (theme-and-variations and magnetic tape music respectively), then there is the title of an institutional lecture series, and a mesostic string which is itself a 'literary' form. But beyond this simple litany of interweaving media, the question of naming suggests in microcosm a broader problematic of *I-VI*. The relationship between notation, execution, performance and reception is tactically deformed – how do they relate, and which might be primary or privileged, if any? – and without configuring this relationship in some usable fashion it is hard to know what the determinate object under discussion is. The problem is not so much that *I-VI* is 'not just one thing', but rather that it is impossible to say exactly how many things it is. Yet to decide that for the sake of argument *I-VI* is a long poem, or a lecture, a piece of music and so on, is clearly to make a decision, *to do something* in a way that is unacceptable according to that paradigm of successful criticism as 'faithfulness' to text or author. Readers face the difficulty of *how* to refer to the work without changing it, and so making it something they weren't referring to. In fact this task is impossible; the reader is always implicated in the text.

This implication can be seen fairly easily in almost any attempt to 'read' a passage of *I-VI*. Because the compositional procedure has removed a great deal – though of course not all – of the intentional semantic content, recognizing or 'finding' an idea, mycopoetically, in the text which seems of use or interest almost immediately throws the reader-auditor back into reflection on his or her own input. Take these seemingly innocuous lines:

music aNd

arE[34]

On the page, but especially in listening to Cage's reading, the words 'music and art' spring to mind here. There are plenty of suggestive sound-patterns of this kind at work in *I-VI*, along with other conventional aural techniques: rhyme, alliteration and so on. But whether this is properly *technique* or rather mere happenstance is uncertain. It seems beyond doubt that Cage included plenty of these sonic effects by decision, but readers and auditors can never be sure that this particular instance isn't simply a fluke or interpolation, or one that slipped through the matrix. This recognition is necessary, but it doesn't answer the question of what, if anything, is 'found' in the text, or how it challenges an explicative idea of criticism – what constitutes the difference between 'music aNd /**arE**' and 'music

---

[34] Cage, *I-VI*, 222.

and art'? Rather than explaining anything about a text, in noticing that these lines resemble an aurally similar phrase, the critic finds himself writing his own mesostics, as indeed I have done above in substituting Cage's written words for those he spoke. This is criticism in the mode of palimpsest or graffiti – an overlay on an already existing material. Cage's longform mesostics not only heavily mediate a large pool of varied 'source' materials but in turn demand a further mediation on the part of readers, who must risk the textual noise in order to infer the signal. The surface of Cage's text is only the meeting point of these mediations, having no pretensions to transparency or originality in itself.

One of the most insightful recent studies of Cage's aesthetic, Dworkin's *No Medium*, engages extensively with the vertiginous hall-of-mirrors quality his work exhibits, arguing that when we feel ourselves implicated in Cage's pieces we are experiencing the necessary interpenetration and plurality which constitutes all mediation – a collectivity which Cage highlights but which is not *endemic* to his work. Dworkin's central claim is that '[c]ontrary to the casual ways in which we use the term, there is no "medium". No single medium can be apprehended in isolation.'[35] There is no medium in Dworkin's conception, only *media*, and so to mediate is to interact with and to change. Dworkin's book is mostly concerned with works characterized by silence or blankness, and so is very interested in the formative influence the art of Robert Rauschenberg had on Cage's development. In this encounter, Dworkin diagnoses a seminal moment of 'no ideas but in things' realization:

> In part, Cage's insight regarding [Rauschenberg's] *White Paintings* derived from his ability to see through the concept to its material form, heeding Ludwig Wittgenstein's injunction: 'Don't think, but look!' Looking with a careful attention *at* the work, rather than *through* the work to its ostensible message, paradoxically permitted Cage to catch a better glimpse of the ideas at play in the *White Paintings*.[36]

The ostensible paradox Dworkin finds, that for Cage the rawness of Rauschenberg's material, rather than the 'concept' or *description* of his work, is the 'idea' of the white paintings, certainly resembles the experiment-sophistication distinction explored in this chapter. Looking 'at' rather than 'through' seems, on the face of it, to be the only possible response to much of *I-VI* (or listening 'to' rather than 'through'), thereby fitting Dworkin's description of Cage's work, which characterizes it as foregrounding the material of art, short-circuiting that

---

[35] Dworkin, *No Medium*, 28. There are clear parallels here with Latour.
[36] Ibid., 120. Emphasis in original.

material's presumed facility as a semantic or representative 'medium'. Yet the problem remains that such a characterization gives little sense of what it is like to read *I-VI*, in part because its idea of the operation of ideas in the text – and in Cage's work as a whole – is too easy to assimilate; what is the 'material form' of *I-VI* in the first place if, as I have demonstrated, its media are so varied and so protean? Dworkin does not discuss *I-VI*, so these objections do not controvert his position, but they do point to its limitations.

The basic issue at play is *I-VI*'s real unfitness for the strictures of a literary criticism which proceeds by eliminative methods, delimiting 'right' and 'wrong' readings. Dworkin's reading of Cage's work is still wedded to this mode insofar as it posits a set of determinate ideas obscurely located within Cage's work (his particular concern is with *4'33"*) which can be accurately encountered and transcribed. One might well be able to extract from Cage's silent piece a realization that in silence there are always *media*, but this outline tells us nothing about the specific character of those media, or of any given performance of *4'33"*. There will always be more ideas to be extracted from any given instance in a Cage work than an idea or outline of that work can contain or suggest; the experimental actuality of the work will always be more capacious than its sophisticated elucidation or image, the work richer than the rules producing it.

This multitudinousness is perhaps particularly acute in Cage's written work, where the frequently frustrated textual habit of semantic construal is nonetheless continuously active in 'hunting' or 'looking' for ideas, so that even in a work unsuited to traditional poetic interpretation the temptation, or habit, remains. The impossibility of a universal or global reading of *I-VI* in no way detracts from the capacity to generate readings on a local level. So, by way of example, a passage such as this:

> **the** ' pOst-literate
> learN that
> olD
> compEtition is
> fiVe
> Of
> Through
> the mIddle space '
> we will use Our
> **but** remaiNs '[37]

[37] Cage, *I-VI*, 238.

seems ripe for interpretation as a confirmation of the type of reading protocols I have been discussing. *I-VI* is a text which teaches its reader to be 'pOst-literate' insofar as it plays with traditional expectations both of poetic composition and critical reception, emphasizing an inspection of poetic media ('Through / the mIddle space') rather than hermeneutic explication in which critics pit their wits against the text or author ('that / olD / compEtition') in a struggle for mastery.[38] There is no adequate or masterful criticism of *I-VI*; there is only the repeated failure of critical sophistication, which is nonetheless a necessary remnant in the experience of the text ('we will use Our / **but** remaiNs'). An always-inadequate *imitation* of received critical/hermeneutic norms is necessary to any experience of the text, just as the writing may seem here to imitate the 'ideas' which produced it. 'Imitation', significantly, is one of the key terms from the mesostic line around which *I-VI* is constructed, the only piece of text Cage provides in an *uncontroversially* intentional manner. The mesostic line and its spine-words are agents not only of construction but of *instruction* then, suggesting to readers a set of parameters according to which the text can be 'used' or operated, if not exactly understood. To press another keyword from *I-VI*, the line provides a summary of 'method' – a summary which is the only obviously paraphrasable, propositional content of the text. ('Method' indicates an obvious link between Cage and Olson, as a provisional name for their common poetic project or object of obsession – it is not so much that form is 'more important than content' for either writer, and more the case that *content communicates formal axioms* for both, in a reversal of the usual assumption.) The provision of a reading of this short excerpt imitates a traditional hermeneutic protocol, suspending its disbelief, so to speak, in order to dramatize that protocol's productive failure.

That such a reading is almost entirely tendentious is precisely the point – media *simply are* biases, interacting with each other in a continuous interpenetration which renders all interpretation contingent. *I-VI* makes this dynamic explicit only because it gives up any pretence at being anything other than a zone of mediated contention, open for use. Since it is nearly impossible thematically to think about or read the mesostics without finding oneself deforming or extending the text in just such a tendentious way, readers soon recognize how 'ideas' become explicitly biased rather than objective, descriptive or regulatory. Resultantly a reader's first impulse may well be to the reconstruction of method

---

[38] As noted in the previous chapter, Olson came to identify his sense of 'postmodern' with something much like 'post-literary'.

common to most Cage criticism: rather than 'what does this mean', the question becomes how was this made, out of what, and how is it read? This seems to shift the emphasis from 'ideas', 'themes', 'metaphors', 'message' to 'things', 'practice' and McLuhan-sense 'medium' – or, perhaps, to the medium-without-medium which recurs as the persistent dream of post-Objectivist American poetry – but in fact making this critical move only pushes the question of ideas to a different level.

Beneath the supposedly transparent surface of a text operating according to predetermined hermeneutic practices, there exists an array of naturalized reading protocols, those habits and practices of reading which must be learnt before text can be made to signify. Some of these protocols pertain to codicological rules generally applicable within certain languages and cultures – reading a page left-to-right, top-to-bottom in English, for example – and others, more local and time-bound, relate to historical traditions of writing, reception and construal which dictate how a text is to be interpreted and understood at the hermeneutic level. These latter are most clearly at issue within writing designated as poetic or literary – though codicological challenges are also implicated, as with the readable vertical line which runs through a mesostic – and can include both systems of categorization and evaluation as practised by particular critical 'schools' or 'movements', and the manipulations of traditions and genres performed by literary authors themselves. These protocols act as filters on the sensory, *in theory* mediating phenomenal data into construable sense via articulate form and the protocols attached to it.

Though naturalized, these protocols are not in fact 'natural' or 'inevitable' even as they seem to the sufficiently acculturated reader a 'second nature'. Their transformation of the phenomenal into the construable is not automatic; they are the product of a process of learning and of extended experience. As one result of this acculturation, a reader educated or inculcated within a certain tradition might well tend to associate certain words with certain authors or texts: for example, a reader immersed in the canonical works of English writing might find the word 'fool' carries an indelible mark of Shakespeare, even if encountered in a news report or recipe, or that 'chaos' remembers *Paradise Lost* (and perhaps a wreath of similar writings – Hutchinson's *Order & Disorder* springs to mind, as might Shelley's take on or translation of the Miltonic). Each reader differs in the exact composition of this set of personal interpretative protocols (Cage might select Joyce, Stein and Pound), but the soil in which the protocols grow is culturally delimited. Individual words and expressions thus take on determinate associations and determinate content not intimately related to local context. Even posited alone, they carry these associations for the reader thus inculcated. The same can be true even on the 'smaller' or more 'local' level of the phoneme. One example here is 'O/Oh', which has perhaps an air of 'Shakespeare' to it, but which also more generally aligns itself with a loose array of romantic-lyric-expressive-individuated-emotional conceptions of poetry, indeed with a powerful and pervasive set of ideas which may closely resemble what the 'average person' means or understands by 'poetry'. ('O' is in some arbitrary but nonetheless determinate and culturally meaningful way the most 'poetic' phoneme in the language, insofar as it can also be a word and a piece of grammar.[39]) An individual phoneme, presented in a certain context, can evoke a whole range of responses and expectations which cannot be described or intuited in that phoneme considered in isolation from its reader and their particular history, or circumscribed by context. Cage's 'cut-up' writings play heavily on this mechanism; judgement in reading and hearing is associated with acculturated expectations and the various flinches and misfires of hermeneutic habit and education as it attempts to get a grip.[40] The macro-indeterminacy of *I-VI*, as with Cage's other long writings, has on the *micro*-level much to do with the highly determined nature of these local parts. Here the importance of *I-VI*'s context as a set of lectures given to a learned audience can be understood in its full significance. The audience is confronted with the submerged and half-formed ur-protocols of their education. However, Cage's purpose here is as much that of pointing out and *cultivating* the arbitrary determination by or attachment to predetermined 'ideas' of certain verbal materials as it is that of undermining or re-indeterminating (un-determining?) them into granularity or verbal rubble. Notice that under this parts-wholes paradigm, Cage's writing in *I-VI* could be said to be '(de)constituted' by its *missing* parts, which are in the majority; only some, usually small, parts of the source texts are left, and the 'whole' of *I-VI* is (de)composed of these disarticulated – and so in some degree *inarticulate*

---

[39] C.f. J. H. Prynne's 'English Poetry and Emphatical Language', *Proceedings of the British Academy* 74 (1988): 135–69. Prynne's recent work on the role of conception in poetry bears some similarity to what I have discussed as 'protocols of reading': '[t]he reader's role [. . .] is already implicitly conceptualised, sharing this intermediate framework with the poet-author as a territory of the imagination where validation rules can be reformulated or even suspended altogether' (*Concepts and Conception in Poetry* (Cambridge: Critical Documents, 2014), 14). Cage's withdrawal of authority from 'ideas' in his text can be understood as of a piece with this suspension of received protocols.
[40] As discussed, this tendency to investigate the breakdown of language in smaller and smaller parts or articulations reaches its logical conclusion in *Empty Words*.

– parts – a whole of holes. The work thus presents on its surface a constant shimmer or ripple of familiar or construable works whose fully comprehensible bodies are consigned to the textual depths.

As is immediately clear, then, this surface experience of *I-VI* is *almost* entirely sensible rather than sense-making, and finding a critical language for addressing this is not easy. Discussing Gertrude Stein's *Lectures in America*, Jed Rasula notes that she saw in her career 'not a conceptual itinerary' but rather a series of somatic *impressions*; Rasula writes that 'her ruminations help us overcome the idea that there are ideas, and make her work available *as palpability*, for this is how she remembers herself, remembers the event of her writing as the uniquely registered perturbation of a proprioceptively animated person'.[41] This 'perturbation', the small disturbances on the surface, corresponds to the process of ideation as it operates in *I-VI*. To perturb is to unsettle or make anxious – an experience familiar to any reader or auditor of this and many other Cage works. In place of settled and reassuring protocols and expectations of reading, the individual who interacts with *I-VI* must face an initially opaque linguistic surface which is only occasionally perturbed or wrinkled by a coincidence of sense or a memory dredged up by a passing fragment. When listening to or reading the lectures, the auditor/reader may find his or her way into a mode of attention in which what might otherwise strike them as nonsensical and/ or random can be interpreted as meaningful; or at least, the mind grants itself a sort of freedom to *cultivate* meanings out of the textual loam in which it is immersed. This recalls again the 'unknown, unnamed vegetables in the patch' Olson claims will spring from 'Projective Verse'; in *I-VI*, however, it might be truer to say that what is produced is not so much 'unknown' or 'unnamed' as *indeterminated*, freed from the constraints of its source's determinate textual order. In this way sense is not completely vitiated, and ideas can be 'produced', whether by happenstance or synthesis, but *intention* in the Cagean sense is fairly strongly diluted – 'impressions' are like 'ideas' in that both are mental *images*, but 'impression' carries the sense of neither conscious agency (intention) nor regulatory authority usually granted to 'idea'. Recognition of source or canon (archive) here becomes a sort of reader-directed and reader-genetic activity, recalling what Rasula terms 'wreading', a reading which engages the reader as a writerly agent whilst revealing the writer's readerly protocols – readers do not so

---

[41] Jed Rasula, *This Compost: Ecological Imperatives in American Poetry* (Athens and London: University of Georgia, 2002), 166.

much recognize the archive in the words of the lectures themselves (though they may), but rather shape the lectures according to their generic/canonical/archival expectations, as well as according to the ways in which those expectations are systematically flouted or deformed by the text's own operation. Each reading is as a result different depending on experience and expectation but is also constituted by a textual surface of indeterminate impressions or ripples which spur the perturbed audience into ideation.

* * *

It is difficult to become an 'expert' in, or successful critic of, Cage's work. A broad licence to 'find' ideas is issued in *I-VI*, but it is important to recognize where the agency lies in such an activity – in the *impressions* which float past on the otherwise impassive surface of the text. What is finally so unusual about these late mesostics is that, although they appear to obscure meaning, they have in fact no secret code or hidden discourse – the surface of the text is its only available dimension. If *I-VI* licenses critics to be adventurous, it also denudes them of a number of certainties and time-honoured hermeneutic tactics. When Cage's detractors complain that his works are essentially empty, that 'too much illumination and scrutiny would probably cause [them] to shrivel', what they are describing is not in fact the works themselves, which remain always more than any account of them, rather it is the idea of a criticism characterized by study, interpretation and explanation which begins to atrophy.[42] This is why it is so much easier to listen to Cage reading the lectures than it is to read them silently for oneself. In listening, the code-breaking hermeneutic is not brought to the fore as a naturalized type of cultural expectation, of silent reading as riddle-interpretation, as 'slow reading' or 'close reading'; *I-VI* is a perverse poem which it is more comfortable – though not 'more correct' – to receive as environmental sound. In the face of a poetic canon which values what is 'symbolic', 'deep' and so susceptible to 'close reading', *I-VI* is conversely literal, shallow and distant (or rather, its 'depth' is bathetic rather than metaphoric). As a result, any ideas readers can construe from the text are entangled in the impressions marked in whatever small ripples can be found on that surface, in the *pressure* to respond which it exerts again and again on the consciousness despite the seeming dearth of commonsensical semantic communication. It mimics an oracle in at least

---

[42] Edward Rothstein, 'Cage's Cage (1990)', in *Writings About John Cage*, 301–8; 301.

this regard – in order not to fall completely into mysticism one has to interpret one's interpretation *as an interpretation*. The line between criticism and poetry becomes difficult to discern; or rather, that line completely swallows both supposedly distinct activities.

Searching and finding, the experimental as unexpected against the preconception as sophisticated, is at the heart of *I-VI*. Cage's 'ask questions' mantra is in part a cover for the decisions he really does make, but it remains a useful model for the experience of reading the text, and for thinking through the ways in which the text does not so much 'contain' as *challenge* ideas about the reception of poetry and the protocols for reading it. Any attempt to reduce *I-VI* to a roster of ideas it 'contains' neuters the actual experience of reading, as Dworkin argues, 'Poetry may well be "what gets lost in translation", though that phrase should be understood not in the sense of elegiac ruination or privation, but of obsoletion or reverie – in the way one might be lost in thought. Which is precisely the way thought can be found in materials, ideas lodged in things.'[43] This is all very well, but such an objection cannot be allowed to degenerate into condemnation of criticism for committing the 'heresy of paraphrase'. Rather, there is simply no translation, no metaphor, only a process of mediation which puts away the privileged position of 'poetry' imagined as a form of exalted or transcendent truth and meaning, and the role of the critic as a possessor of privileged expertise or insight into this exalted discourse. Cage himself was perfectly relaxed about this putting away: 'As for me, I'm not so inclined to read poetry as I am one way or another to get myself a television set, sitting up nights looking.'[44]

---

[43] Dworkin, *No Medium*, 124.
[44] Cage, 'On Robert Rauschenberg', 105.

6

Models and mereology

The diverse work of the artists and scholars who congregated at Black Mountain through the 1930s, 1940s and 1950s was nonetheless united in being haunted by the spectre of *material*, by a quest for the 'object' or 'stuff' of artistic activity, its basic subsistence or smallest unit.[1] Though in the poetic context this concern certainly had very deep roots in several traditions, it became especially visible with the advent of modernism, and with the Objectivist, Cubist and Dadaist impulses variously given birth to thereby. By the middle of the twentieth century this question of poetic materials, and its corona of related issues, had become well-absorbed into poetic practice whilst remaining at the forefront of some of the more radically experimental trends in poetics. Under this conception, poetics could be understood as a mode of investigation or research *into poetry*, much as a composer might have to research and design a novel instrument in order to realize a proposed composition: 'poetics' and 'experimental poetics' are then construed as near synonyms. The question poetics then asks is: What works? And so, by extension: what is necessary? What is the basal unit out of which poems are made?

Cage pursued this line of inquiry by whittling away at sensory data, relying on smaller and smaller pieces of sound or text until he arrived at *Empty Words*, at a poetry constructed of phonemes alone (or, more properly, phonemes and a listener/reader). Olson, meanwhile, attempted to locate the smallest part of his poetry in the 'facts', the concrete objects of experience, which his writing is both built on and communicates. Even that supposedly essential Olsonian entity, breath, is itself a 'fact' in this sense, an action and an achievement, given

---

[1] For accounts of the importance of material conceptions of artistic practice in the daily activities of Black Mountain, and particularly of the centrality of Albers's *matière* studies, see Michael Beggs, 'Joseph Albers: Photographs of *Matières*', in *Leap Before You Look*, 86–9; and Jeffrey Saletnik, 'Bauhaus in America', in *Leap Before You Look*, 102–5. For a recent assessment of Olson's connection to the mid-century American artworld, see Mark Byers, *Charles Olson and American Modernism: The Practice of the Self* (Oxford: Oxford University Press, 2018).

rather than made. Towards the very beginning of *The Maximus Poems*, Olson writes that, in this work

> the underpart is, though stemmed, uncertain
> is, as sex is, as moneys are, facts!
> facts, to be dealt with, as the sea is, the demand
> that they be played by, that they can only be, that they must
> be played by, said he, coldly, the
> ear![2]

'Fact' of course has a long generation in Olson's work, appearing as early as *Call Me Ishmael*; here it could be read as the undergirding of his poetic. But it is crucial to note that the specific object of which 'fact' is the 'underpart' in this passage is not clearly stated: it could be the bird's nest which functions as the blason for this first section of *Maximus*, or it could be the statue of the Virgin Mary which occupies the previous lines, or, most likely of all, it could be both. This unclearness is characteristic not only of the thoroughgoingly paratactic logic of Olson's writing but of its temperamental construal of the relations between parts and wholes in poetic composition. Though presenting himself as a poet of metaphysical scope and speculative ambition, determined to create a poetry 'Equal, That Is, to the Real Itself', Olson is also deeply invested in a validation of specificities or particulars, so much so that he repeatedly labels himself a 'particularist', and his method 'particularism'.[3] Though his interest in what Blake might call 'minute particulars' is commonly acknowledged in the extant criticism, there is little concomitant consideration of the way in which Olson's particularism is in tension with the cosmic aspiration, or 'will to cohere', which is an equally important aspect of his poetics.[4] In other words, there is as yet no usable account of how parts and wholes interact in Olson's work, or on what basis their structuration proceeds. Despite certain similarities, Olson's position is not in fact identical with Blake's ethically suspicious treatment of the general; at any rate, Olson's encounter with Blake would almost certainly have been mediated via Whitman, who is more a poet of the whole than a poet of parts, given to universalizing speculation. There is a universal and holistic

---

[2] Olson, *Maximus*, 6.
[3] Charles Olson, 'Equal, That Is, to the Real Itself', in *Collected Prose*, 120–5. For an early use of 'particularism' as against the 'general', see 1951's 'Human Universe', in *Collected Prose*, 155–66; 156.
[4] See William Blake, *Jerusalem* in *The Complete Poetry and Prose*, ed. David V. Erdman (New York: Anchor, 1988; first published 1965), 144–259; 205: 'Labour well the Minute Particulars, attend to the Little-ones' and 'He who would do good to another, must do it in Minute Particulars / General Good is the plea of the scoundrel hypocrite & flatterer'.

aspiration in Olson's poetry which, whilst immediately evident to most readers, is not easily reconciled with his insistence on the significance of the partial and the local, with the peculiarity of a perception or the contingent ephemera of an archive. Where Blake's *Jerusalem* proposes that 'The Infinite alone resides in Definite & Determinate Identity', I have argued that Olson's work is committed to the *indeterminate* and *indefinite* in the longform as clearly as it is to the particular.[5] What is then at issue in *Maximus* thus considered is something like a reconciliation of the local with the global, the part with the whole, in a way which does not reduce one to an aspect of the other – an issue which itself stems from and brings to the fore what might be considered the inherent contradictions of Blake's 'Minute Particulars', which seek to unite diverse particulars through their sheer particularity in a sort of transcendental gesture: to create a 'universe of parts'. In Olson's writing this tension is clearly evident, and directly addressed.

It has been recently and convincingly argued that, along with the continuing influence of modernism's material interest, the foundationally focused poetics which began to emerge in the middle twentieth century were also responsive to proximal historical pressures, especially to the ascendency of atomic science and an accompanying 'atomic culture' in the United States, which itself was a response to the imperious and terrifying power of the American nuclear technology which put an end to the Second World War. In the 1950s, the structure of nature was more easily identified with mushroom *clouds* than the edible kind Cage enjoyed, and resultantly,

> A poet might reasonably conclude that a poetry curious to reveal more about what is not well understood should be investigating not only the politics of nuclear energy but also the energy and particles that make poetry and its world possible. Perhaps even poetry could be analyzed into fields and fundamental units.[6]

Here I want to use the idea of the 'atom' in its original sense, as simply the smallest part of an entity (from the Greek *atomon*, uncuttable or indivisible), concerned precisely not with its splitting – though, as Middleton argues, there were important poetic ramifications to this ambivalent breakthrough – but rather with its subsisting or subsistent and coagulating character. Both Cage and Olson are in various ways concerned with the 'atom' of poetry as a basic building block. Simultaneously theirs is writing which operates in 'fields', between and

---

[5] Ibid.
[6] Middleton, *Physics Envy*, 108.

across atomic entities. Each body of work is characterized by mereological experimentation – a play between parts and wholes which stresses and tests the varieties of textual determination and indetermination producible out of lengthy poetic forms containing highly heterogeneous and not always clearly delineated or clearly reconciled materials.

The reconciliation of the general/particular, global/local, whole/part in poetry is at stake in Olson's work on various discursive, symbolic, structural and generic levels, perhaps most plainly in the complex machinations surrounding scale which *The Maximus Poems* is/are particularly fond of. Dimensionally peculiar expressions – 'he with a muscle as big as his voice', for example – are a common feature of the book, and incubate the reassessment of scalar and mereological relations which appears at all levels of the text.[7] To thus overturn fossilized conceptions of poetic scale is, amongst other things, directly to enter into a fractious conversation with the epic and long-poem traditions, and this Olson surely and explicitly does, hoping as he did to rebuild the epic from *The Waste Land*'s despairing rubble by his 'hunt among stones'.[8] At the same time, this desire to reunify poetry after the traumatic blow of modernism, in the face of the fissive energy of the dawning nuclear age, came into an alliance with a newly optimistic counterculture gearing up for the idealism of the 1960s. Rukeyser wrote in 1949 that '[t]he work is what we wanted, and the process. We did not want a sense of Oneness with the One so much as a sense of Many-ness with the Many. Multiplicity no longer stood *against* unity'; Olson similarly appended an epigraph to the first volume of *Maximus*, along with the dedication to Creeley as 'the Figure of Outward': '*All my life I've heard / one makes many*'.[9] The *Maximus Poems* operates under the sign of these dual motions, of the proliferation of parts and of the gathering of everything into one extrinsic 'Figure'. The articulation and combination of these tendencies as more than sheer paradox is a major motor of Olson's formal achievement.

***

Olson's 'particularism' was matched, from its earliest beginnings in his essays and his letters to Creeley, with an insistence on 'coherence', on juncture and

---

[7] Olson, *Maximus*, 11.
[8] Eliot, *The Waste Land* in *The Poems of T.S. Eliot*, 53–77; 55; Olson, 'The Kingfishers', 93.
[9] Rukeyser, *The Life of Poetry*, 207; Olson, *Maximus*, 3. Emphases in original. See for comparison the semi-official motto of the United States, stamped into all coinage: *E Pluribus Unum*.

organization, if not exactly clarity or consistency. This might seem superficially to fly in the face of a poetry which is in many ways deeply *in*coherent, on occasion almost to the point of stuttering silence; yet, as early as the 1951 essay 'The Gate and the Centre', Olson was already anxious to emphasize the centrality to his developing poetics of what he repeatedly referred to as the 'will to cohere'.[10] By this somewhat obscure formulation Olson meant a rejection of post-Socratic civilization, here associated with overdetermination, generalization and an excessively 'critical' approach to history and historiography, which reduces its potential for poetic 'use' to a litany of inert data – 'classify, boy, classify you right out of existence', as he ventriloquizes Socrates – a position which parallels Cage's critique of sophistication in many aspects.[11] In place of this, the 'will to cohere' names a euhemerist view of history with perennialist ambitions which looks back to a pre-Socratic age when 'a city was a coherence which, for the first time since the ice, gave man the chance to join knowledge to culture and, with this weapon, shape dignities of economics and value sufficient to make daily life itself a dignity and a sufficiency'.[12] This joining of knowledge to culture would serve to heal the schism between philosophy and poetry, making the latter properly a producer of knowledge rather than its mere reflector (or *de*flector). More directly, it would also validate a formally adventurous, cross-pollinating, thoroughly interdisciplinary writing practice, 'some sort of epic' which refused to surrender knowledge wholly to the experts. Along with this came a peculiar political vision, in which the city of Gloucester was mapped imaginatively onto various polities from the ancient world, and separated from the contemporary United States. Urban geography becomes the fusing point of the local and the global.

The city is one of various vehicles Olson employs for thinking through coherence and particularism, and the difficult, contentious relationship between parts and wholes which these two commitments make inevitable. *Maximus* is from its earliest pages profoundly worried by the possibility that it could just break apart, or break down, under its own weight, momentum or lack of consistency. In 'Letter 7', brooding on boat building and carpentry, Olson sees

---

[10] Charles Olson, 'The Gate and the Center', in *Collected Prose*, 168–73; 170, 172. See also Olson, 'The Present is Prologue', 205–7; 206. c.f. Pound, *Cantos* CXVI, in which the poet laments the final failure of his project as a failure of coherence (816).
[11] Olson, 'The Gate and the Center', 168.
[12] Ibid., 170.

in the practice of caulking a ship a suggestion for handling the difficulties in his own construction, noting

> How much the cracks matter, or seams in a ship, the absolutes
> of swelling (the mother), of weather (as even in machine parts,
> tolerance
>
> Only: no latitude, any more than any, elite. The exactness
> caulking, or 'play', calls for, those
> millimeters[13]

The gaps between the planks of the hull cannot be allowed to be too large, lest the vessel sink, but by the same token they require a certain degree of give in order to ride out 'weather' and 'swelling', as Olson has it. 'Exactness' must be met with 'tolerance'; the structure must be neither too loose nor too tight but allow for a certain degree of what Olson terms 'play' and what I have here been referring to as indeterminacy. That is, an overdetermination or rigidity of poetical structure would lead to its failure, as would too complete an indeterminacy. The sweet spot is small, a matter of 'millimeters'. In its most basic formulation, the problem facing Olson is that of deciding *how diffuse* to make his material, how close the logic of the work needs to be. This is, even more so, a problem for his readers: without reliable, predetermined categories and scales against which to judge the work, navigation can be difficult. As Olson writes in Volume II, knowing 'where you are' or 'what you are in' when reading Olson is itself a question meriting some degree of mereological consternation:

> it isn't so decisive
> how one thing does end
> and another does begin to be very obviously dull about it[14]

If indeed it is the case that our understanding of *how to read* Olson remains limited, for all of the scholarly and poetic interest his work has accrued, then it is my contention here that the indeterminate relation of parts and wholes which *Maximus* is particularly invested in is a major source of this readerly perplexity.

The basis of this difficulty consists in Olson's writing being subject to an unusually acute set of mereological problems – problems of the relation between parts and wholes – such that the great proliferation of small, gritty, factual,

---

[13] Olson, *Maximus*, 36.
[14] Ibid., 331.

detailed readings or researches which one can make of/into his voluminous works are not obviously or easily related, or even relate*able*, to the experience of reading his work in macrocosm. Whilst part-whole relations are clearly of relevant concern to any reading of any text, and become increasingly so as a text becomes increasingly lengthy, I claim here that for Olson this tension is central. One way of understanding this is through the lens of Olson's deep interest in the large, the vast, the cosmic. In *Call Me Ishmael* Olson writes, 'I take SPACE to be the central fact to man born in America from Fulsom Cave to now. I spell it large because it comes large here. Large and without mercy.'[15] This has been taken as something of an axiomatic statement by most readers of Olson. Insofar as he is read as, and understood himself as, an 'American' poet, Olson has also been read as a poet of bigness, 'projective size', leading to a critical preoccupation with what Keston Sutherland has referred to as the 'question of size' in Olson's writing: How big is a poem and how big can it be?[16] This question of scale will be reprised here, but reinterpreted as instigating an investigation into the role of the *small* in Olson's writing. This is useful both as a corrective to what has become something of a dogma in Olson studies, and because a counter-intuitive attention to size as *smallness* highlights the mereological tensions which make reading Olson, and accounting for reading Olson, so difficult and so frequently baffling. This section will focus on a small 'theme' or cluster of 'thematically' small objects in the very big *Maximus Poems*, these objects being *models* or *miniatures*.

    The majority of this analysis concerns itself with a reading of one bit or part of *Maximus*, from near the end of the posthumously published *Volume III* (1975). To write 'part' seems loose, but in a sense the question of how to term the units of *Maximus* is precisely the mereological problem which is being described here. It is part 'II' of a five-page section called '<u>Golden Venetian Light From</u> / <u>Back of Agamenticus Height Falling</u> / <u>Like Zeus' dust All Over the River & marsh as</u> / Night Falling Saturday June 28th 1969 on / Gloucester / <u>Ripping Red River</u>' (itself a suitably immoderate title), which might well be understood as a constituent 'poem' of *The Maximus Poems* if it were not for the fact that so much in the book is not obviously part of a single or unique 'poem' at all. The question of whether *Maximus* is one poem or many, an epic or a sequence, or all, or none, is very much to the point: When we read *Maximus*, or a part of *Maximus*, what

---

[15] Olson, *Call Me Ishmael*, 11. Emphasis in original.
[16] Keston Sutherland, 'XL Prynne', in *Complicities: British Poetry 1945–2007*, eds. Robin Purves and Sam Ladkin (Prague: Literraria Pragensia, 2007), 43–73.

in fact are we reading?¹⁷ Here I will continue to talk about 'sections', 'parts' or 'bits' on the basis that these non-technical words do not overdetermine what is a deeply *in*determinate set of relationships. Part 'II' of the section begins with a characteristically Olsonian invocation to view the landscape:

> Look at the size of those Blackbacks & bossing it
> over the normal Gloucester gull on the marsh – 4 of them,
> 1 Blackback & 3 mature regular gulls, like
> water-fowl, & swooping low over the river & calling
> strongly when in the air, back of the 'homes' of my 1st
> Poems – the Frazier Federal*
>   double & 4 masted was it Brooksie called the proud Monster Federals
>
> and the Aunt Vandla gambrel (also enormously overdone and so like
> that model toy steam shovel I bot the Waiting Station for Chas Peter's
> 1ˢᵗ Christmas Gloucester (age almost 3) and I stood naked in a
> rage both fr. tiredness (& from damn) and the goddamn toy
> it wasn't one it was a goddamn literally practically <u>exact</u>
> model crank-crank & all that shit in the world: it was too much
> both for him and myself, and his mother like any mother
> doing that thing all from love, that somehow
> the goddamn thing might satisfy. Bullshit, it won't if it don't, and
> forever!
>
>   *   They both curiously
>   have a goddamn built on
>   Blackblack solarium or some shit extra smart
>   modern kitchen or little chincapin of
>   themselves both of them. That's curious
>   what with one with a hip roof & the
>   other with that doll of the gambrel roof
>   of my Aunt Vandla's toy village.¹⁸

This is a complex passage, particularly with regard to questions of reading understood either hermeneutically or as a matter of physical-performance pragmatism (how are readers to handle the asterisk?), but what I want to focus

---

[17] See M. L. Rosenthal and Sally Gall, *The Modern Poetic Sequence: The Genius of Modern Poetry* (Oxford: Oxford University Press, 1986), which argues that *Maximus* is 'part lyrical sequence and part didactic poem' (339). In what sense can these two categories really be understood as distinct or exclusive?

[18] Olson, *Maximus*, 614. Emphasis in original.

on is the two types of, or two attitudes to, models on display in this passage. The models Olson is remembering here are both dispersed and adjacent, in time and in place, according to a typically looping, paratactic logic: readers are presented with the cardboard model village Olson's Aunt Vandla gave to him during his childhood in Worcester, Massachusetts, likely sometime in the mid-tens to early twenties, but which here reminds him of the houses of Kent Circle, Gloucester before him as he writes in June 1969 (Kent Circle is the area of Gloucester in which Olson wrote his first poems in the early 1940s, whilst staying with his mother; Olson seems to suggest that the model village was based precisely on these particular houses), and then with the 'toy steam shovel' – though significantly it is *not* in fact a toy, as the poet notes – which Olson bought his son from a Gloucester convenience store in 1958-ish, but which is called forth by the thought of the parts of the houses (the gambrels) which themselves remind Olson of the model village and of models more generally. What is presented in this passage is a tightly bound but open-ended system in which models, or the *idea* of models, is/are highly resonant, associative sorts of objects, able to pack a lot of reference into a seemingly small space. There is a sort of recurring Russian-doll logic at play here, as the 'real thing', the house in front of Olson, remembers or bodies-forth the model, whilst that model nevertheless 'contains' the house in its pure or pseudo-Platonic form, without 'shit extra smart' extensions and accidents, the 'goddamn built on' aspects which Olson here condemns. Each is paradoxically a 'part' of the other's 'whole'. In this way models are oddly idealized, as objects characterized by purity or straightforwardness, 'model pupils' for the poet's pedagogic purposes. At the same time, models are things that do not 'satisfy' in this passage, which are, as Olson writes 'enormously overdone'.

A problem of scale is clearly written into this phrase: 'enormously overdone'. The reference is shared between the gambrel roof of the building observed and the model steam shovel, and indicates an ornateness, fussiness or overprecision which Olson dislikes: 'it was a goddamn literally practically <u>exact</u> / model crank-crank & all that shit in the world' he says of the steam shovel that was not a toy and so of no use to his son – or, by extension, to him. 'Exactitude' is the pressure point here, underlined with a sort of repulsed vigour, the overzealousness warned of in the discussion of hull building, which makes the vessel brittle: 'crank-crank' is work, not play. His rage against the federal architecture of Kent Circle is fuelled by the degeneration of the real houses away from the models he remembers from childhood: they are now in possession of various add-ons which complicate Olson's cardboard remembrances.

This is not the first time Aunt Vandla and her model houses have appeared in *Maximus*. It is the third iteration, the model houses appearing once in both the first and the second books as well, so that by this late point of the third book readers have been trained to associate Aunt Vandla and the Kent Circle houses with these models; thereby Olson's seeming disappointment at the change (or degeneration) of the full-scale houses in *Volume III* is in some sense shared by his readers. They are at best 'curious' lookalikes or half-made images of the models readers have been made familiar with. In a strange reversal, the real buildings are presented as the Potemkin village, as a disappointment of expectations. Being 'enormously overdone' in this context means being out of scale, out of whack with what has come before or what is connected. Here the relationship between the full-scale house and the miniature house is one of disconnect, but in the other instances of the Vandla-Federal-model village complex, the model and the full-scale are run oddly together:

> When I woke
> in the toy house I had headed for, the look
> out my window
> sent me, the whiteness
> in the morning sun, the figures
> shovelling
>
>   I went home
> as fast as I could,
>
> the whole Cut
> was a paper village my Aunt Vandla
> had given me, who gave me,
> each Christmas,
> such toys
>
> As dreams are, when the day
> encompasses. They tear down
> the Third Ave El. Mine stays,
> as Boston does, inches up.[19]

This is from a part of *Volume I* entitled 'The Twist', which is again a dream-narrative. Here the poet *inhabits* the model village, which maps itself out and across the expanse of Gloucester. The Cut is a small channel and canal which

---

[19] Ibid., 89.

separates Cape Ann from the mainland; Kent Circle is on one side of it. The toy is expanded in scale both from the miniature to the inhabitable and from the specifically located to the generally spread, so that the federal-style houses appear on both sides of the Cut. Not only are the models thus expanded in the dream, but they are likened to dreams or agents of dreams themselves: 'such toys // as dreams are'. Both models and dreams enact a manipulation or mutation of scale, exaggerating and transforming their objects.[20] Again, one could read this as a dismissal of models – they are like dreams that dissipate 'when the day encompasses', when matched to reality. But what I want to pressure here is the close identity Olson seems to be proposing between dreams, models and poems. If a model can be understood as a *dream* or *abstraction* of a full-scale counterpart, then it follows that a dream poem is a dream's model, that such a poem not only can but in some sense *must* inhabit these sorts of abstractions or out-scale models in its dealings with the 'full-scale' or the real, with the critical commonplace of Olson's troping of the big or cosmic. Here 'abstract' is used not to indicate 'theoretical' or 'conceptual' so much as it is in its etymological sense of 'drawing away', of one thing contained in a thing of lesser scale. So, in the second appearance of the model village, in *Volume II*, a brief part entitled 'Kent Circle Song', the full-scale street is 'My Aunt Vandla's / village', and also a gingerbread house – the miniature subsumes the full-scale, the map becomes the territory, and Kent Circle is an *expression of a model village*, at least for the poem.[21] Again, 'Kent Circle Song' makes use of two simultaneous columns, which juxtapose the more mundane description of Aunt Vandla and her toy village in the left column with a folkloric Hansel-and-Gretel version in the right, suspending each in relation to the other. Olson is *in* the gingerbread-paper-toy village, and the model *is* the dream *is* the poem, or at least a separation between the three is not rigorously enforceable. Without wanting to be too forceful in claiming that dreams are 'real', what I want to suggest is

---

[20] Or parallel the structure of myth: another repeatedly encountered piece of *Maximus* material concerns the Algonquin myth of 'he-with-his-house-on-his head', in which the narrator encounters a man 'carrying his house on his head'. Having traded a raccoon skin for the house, the narrator is surprised to find it is 'light as a basket', and in possession of 'so many rooms and such good furniture', and carries it off. Later he puts down the house, goes inside and sleeps, only to awaken transformed into a partridge, with his bed a blanket of snow and the house a forest. The size relation between man, house and world is fundamentally indeterminate and shifting, dreamlike, in the mythic narrative. See *Maximus*, 201 and also 311.

[21] Ibid., 303. Earlier in 'The Twist', an ex-girlfriend is also implicated in the model-house nexus: 'She was staying, / after she left me, / in an apartment house / was like cake' (87–8); a further reference to Aunt Vandla, on the page of *Volume I* entitled 'Maximus, to Gloucester', similarly reads, 'lawd, how the house had been inflated / in my mem-o-ry' (110).

that models are used here to provide a formal and essentially mereological way of thinking about relationships between poems and worlds. Insofar as they embody the principle of representation – of the 'goddamn literally practically exact', as *Volume III* has it – Olson rejects models (the steam shovel); but insofar as they are tools for imaginative expansion, repurposing and even play (the cardboard village) they are poetically useful. There is a tension at work in Olson's long poem between the synecdochic relationship of the model to the full-scale and the mereological relationship of the part to the whole – *Maximus* is especially interested in engineering instances in which these synecdochic and mereological relationships are blurred.

Here it is important to clarify that though the map-territory, model-object relation is not usually synecdochic in the sense that the arm-body relationship can be expressed as a synecdoche, it can nevertheless be the case that a model is synecdochic if the object modelled is *global*, that is, if it is a model of an object that necessarily *includes itself*. So, it is possible to read a map of Cambridge in Leeds, and in this instance the relation is not synecdochic; but a map of the world *is* a synecdoche insofar as – under terrestrial circumstances – it is a map of a territory it is inside, and within which it can be imagined that the map itself might be mapped if the cartographic process were to possess sufficient granularity. This auto-synecdoche can also be seen in works which map or model their own formal or generic worlds, as shall be suggested.

Maps are, of course, kinds of models, abstractions of a territory.[22] *Maximus* has often been compared to a map, both of Gloucester and of some more private cosmological system; Olson's mappemunde, to include his being.[23] Where in this example the individual is proposed as a mappable part of the world, a few pages later the world itself is the individual, and the city just its part: 'The earth with a city in her hair / entangled of trees'.[24] The 'maps' being imagined here are not scale replicas in supposed something-to-one correspondence with the territory; they are in a looser and more contingent relationship with the landscape, including themselves. They are abstract, then, but they do *model* the landscape as Olson experienced it (and it is detail of experience, rather than exactitude of objective record, which matters here). Resultantly it is tempting to prefer the

---

[22] For a concrete example of this thinking in Olson's writing, see *Maximus*, 150 and 156, on which Olson uses the space of the page to map out distances between parts of the town in number of paces, and draws or traces the coastline of Gloucester's Western Harbour in typed numbers. The map here is necessarily not to scale – it preserves its capacity to model without being over-exact.

[23] Ibid., 257.

[24] Ibid., 289.

language of models over maps when discussing *The Maximus Poems*, at least insofar as 'model' suggests a metonymic relation which is more indeterminate than the schematic, faithful transposition of scale which is generally associated with maps in an age of scientific cartography. *Maximus* can be read as a model village, a site of flexibility and play.

Because models in the Olson-approved sense are not properly speaking adjudicated according to faithfulness of detail, and, indeed, because an overprecision of detail is taken by Olson as a defect, detailed close-reading of the *Maximus* model, of a sort I have attempted here, starts to look dubious, less flexible cardboard village and more muck-raking steam shovel. The 'Muck-rake' makes for a suggestive commentary on the shortcomings of Butterick-style annotative scholarship, which for all its virtues runs the risk of focusing on detail to the exclusion of overall interpretation or reflection on readerly experience, on parts considered without the whole.[25] It remains unclear what the *specifics* of each part have to tell us about the whole – the foregoing discussion concerns models, and two particular model-objects in the toy village and the steam shovel, but many readers could go through *Maximus* without ever once noticing what are essentially minor parts. Clearly, this reading leaves a lot of other material which is equally part of *The Maximus Poems* out, and however illustrative it is of various difficult dynamics integral to a reading of *Maximus* as a whole, another reader could just as easily find another 'part' with which to contradict, de-emphasize or refocus this analysis. Again, traditional critical modes, if not completely vitiated, are subject to unforeseen consequences and unhelpful blindnesses in the face of this kind of textual indeterminacy. The close-reading model is hard to sustain in a textual situation where many of a text's most important dynamics operate not within parts or details but across and between them, often at very great distance or remove. Criticism struggles compellingly to demonstrate this mereological operation. The coherence of the reading, like the coherence of the work, remains very much at issue.

***

---

[25] For the original instance of the 'Muck-rake', see John Bunyan, *The Pilgrim's Progress: From This World, To That Which Is to Come*, ed. Roger Pooley (London: Penguin, 2008; first published 1678), 201–2; instructively:

> There was a man who could look no way but downwards, with a Muck-rake in his hand. There stood also one over his head with a Celestial Crown in his Hand, and proffered him that Crown, for his Muck-rake; but the man did neither look up or regard; but raked to himself the Straws, the small Sticks, and Dust of the Floor. (Emphasis in original)

In thinking and writing about genre, the word 'model' tends to signify rather differently from the way in which it has been used here. Generally in poetic contexts a model is a predecessor or a precursor, one whose influence forms a part of the current practice. In a counter-intuitive way, the poet is the replica of the model in this relationship, 'modelled on the model'. Olson is no exception in this regard. In his study *Olson's Push*, for example, Sherman Paul uses the word 'model' in precisely this sense, intermittently naming Apollonius of Tyana, Pound, Rimbaud, Melville, Dostoevsky, Lawrence and Whitman as Olson's pre-eminent models.[26] To this list might be added Edward Dahlberg, Keats, Carl Ortwin Sauer, Homer and doubtless many more. It is worth noting the formal variety of these models: epic and lyric poets, novelists, playwrights, scholars, philosophers and authors of non-fiction. The adventure and potential incoherence of Olson's writing is in some degree a function of his thoroughgoing interdisciplinarity, reinforced at Black Mountain and the constant companion of his later life. To make a coherence out of such diverse influences required a new and capacious account of genre, and this Olson attempted to provide in his teaching and theoretical writing, but most importantly and effectively in *The Maximus Poems*. It is telling that, though Olson wrote a large number of stand-alone 'poems' in a vaguely lyric mode, few of these have attracted the attention of either readers or critics – notable exceptions, including 'The Kingfishers' and perhaps 'In Cold Hell, In Thicket', are themselves considerably more substantial than the average lyric. Only 'The Librarian' has attracted any major attention as a short poem, and in many ways this, too, is an outlier. *Maximus*, on the other hand, marks Olson's signal achievement in the eyes of almost all readers, and it is the argument here that this success consists, at least in part, in how it successfully expands the purview of the long poem without completely exploding its formal coherence or usefulness, thereby providing Olson with an outlet for his mereological experiments which shorter forms were incapable of containing and for which the epic in its traditional guise was no longer available.[27] In so doing, the book severely stresses the categories in which it might be put, even to the point of making the work's unity seem questionable, even arbitrary.

---

[26] Sherman Paul, *Olson's Push: Origin, Black Mountain and Recent American Poetry* (Baton Rouge and London: Louisiana State University Press, 1978), 27, 73, 92, 116.

[27] For a classic account of *Maximus* as a paradigm-changing work which validated the poetic use of materials from diverse and heterogeneous fields, and its impact thereby in Britain, see Eric Mottram's 'The British Poetry Revival, 1960-5', in *New British Poetries: The Scope of the Possible*, eds. Robert Hampson and Peter Barry (Manchester and New York: Manchester University Press, 1993), 15–50.

In philosophical mereology, much debate revolves around the degree to which wholes variegated beyond a certain degree constitute wholes at all. Certain proposed 'wholes' appear intuitively inadmissible if they seem somehow 'too large, or too heterogeneous in composition'.[28] A whole which is composed of too various a list of ingredients can be dismissed as a fiction; wholes must have parts which are in *some* relation with each other. On the other hand, it is less than clear what is meant by 'part' in many instances: 'It emerges that "part", like other formal concepts, is not univocal, but has analogous meanings according to whether we talk of individuals, classes or masses.'[29] Crudely put, for an arm to be a 'part' of a body is not the same as for a sentence to be a 'part' of a novel; each is a different relation from a poem's being 'part' of a genre. This fairly commonsensical insight has a number of ramifications, primarily that the natural-language concept of 'part' has several analogically related but by no means identical senses. Though 'there are a number of distinct concepts of part, some of which possess formal analogies to others, [...] it is highly doubtful whether these are all restrictions of some single, overarching part concept'.[30] Neither 'part' nor 'whole' are stable concepts, then; rather they are mutually reinforcing, with the type of whole determining the kind of part and vice versa. In a certain way, the problem of mereology is a problem relating to the genitive case, to the secrecy of the word 'of' in the sentence 'x is a part *of* y'. When, as has been common here, one writes that some page of writing is a 'part' of *The Maximus Poems*, the difficulty does not belong to the 'whole', which clearly refers to the book in the hand, nor necessarily to the 'part', which is not a rigid designator, and can be used in several senses as context allows or dictates. Rather the problem is precisely located in the *relation* 'of', which requires some maintenance and an at least minimally specific set of rules for how to interpret that relation. In traditional poetic formalisms, this relation has been more explicitly structured: long poems are made of books, cantos and so on; poetry can be conceived as made of stanzas or lines; all of these are known quantities. One of the perverse consequences of Olson's tying of the line to breath in 'Projective Verse' is that by *naturalizing* rather than *formalizing* the line, Olson makes it no longer a usable unit of formal

---

[28] Peter Simons, *Parts: A Study in Ontology* (Oxford and New York: Clarendon, 1987), 87–8. Simons's is a discussion of the modern field of mereology; for a survey of the philosophical history of thinking about parts and wholes before Stanisław Leśniewski coined 'mereology', see Jonathan Barnes, 'Bits and Pieces', in *Matter and Metaphysics*, eds. Barnes and Mario Mignucci (Naples: Bibliopolis, 1988), 223–94.

[29] Simons, *Parts*, 2.

[30] Ibid., 106. Barnes suggests, for example, that there are two basic types or kinds of part, 'real parts' and 'logical parts' ('Bits and Pieces', 236).

measurement; the line becomes less distinctively a formal feature of the poetry. Because *The Maximus Poems* dispenses with these received building blocks – as do Cage's *I-VI* and *Mushroom Book*, though in respectively different ways – the relations between parts and wholes are rendered indeterminate. This is why questioning what the base or 'atom' of poetry might be generates the set of mereological questions that have been described here: dismissing the set of received 'parts' out of which writing is said to be constructed destabilizes the mutually reinforcing relation between parts and whole. Because the word 'part' has necessarily contingent meanings, 'it is difficult [. . .] to set firm limits to the intuitive concept of a *part*; indeed, it may be doubted whether this concept has firm limits'; rather than settling into a new determination, the hunt for poetic fundamentals will always produce mereological indeterminacy.[31] Indeed, it is evidently the case that Olson developed no especially stable answer to the question of poetic fundamentals, and nor did Cage – each is in an experimental mode, 'hunting' for the atom, and neither ever settles entirely on a result. This in no way undermines their work, but it does mean that poetic mereology cannot be merely reconstituted around a newly discovered and determinate part-whole relation. A new approach is required.

In this context, it is useful briefly to consider the influence of Alfred North Whitehead on Olson.[32] Whitehead is an important forerunner of the formal development of mereology as a philosophical discipline; the term itself was coined by the Polish mathematician and philosopher Stanisław Leśniewski in 1927. As Peter Simons notes, Whitehead's proto-mereology was unusual in that it was essentially 'atomless', without any lowest or smallest fundamental part, or necessary largest whole: 'That the world is "open" both above and below seems to have been something which Whitehead found self-evident, for he gives no arguments for it.'[33] Without making too strong a claim for the formal instrumentality of Whitehead's thought for Olson's work – *Maximus* was already well under way by the time the poet became seriously interested in the philosopher – there is a suggestive conceptual resemblance between Whitehead's atomless ontology and Olson's formal indeterminacy. Both are concerned with *process* in a way which destabilizes substance or material, and which therefore

---

[31] Simons, *Parts*, 34.
[32] See the NET film on Olson, in which the poet briefly discusses 'my great master, and the companion of my poem, Mr. Whitehead'.
[33] Simons, *Parts*, 83.

means parts are never in set, but rather in shifting relations to one another. Where Whitehead was working on a metaphysics, Olson was developing a longform poetics capable of collating the heterogeneous particulars of reality in an overarching formal whole. Simultaneously, Olson wanted to write a poem which formed a 'part' (but also the *root*) of a revivified epic tradition. Without recourse to determinate conceptions of part with which to build either, Olson had to develop a more experimental approach to making his work cohere.

For readers, the question is not one of constituting but rather of *naming* parts of *The Maximus Poems*. This requires the development of a usable definition of 'part' which would allow for the modelling of the work necessary to begin to read it and talk about it productively as a whole, rather than merely as a set of disconnected pieces, which would allow it to be accounted for both as a work with an intrinsic integrity and with a context in a tradition. The relation of part to whole in any given reading of the volume requires an intermediary or vector for interpreting a local reading as part of a global structure, even if the local reading is recognized as necessarily contingent. To this end, it is worth investigating Olson's own manifest usage of the word 'part'.

* * *

As has been discussed, *The Maximus Poems* is a work much preoccupied with the possibility of its own formal dissolution. The threat is on two fronts: from a house-of-cards collapse, the result of overwhelming particularity, and from an excessively rigid structure in which the work as a whole overdetermines what it contains or what can be included in it.

Here it is productive to return to Gloucester, model village. Many of the formal anxieties which possessed Olson's writing practice were played out in one way or another in his presentation of and reflection upon the city. The problems he diagnosed in the urban space and the problematics of his literary production are mutually reinforcing, and the proposed solution to one is the proposed solution to the other. So, in a late section of *Volume III* entitled 'December 18th', Olson bemoans what he sees as the homogenization of America, and the absorption of Gloucester into the nation at large ('now indistinguishable from // the USA') in terms which can be read as a set of formal complaints:[34]

---

[34] Olson, *Maximus*, 599.

> oh Gloucester
>
> has no longer a West
>
> end. it is a
>
> part of the
>
> country now a mangled
>
> mess of all parts swollen
>
> & fallen
>
> into
>
> degradation, each bundle un-
>
> bound and scattered
>
> as so many
>
> units of poor
>
> sorts and strangulation all hung up each one
>
> like hanged
>
> bodies[35]

In this section, the model village has ceased to be a useful tool and become merely an empty cypher: 'what was Main // street are now /// fake gasoline station // and A & P supermarket'; the natural world reflects the poet's gloom: 'nature is // effected by // men is no more // than man's // acquisition or improvement'.[36] The source of this discomfiture is expressed as a spoilage of scale and of relation, such that the part of Gloucester previously known as 'West' is no longer identifiable or distinct from the great mass of the land, and the localities of the nation are no longer bound together by anything more than their own sickly tumescence.[37] The 'part' which West Gloucester now is of the nation is an unarticulated and indistinct one, fully homogeneous, whilst the nation is reduced to a ragbag of 'parts' – a 'mangled mess' governed by identikit corporatism. There is an ambivalent destruction at

---

[35] Ibid., 597.
[36] Ibid., 597–8.
[37] It is of interest to note that Kent Circle, the location of Aunt Vandla's model village, is in West Gloucester; the degeneration of the real houses away from the familiar models seems to have been part of what Olson saw as a wider national process of homogenization and generalization.

work, the parts of the town, as of the poem, 'un- / bound and scattered' but also 'bound and scattered', subject both to centrifugal and centripetal forces. Perhaps most noticeable is the diagnosis of strangulation, and more particularly of hanging; a hanged body exemplifies the 'both too tight and too disconnected' problem, the neck connected too tightly to one point and not to any other. The hangman's noose is specifically measured in order to have absolutely no give, no 'play', precisely in order that something snaps. This is an image of formal derangement as much as it is of political malaise, and shows Olson's mereological thinking in an especially melancholy mode, depicting a state of failure. 'Parts' here are simply what is left over from the failure of poesis.

Here 'part' seems to carry a sense of discarded or dead 'body parts', a lexical suggestion which chimes with the diseased cast Olson gives to Gloucester in this passage: 'swollen', 'degradation', 'mangled' and so on. The disconnection of parts is framed as a mutilation, the body of the text reduced to a corpse. This is mutilation both of expression, of poetry's ability to say anything specific or particular at all, and of form, which is overrun entirely by inarticulate 'units' in possession of no structure or syntax. Discussing Robert Kelly's *The Mill of Particulars*, Rasula has pointed out the bacterial or immunological paradigm according to which linguistic particulars are commonly treated, writing that

> Language is inconceivable without a granary of words, a 'mill of particulars' in [Kelly's] parable. But particularity can run amok without an informing pattern, a disposing matrix. The pestilential vision of parts overrunning the whole.[38]

As I have discussed, the informational and its undoing is a key dynamic in Olson's writing. A subversion of knowledge with information by the archival mode is matched by a rejection of *per*formance, in the sense of a complete provision of form, in favour of an 'informance' which is a process of *putting into shape* in a set of contingent and reversible ways – such that informance works at times in tandem with *de*formance, the destabilizing and degradation of form seen in Cage's mycopoetics, or in Olson's own dissipative, high-speed writing. The informational is evoked and subsequently deranged. For Olson, then, the 'pestilential vision' of particularism is a danger not entirely to be rejected. As has been noted, Olson's poetics requires a *degree* of formal dissolution to function but is also predicated on some speculative coherence in even these dissolute structures. The development of a concept which allows this dissolution to contain a productive force is nonetheless an integral challenge for Olson's readers.

---

[38] Rasula, *This Compost*, 145.

One of the more well-known sections or parts of *Volume II*, entitled 'MAXIMUS, FROM DOGTOWN – I', concludes with a pragmatic moment of reconciliation between the homogenizing and the dissipative, locating both in an organismic conception of the body. The sailor Merry, who might be said mythologically to 'represent' a conflict between individual ambition or pride and a broader metaphysical unity, having been torn into pieces by his own bull, is left to rot, and covered with flies:

> Then only
> after the grubs
> had done him
> did the earth
> let her robe
> uncover and her part
> take him in[39]

This is part of a system of concentric wholes which 'MAXIMUS, FROM DOGTOWN' proposes, with the individual body being reintegrated into the earth just as the earth is an emanation of the sea, seen as 'the thing which encloses / every thing'.[40] The pestilential, degrading work of the grubs, which break down the body into even smaller pieces than the bull enabled, paradoxically facilitates its reintegration into the earth. In other words, a structure is created which allows parts to individuate and then be taken back in by the whole, making radical individuation the parent of unity. Analogically, it becomes possible to think of part-whole relations within *Maximus* not as static and hierarchical, but rather as contingent, fungible and processually determined. A part need not be in one predetermined relation to a whole but can be conceived of as caught up in a process of mereological formation and dissolution which is manipulated by readers. Readerly attention brings certain parts 'into focus', drawing them out from the whole, but does not accord them absolute pre-eminence as a result. Here Retallack's figure-ground shift is enacted not so much by foregrounding the suppressed background but more exactly by making the 'foregroundedness' of the foreground a merely pragmatic and transparently arbitrary positioning active at any particular moment of reading. The reconciliation of part and whole is not governed by a static concept of either, but instead functions according to a

---

[39] Olson, *Maximus*, 176.
[40] Ibid., 172. Emphasis in original.

conception of mereology as always processual. Parts and wholes structure each other mutually; they also keep each other moving.

Here the actual mereological import of Olson's much-vaunted breath-poetics becomes clearer: the part-whole relation, when sufficiently indeterminate, as in *Maximus*, is a matter of positioning, manipulating the perspectival attitude taken to the text by various manipulations of physical disposition – Olson's deep interest in the idea of 'landscape' as a positional, point-of-view experience of the world is also relevant here.[41] As such the contingent length of the line as envisaged in 'Projective Verse', meted out by the breath rather than according to a predetermined metrical, temporal, sonic or spatial scheme, forms and reforms part-whole relations between line and word, line and page, line and poem and so on without allowing that relation to settle or become *too* coherent. The body is itself a useful model for this mereology insofar as its capacity for movement, growth, decay and death means its parts are in no static relation to its whole, even if during the body's life certain patterns do emerge and become evident. The human body is where the mereological problem starts from in Olson's schema, as the relation of individual to landscape forms the part-whole relation *in nuce* and ab initio (similarly, Barnes notes that the philosophical discourse on part-whole relations emerged in the ancient world as an essentially ethical-ecological question of the relation between human individual and cosmos).[42] Use of the term 'part' in *The Maximus Poems* almost always indicates a part *of a body* for Olson, or is conflated with the body as a whole such that 'part' is itself a synecdoche for 'whole'. Indeed, Olson proposes the body as a model for a cosmological mereology. In Volume 3, as part of a three-page section discussing 'Enyalion', an ancient war god, Olson makes this link explicit.[43] Having described how the god 'goes to war with an image' and 'takes off his clothes // wherever he is found', the poet then writes that Enyalion 'is in the service of the law of the proportions // of his own body'.[44] The figure of the god is set against the image – Enyalion is not an idea but a set of relations, relations which are expressed in the body as in the world. The section ends proclaiming

---

[41] See, for example, the untitled section of Volume II which begins 'out over the land skope view as from Alexander Baker's still', in Olson, *Maximus*, 296.
[42] Barnes, *Parts*, 255.
[43] 'Enyalion' seems to be Olson's rendition of the ancient Greek entity 'Enyalio' or 'Enyalios'. Appropriately enough for the argument here, it is not clear whether Enyalios was a facet (or part) of the war god Ares, or a deity in his own right who simply shared some of Ares's attributes; Homer attests to both usages in the *Iliad*.
[44] Olson, *Maximus*, 405–6.

> the rule of its parts by the law of the proportion
>
> of its parts
>
> over the World   over the City   over man[45]

The world, and by extension the long projective poem, is not to be understood as made in the image of the body but rather according to the proportions which pertain between its parts and its wholes. The relation between city – here always implicitly Gloucester – and world is understood by Olson as governed in the same way as the relation between the city and the citizen, or between a body part and a body as a whole; that is, according to a scheme which allows the merely local to be interpenetrated with the global without losing its particularity via application of a contingent and perspectival attitude to the interpretation of the sensory, an attitude as applicable to reading as to any other mode of perception.

Here, then, a suggestion might be extrapolated for a reading practice which could account for the difficulties inherent in making a reading of a part of *Maximus* in a way which is coherent with the rest of the work. The fact is that any reading of such a lengthy and heterogeneous work must of necessity be a product of a somewhat *partial* reader, both in the sense of being a reader with ulterior motives or prior commitments, and of being incapable of accessing anything but a part or scattering of parts of the work, since powers of recall and synthesis are not perfect. This can be embraced as a potentially fruitful approach to encountering a work whose extreme internal variance is difficult to fully comprehend, and simultaneously as a good window back into earlier longform works which whether by narrative or intellectual overdetermination can seem like rather stolid and forbidding monoliths. For Olson this partiality is intrinsically related to the local and the somatic, but also to the way in which the global and cosmic is intuited, since, Paul has written,

> the correlative of the particular [in Olson] is 'human sense' ('objects as they present themselves to human sense'), and Olson also found the impressive clue to this in the Maya, specifically in the way, to use his striking metaphor, they wore their flesh.[46]

---

[45] Ibid., 407.
[46] Paul, *Olson's Push*, 85.

However partial, opportunistic and idiosyncratic Olson's sense of Mexican culture was, there is a useful indication here of the way in which he seemed to think of 'flesh' as precisely that which individuates *and* that which brings us into coherence with the rest of the species, with nature and with the world.[47] If its unsoundness in the face of pestilence or degradation makes it an unstable foundation on which to base a poetics, that instability allows the writing's mereological relation to be both particular and coherent. It licenses the partial reader to manipulate the part-whole relation in order to create a number of otherwise impossible readings and effects, and repeatedly sidesteps the re-imposition or renormalization of texts according to predetermined protocols for reading and writing. The poem avoids the Blakean moralization of particulars and becomes instead a tool for the discovery of and attention to the reader's own particularities. In the early Volume I part entitled 'Letter 6', Olson provides a proleptic account of the poetic mereology *The Maximus Poems* will go on to develop and inhabit:

> There are no hierarchies, no infinite, no such many as mass, there are only
> eyes in all heads,
> to be looked out of[48]

The book's thinking of smallness alongside rather than merely within largeness, and of part-relations as shifting and perspectival, allows for a coherence of 'many' which does not make of them a homogeneous 'mass'. It allows each part of a lengthy form to give play to its proper character without thereby vitiating the wholeness of the work as part of a tradition of long and internally variegated poetic productions.

* * *

Variegation is clearly a central characteristic of Cage's work, in this sense; his are texts composed of multiple sources, arranged in such a fashion as to recolour those sources, making them different from themselves as well as different from each other. This makes his mesostic texts, especially, seem almost completely resistant to paraphrase or conceptual delineation by readers. This can be understood as an especially severe type of the mereological problem

---

[47] For the most extensive account of the shortcomings of Olson's Mexican thinking, see Yépez, *The Empire of Neomemory*.
[48] Olson, *Maximus*, 33.

which has here been discussed. In some degree, Cage's mesostics are content in this variegation, seemingly unconcerned with Olson's 'will to cohere'. Peter Jaeger suggests something like this when he writes that '[Cage's] texts say no to interpellation // by refusing to cohere at a thematic level'.[49] Whilst it is certainly true that what might be termed the rhetorical incoherence of Cage's writings developed a pronounced political, anarchistic flavour as his career progressed, Jaeger notes that this refusal of thematic coherence, the creation of a 'radical subject as void, with nothing to say', is nevertheless not a refusal of coherence tout court.[50] If there were no coherence whatsoever within Cage's texts, then how could we tell one piece or part of his writing belonged to one text and not to another? It seems obvious that, despite their shared sources and, in some degree, their shared methods, anyone broadly familiar with Cage's work could tell the difference between a section of the 'Lecture on Nothing', *Mushroom Book* and *I-VI*; even marking distinctions between more similar texts, *I-VI* and *Composition in Retrospect*, for example, is far from impossible. If this were not the case then the writings' complete and utter incoherence would become itself a form of complete homogeneity, in which no differences between parts could be articulated at all, where there would be no particulars to attend to. For there to be textual particulars of the sort a Cage-like attention is meant to be paid to, there must then also be articulable coherence on the level of textual wholes. A model for this in Cage's writing can be found in his essay on Robert Rauschenberg, in which he describes the painter's canvases as exhibiting a characteristic sense of 'the over-all where each small part is a sample of what you find elsewhere'.[51] A sample does not delineate the whole, but only suggests it – as a form of synecdoche or model – so the part in this description is *indicative of* but not yet *identical with* or *determinative of* the whole. This is a model of coherence, and one apt to Cage's own compositional methods in that any given 'part' manifests itself in his work in a number of not-quite identical ways, but it is a troubling one, since it still leaves the whole to be constituted out of the extrapolation of parts.

The question of part-whole relations has in fact been discussed fairly frequently in Cage scholarship, if not exactly in the terms employed here. Generally speaking the issue has been framed using Cage's own language of the 'global' – as when he describes himself in composing *I-VI* as being 'in a global

---

[49] Peter Jaeger, *John Cage and Buddhist Ecopoetics* (London: Bloomsbury, 2013), 128.
[50] Ibid.
[51] Cage, 'On Robert Rauschenberg', 100.

situation' regarding his sources, meaning the text can be selected from any part of the whole – and so counterposing to this the 'local' as part.[52] Perhaps the key contribution to this discussion can be found in Daniel Herwitz's essay 'John Cage's Approach to the Global', wherein he argues that the mereological scheme of Cage's mesostic poetry mirrors a cosmopolitan politics in which the binding force is the toleration of difference, allowing each part to be equal within the general heterogeneity. Like Jaeger, Herwitz sees in this a resistance to orthodoxy and authority in interpretation, writing that

> [t]he structure of Cage's mesostics aims to put what Wittgenstein would call a 'full stop' (in the *Philosophical Investigations*) to meaning, textual imposition, and the desire for world control, thus freeing us to let the complexities of the world just be, and allowing us to bond in the midst of our various differences.[53]

Whilst there is much to agree with in this account, it leaves untouched the question of how this interpart toleration plays out as a pragmatic readerly problem: if nothing at all is being imposed by the text, then it is unclear what, if anything, readers are supposed to be paying attention to. Simply restating Cage's anarchistic sentiments as a set of presumed intentions does not solve this problem, even if it does provide a handy explanation of the textual heterogeneity readers encounter. In short, without some governing principle or set of readily available protocols, the mesostic text would be rendered a mere accumulation or heap of verbiage; it would certainly not be as interesting and engaging as it is. If, to follow Herwitz's example, listening to *I-VI* can be understood as a 'disciplined form of engagement' – and it can – then from what does this discipline emerge if not some global, governing function which organizes that attention: that is, from a new protocol which supersedes the old unity of part and whole as constituting authorial intention and thematic coherence.[54]

I-VI itself spells out no incontrovertible answer to this problem. It is in the very nature of its heterogeneity that it 'says' nothing obvious or univocal in a semantic sense, but rather is forever in the process of undercutting and realigning its semantic resources into new formations. However, this is not the 'full stop' to meaning Herwitz diagnoses via Wittgenstein. Cages texts can, like Rauschenberg's canvases, still be suggestive even if they do not hold out the possibility of stable signification and interpretation, and meanings can be

---

[52] Cage, *I-VI*, 2.
[53] Daniel Herwitz, 'John Cage's Approach to the Global', in *Composed in America*, 188–205; 194.
[54] Ibid., 197.

taken pragmatically from the text which can then function as usable guides. For example,

>   If we could grasp the whole '
> oN
> makEs
> worlD
> of **It**
> a flaSh[55]

The whole grasped by readers is the book itself, the physical manifestation of the work. The 'flaSh' remembers the energetic speed of the flipbook previously discussed. Reading, this interpellation of the text suggests, is bounded not primarily by meaning or the hermeneutical impulse, but first and foremost by the shape and formulation of the text itself. To grasp the whole, readers must first grasp the volume, grasp the way in which the material book (its dimension, weight, scale) determines the fate of the work it contains.

A similar mereological suggestion can be extracted from the second volume of *Maximus*, in which a characteristically cryptic page connects Olson's cosmological musings to the construction of his book. The page runs, in whole:

> I looked up and saw
> its form
> through everything
> – it is sewn
> in all parts, under
> and over[56]

Before signification, before interpretation – 'through everything' both in the sense of 'beyond' and 'throughout' – the form of the work is discerned in the codex itself, the stitched pages of the book understood as possessing physical as well as thematic dimension, an 'under' and an 'over', pages above and below. The conceptual whole of the work might be no more than the book itself, which constitutes a set of reading protocols, limiting problems merely by the arbitrary closure of its covers. One innovation of the codex was in its capacity both to compress textual space, to contain a lot in a relatively small volume, but also to be moved, to skip between locations and archives. A scroll too has volume,

---

[55] Cage, *I-VI*, 220.
[56] Olson, *Maximus*, 343.

but that volume is organized in a different manner. Rather than as a continuous unrolling, the codex institutes the page as the primary site of writing and reading, thus providing the basis in which familiar codicological protocols (left-to-right, top-to-bottom, recto-verso-recto and so on) make sense, and thereby also constituting the challenge to those protocols which both Cage's and Olson's poetics are engaged in. In a codex, there are many pages, parts split apart, but precisely due to this disjunction of what, in the scroll, had been one unfolding whole the codex is more moveable, more malleable and ultimately more durable. In his discussion of Ingarden's model for indeterminacy in *The Act of Reading*, Iser notes that the constitution of the text requires both parts and a whole, and a flexible but forceful relation between them, if the text is to be a text at all:

> But if the work is to come together in a polyphonic whole, there must be limits to the tolerable level of indeterminacy, and if these limits are exceeded, the polyphonic harmony will be shattered or, to be more precise, will never come into being.[57]

The mereological relation is then characterized by 'tolerance' in the sense outlined in Olson's shipbuilding model – a structural flexibility between parts which allows for the pragmatic shifting of the whole, a 'play' which will preserve it and open it for navigation. Both the writings of Cage and of Olson possess this property, being able to morph or 'give' around the various uses readers might make of them without thereby vitiating their coherence entirely. In this context the concept of textual 'play' can be understood not only as anthropologically and psychologically but also as structurally meaningful in the consideration of longform poetic texts.[58]

---

[57] Iser, *The Act of Reading*, 172.
[58] For the classic account of textual production as a form of play, see Sigmund Freud, 'Creative Writers and Day-Dreaming', in *The Freud Reader*, ed. Peter Gay (London: Vintage, 1995; first published 1989), 436–43.

7

Typos

Towards the denouement of Melville's fifth novel, *White-Jacket* (1850), the eponymous narrator falls from his post on the rigging of the USS *Neversink* into the Atlantic Ocean, 'into the speechless profound of the sea'.[1] Certain of death, and tired of the miserable life afforded him aboard the navy frigate, White-Jacket surrenders himself to the waves:

> The horrible nausea was gone; the bloody, blind film turned a pale green; I wondered whether I was yet dead, or still dying. But of a sudden some fashionless form brushed my side – some inert, coiled fish of the sea; the thrill of being alive again tingled in my nerves, and the strong shunning of death shocked me through.[2]

This passage, along with much of the rest of the novel, contains plenty which Melville would expand on in *Moby-Dick*, published in the next year. But it is also the source of an unusually influential instance of critical misprision, perpetrated by one of Melville's most important advocates and rediscoverers, the Americanist F. O. Matthiessen, in his book *American Renaissance* (1941). Matthiessen, in the course of his lengthy and seminal study, provided extensive commentary on Melville, who had been much neglected in the States after his death and had only just begun to re-emerge as an object of scholarly and critical interest (Matthiessen, Olson's doctoral adviser at Harvard, borrowed from his student's recent bibliographic discoveries for his chapters on Melville).[3] Although paying the lion's share of his attention to *Moby-Dick*, *American Renaissance* contains a number of comments on other of the novelist's works, including this, on *White-Jacket*:

---

[1] Herman Melville, *White-Jacket: Or the World in a Man-of-War*, in *Redburn, White-Jacket, Moby-Dick* (Cambridge: Library of America, 1983), 341–770; 762.
[2] Ibid., 763.
[3] Though not himself a modernist writer, Melville's reception has been significantly inflected by enthusiasms of his modernist readers in the early twentieth century, giving him a proleptic modernist quality shared also with Emily Dickinson.

[. . .] hardly anyone but Melville could have created the shudder that results from calling this frightening vagueness some '*soiled* fish of the sea'. The *discordia concors*, the unexpected linking of the medium of cleanliness with filth, could only have sprung from an imagination that had apprehended the terrors of the deep, of the immaterial deep as well as the physical.[4]

Matthiessen's error of reading is clearly of a rather embarrassing nature, especially given his insistence that 'hardly anyone but' Herman Melville could have produced such an expression when in fact it was precisely Melville who did *not* do so. The word which Matthiessen praises so highly here was instead a publisher's typo, and so what might seem to be the 'overinterpretation' he committed has become something of a cautionary tale, which Steven Mailloux discusses as part of an article which considers the archival problems posed by typographical error and uncertainty:

> As many of you know, Matthiessen makes a rather egregious scholarly error here, for he carelessly reads a typo for the truth. Melville almost certainly wrote 'coiled fish'; this is what appeared in the first edition, and it was some unknown compositor who miscopied this as 'soiled fish' for a later reprint of *White-Jacket*. Matthiessen's archival negligence in relying on a popular reprint edition has often been used by textual scholars as a warning to would-be interpreters who ignore the textual history of the version they are using in their critical studies.[5]

There is some irony to Matthiessen's having allowed such an oversight to enter into his study, considering the extreme diligence with which Olson, his student and researcher, tracked down and attended to Melville's own books, marginalia and manuscripts; Olson was able to identify some items from Melville's library merely by recognizing the marginal handwriting, for example, and would have been unlikely to fall for the misprints of a poorly edited trade copy. But, on the other hand, given Olson's long-nurtured contempt for the critical industry which grew up around Melville, the poet might have appreciated that irony for being at least more imaginative than the 'definitions so denotatively clear' which he felt characterized institutional scholarship and its 'niceness'.[6] And for all the undoubted mistakes Matthiessen makes in this small moment, it is tempting

---

[4] F. O. Matthiessen, *American Renaissance: Art and Expression in the Age of Emerson and Whitman* (London, Oxford and New York: Oxford University Press, 1968; first published 1941), 392. Emphasis in original.
[5] Steven Mailloux, 'Archivists with an Attitude: Reading Typos, Reading Archives', *College English* 61, no. 5 (May 1999): 584–90; 585.
[6] Olson, 'Letter for Melville', 234, 237.

nonetheless to agree with him that 'soiled fish' *is* better than 'coiled fish', and somehow more Melville-like than Melville himself manages to be in the 'correct' text of *White-Jacket*. What Mailloux calls the 'truth' of the text seems rather humdrum in comparison.

The typo releases Matthiessen from the mere determinacy of Melville's text; the question here is directly one of authority, of intention and its misapprehension not only via readerly misprision but via the shifting substrate of the text itself, revealed to be neither as solid nor originary as naturalized reading protocols teach us to believe. The 'coiled fish' becomes a 'soiled fish', not a determinate object of discussion and analysis but rather a suspended relation – readers having encountered 'soiled', 'coiled' never quite settles back into its authority, however 'correct' or 'intentional' it may be. Through the typo, Melville's text indeed takes on a 'fashionless form', outside of the purview of editors or the authority of the novelist, becoming oddly unmade. The moment functions in a manner analogous to Cage's conception of 'surprise', as what was expected turns into something else, Matthiessen's *discordia concors* restructured around the textual slippage.

Here I want to consider the role of the 'typo' in the determination and indetermination of reading, primarily through an inspection of the 2001 text of one of Cage's later lecture-poems. Cage's work poses a number of problems for textual editing, as a result of both his objections to authorial intention – objections which seem to *license* error, and which have been well-rehearsed in earlier chapters – and, contrastingly, his overriding interest in *details*, which indicates an author and an artist unlikely to produce errors or slips in an *unconsidered* or *unrecognized* way, even if certain details seem inexplicable or arbitrary to his readers. For Cage, poetry is composed of language and attention, and the latter ingredient makes errors of *in*attention, of the type committed by the editor of *White-Jacket*, both less likely and more pressurized. Reading Cage for typos, then, is a rather different kettle of fish than is the case with Melville, and the endorsement or censure of textual slips has rather different stakes.

* * *

Cage's *Anarchy* is a mesostic lecture-poem on various anarchist themes (and variations) drawn from a selection of the poet's favoured anarchistic texts, some his own and some by friends and predecessors. The usual suspects – Thoreau, Buckminster Fuller – return to the field, and some new faces emerge – Tolstoy,

Emma Goldman and other anarchist writers. As ever, Cage quotes from his own archive liberally, with particular emphasis on text from the long-running *Diary* sequence. *Anarchy* is notable for being, at about eighty pages, the longest mesostic sequence Cage had written up to this point in his career – the Norton Lectures were yet to be produced – and for being the most *explicitly* political poetry he ever composed. Where he would later describe *I-VI* as a set of variations where 'the theme is not given', *Anarchy* is in possession of an unusually particular focus.[7]

It is worth briefly outlining the composition, performance and publication history of the text, which is complex and not clearly stated in any of the textual variants. Cage composed *Anarchy* at home in New York City in January 1988, and its inaugural performance was given in Middletown, Connecticut in February of that year, as part of an event organized by Wesleyan University ('John Cage at Wesleyan'). Confusingly, Cage subsequently presented a 'A Lecture on Anarchy' at the Slee Concert Hall in Buffalo, New York, on 14 March, as part of the 'North American New Music Festival'. The latter seems to have been a performance of the same text presented in Middletown, since the programme for the event consisted of a handout detailing a number of the source texts used in *Anarchy*. The first published text of *Anarchy* was made available in late 1989 in the *Bucknell Review* 32.2, as part of the special issue *John Cage at Seventy-Five*, edited by Richard Fleming and William Duckworth. This edition of the text is now difficult for readers to access: the journal number was never reissued or digitized, and the *Bucknell Review* ceased publication in 2004. As a result, and as part of its attempt to produce accessible editions of all of Cage's major writings, Wesleyan University Press, which had not taken up the opportunity to publish the text after its first performance, reissued *Anarchy* as a solo volume in 2001, without any of the accompanying material from the *Review* version. Wesleyan's *Anarchy* is now the only readily available edition, and is the one I will focus my attention on here, with brief references to the *Bucknell Review* text.

In compositional terms, *Anarchy* bears a fair degree of similarity to *I-VI*, though with important distinctions. It is a sequence of twenty mesostics of varying lengths, drawing on thirty quotations which form the 'maximum source' for the poem.[8] The number of sources each of the twenty mesostics employed to populate their wing-words was determined by way of Andrew

---

[7] Kenneth Silverman, *Begin Again: A Biography of John Cage* (New York: Knopf, 2010), 378; Cage, *I-VI*, 335.
[8] John Cage, *Anarchy* (Middletown: Wesleyan University Press, 2001), v.

Culver's programme *IC*, which simulates the coin-toss number selection of the *I-Ching* – some mesostics use several source quotations, some only one. Similarly, the particular sources to be used in the wing-words were determined by *IC*. Unlike *I-VI*, the mesostic line was not set in advance, and each of the source texts, as well as the names of their authors and the titles of the books they were from, were put into a pool and selected via the *IC* procedure. This led to greatly varying lengths between the mesostics, with some being less than a page long, and some much longer; mesostic 5, the longest, runs to fifteen pages. Where the chance operations resulted in the duplications of strings – the same mesostic line appearing twice – Cage made the multiple into a single-string 'renga' which he describes as 'a single poem composed for a plurality of poems'.[9] These 'renga' are marked with an asterisk after their number ('17*'). The wing-words which were to populate these mesostic strings were then selected by Jim Rosenberg's programme MESOLIST, updated by Culver so that, as was later the case with *I-VI*, it would be 'global with respect to [the] sources' – that is, so that the characters selected could be of any number and the lines potentially longer than previously possible – and also via *IC*.[10] The most significant formal differentiation between *Anarchy* and *I-VI* is that whereas the latter operated according to the 'one hundred per cent' mesostic formula, in which between two letters of the mesostic string, say 'A' and 'S', neither letter is permitted to appear, the former employs the 'fifty per cent' mesostic rule according to which the second letter may not appear between itself and the first, so that between the two 'A' is permitted but 'S' is not. As a result of these rules, not all string letters could be assigned words, so some letters are missing in the strings, usually infrequently used letters like 'X'. This occurs in seven of the mesostics. Stanzas, indicated in the standard way, by a blank space between lines, appear to have been formed according to Cage's sense of the text in spoken performance, by 'space, a full stop, a new breath'.[11] As with *I-VI*, use of an inverted comma (‘) signifies a small pause, though these are much less frequent in *Anarchy*. As a final difference, it is important to note that *Anarchy* was composed using Cage's IBM PC, but that he did not yet possess the Compaq PC he employed alongside the IBM machine in producing the Norton Lectures. All of this is explained in

---

[9] Ibid., vi. By this Cage seems to have been suggesting that the renga mesostic was a contribution to a hypothetical collection of mesostics on the same string, in the same way that Japanese renga were often written by 'circles' of correspondents.
[10] Ibid., vi.
[11] Ibid., vi. By 'full stop' Cage means a stoppage in speech, not the punctuation mark.

a piece of introductory and explanatory prose at the front of the text, and the full sources are presented. Though the details are exhaustive, they are difficult to grasp with regard to their implications for the text – Cage, as ever, provides trickily opaque explanations, but it is important to consider them, both because they reveal something about the different quality *Anarchy* has when compared to Cage's other mesostics, particularly *I-VI*, and because, as I shall discuss, for Cage detail was central to the nature of the work as he practised it.

Generally speaking, *Anarchy* makes more 'sense' than *I-VI*. There are several possible reasons for this, including potentially Cage's own will to make it so, but it is likely that the two main contributing factors are the relative homogeneity of the sources in terms of their theme – by contrast, Cage spoke of the 'non-homogeneity' of *I-VI* – and the greater latitude granted by use of the 50 per cent rather than the 100 per cent rule, which allows for longer and so more syntactically traditional wing-lines, and so for greater range of choice.[12] The result is that, despite the variety of chance procedures which went into the production of the text, sequences of lines still emerge which appear to closely track Cage's own views on anarchism. For example this, from mesostic 5:

society's
Different from
goVernment[13]

The 'point' being made, of course, is that per Cage's own techno-anarchist proclivities, once the correct technologies have been put in place, and the correct programmes devised, self-organizing structures can be relied upon to produce their own forms of usable sense; there is little need for an author, and so, analogously, little need for governments or kings, as the source texts assure us in their various ways. Cage's mesostic poetry forms, dissolves and reforms all kinds of fragile and flexible societies under a (fairly) anarchic authorial regime, and much of the pleasure to be drawn from these texts consists in watching these contingent relations between language unfold and resolve in the process. Readers can construe these relations in various ways, creating new and unexpected connections for themselves, without feeling bound by faithfulness to authority. Cage hoped for 'a language in which people can read in their own

---

[12] Silverman, *Begin Again*, 378; Cage, *I-VI*, 6.
[13] Cage, *Anarchy*, 23.

way, no matter where they come from'.[14] Textual government, it might seem, has been all but abolished.

But what happens when the stable stock of text in which this liberated reading happens is *de*stabilized, when the authority of the publisher is brought into question? Much of the confusion evinced in the face of Cage's writing tends to find in it a huge crop of details which are unsatisfactorily articulated or linked; and if these details are called into question then a whole new raft of problems appear. This is the case with the Wesleyan reissue of *Anarchy*, which is riddled with typographical errors, some of them obvious, and some less so. Whilst some of Cage's textual productions, for example, *Empty Words* or *Mureau*, which make use of language broken down to letter and phoneme, make the identification of typos nigh on impossible, *Anarchy* is sufficiently sense-making, clearly enough rule-bound, and composed of a small enough pool of source texts, that the discovery of typographic errors in the mesostics is eminently possible. The detection of typos in the prose introduction is obviously fairly straightforward, and in fact most of the errors in the Wesleyan edition are to be found there. Whilst this chapter will not go exhaustively through every typo in the 2001 text, it will discuss a selection, some clear-cut and some less so. The challenge posed to readers by these wrinkles of detail gets to the heart of the difficulties and pleasures afforded by the mesostic.

The first class of typo I will discuss are those found in the vertical mesostic string, of which there are either one or three. Perhaps the simplest example is to be found in mesostic 2, in which the part of the string which reads 'Problems of governments are not inclusive enough' – from Cage's *Diary* of 1968 – renders 'inclusive' thus:

> reaIIze the
> oNly one
> a plaCe that works
> and peopLe
> abouT
> dad'S
> development whIch has
> Voting on
> all thE[15]

---

[14] Richard Kostelanetz, *Conversing with Cage: Second Edition* (New York and London: Routledge, 2003), 143.
[15] Cage, *Anarchy*, 2–3; ix.

'inclusive' becomes 'INCLTSIVE'; this seems a clear-cut typo, in which the wing-word 'about' has been moved left one space from its correct position, so that a capitalized 'U', which would satisfy the string, is rendered as a capitalized 'T', producing the nonsense-word. In fact, corroboration against the 1989 text confirms that the line 'should' read 'aboUt'.[16] This typo seems to be the product of a typist's error in the production of the Wesleyan text, an easy one to make considering the deeply unorthodox *mis-en-page* and capitalization rules which the mesostic form operates in accordance with. If you type out enough mesostics, one is sure to slip through the net. Though making no difference to those who heard Cage read the lecture either way, this kind of typographic error is relatively easy to detect for readers as they follow the mesostic line along with the wing-words.

What appears to be another instance of exactly this error can be found a few pages later in mesostic 3. The section of that string which reads 'they sit at the crossroads of African villages' in the introduction's source collection is rendered like this:

> aRe
>
>   Order
>   cAn
>   orDer
>   So
>   Not
>   Anything can
>   Function
> we aRe not
>   In
>   funCtion
>   thAt's
>   thiNgs[17]

'crossroads of African' becomes 'CROSSROADSNAFRICAN', in which the 'N' seems to be misplaced. In the source text, provided at the start of the book, the text for this mesostic string reads, 'We'll take the mad ones with us, and

---

[16] John Cage, 'Anarchy', *John Cage at Seventy-Five: Bucknell Review* 32, no. 2, eds. Richard Fleming and William Duckworth (Lewisburg, London and Toronto: Bucknell University Press, 1989), 119–208; 130. Hereafter *Bucknell Review*.
[17] Cage, *Anarchy*, 11.

we know where we're going. Even now, he told me, they sit at the crossroads of African villages regenerating society. Mental hospitals: localization of resources we've yet to exploit.'[18] It appears at first glance, then, that the capitalized 'N' of 'Not' is incorrect, and, as with 'INCLTSIVE', the letter next to it, 'O', should have been capitalized in its place, producing 'nOt' to form the word 'OF' in the string, where 'F' has presumably been supressed because no words could be found to suit the rule. But the ultimate source of the quote, again the *Diary* of 1968, has it as 'crossroads *in* African villages', which would make the 2001 source text incorrect, but the mesostic properly formed.[19] Cross-referencing with the 1989 text shows that the mesostic is the same as in the Wesleyan edition, the line reading 'Not' not 'nOt', but that the source text in the first edition also reads 'crossroads *in*' not 'crossroads *of*'.[20] Again, then, this seems to be a compositorial typo in which transcribing text leads to the replacement of one appropriate preposition with another. Cage's 'empty words', words which only usually bear sense in context but which he was characteristically interested in raising to equality with 'full words', are the ironical source of this error; the dangers of misidentifying or underestimating these small bits of language is amply demonstrated.[21]

As has been noted, the majority of typographical errors in the 2001 Wesleyan edition of *Anarchy* are to be found not in the undoubtedly more typographically complex mesostic texts but in the orthodox prose which proceeds them. Whilst this certainly indicates that the text might have been more carefully edited, it also creates for readers an expectation of typographical oddity from the very outset which becomes a constant companion in the reading process. It is a frequent tactic of Cage's to preface his writings with explanations of method, which, as I have discussed, themselves often serve up a partial and misleading version of what the work is 'about' or what it is like to read. As with the method-mania which these prefaces puckishly induce – threatening always to turn reading Cage into an inquisition of his technical rectitude – the unforced errors represented by these typos suggest to readers a set of protocols which they cannot easily

---

[18] Ibid., vii.
[19] John Cage, 'Diary: How to Improve the World (You Will Only Make Matters Worse) Continued 1966', in *A Year from Monday: New Lectures and Writings* (London: Calder and Boyars, 1968), 52–69; 59. Emphasis mine.
[20] Cage, *Bucknell Review*, 124, 138.
[21] On 'empty' and 'full' words, their genesis in William McNaughton's characterization of Chinese linguistics, and Cage's interest in them, see Kostelanetz, *Conversing with Cage*, 147–8, especially, 'I would like with my title [*Empty Words*] to suggest the emptiness of meaning that is characteristic of musical sounds'.

escape or put out of mind, just as 'coiled fish' will never not be somewhat 'soiled' by the editor's intervention and Matthiessen's riff upon it. 'inclusive' is hard to finally disentangle from 'incltsive', however 'incorrect' readers know the latter to be. The expanse of the text is thus infected with this tiny moment.

The typographical errors in the Wesleyan edition thus inculcate a form of typographical suspicion which encourages readers to attend especially fastidiously to the letters which make up the words of the text, rather than skimming over and resolving words in the usual manner. The destabilized text becomes subject to a denaturalized and sceptical lettristic reading protocol. Even where the text is 'correct', doubt creeps in. So, for example, Cage's anecdote concerning his inventor father, from the *Diary*, which reads in part, 'Dad's airplane engine, 1918, flew to pieces before it left the ground'.[22] Though this text is correct in both editions, readers might wonder whether the 'f' of 'flew' might not be a typo, since 'blew' seems more idiomatic, and 'f' and 'b' are sufficiently close together on a QWERTY-configured keyboard for the slip to be feasible. In a similar mode, the line from mesostic 2, 'the maRvelous', which is identical in both texts, seems unusual to British eyes, since in British English the word 'marvellous' has two 'l's. This hypersensitivity to the details of text extends to a scrutiny of the mesostic rule and the string line, which, whilst more difficult to check, itself suggests a few false starts on the discovery of typos. For example, this, again from mesostic 2:

> thE
> fOr '
> iF
> S[23]

Here the final line, 'S', isolated at the end of a short stanza, stands out as a potential error either of typography or of composition, since 'S' in its own right is not a word ('A' and 'I' appear fairly frequently in Cage's mesostics but are obviously uncontroversial even if almost impossible to assign to any particular source). Yet a return to the source texts proves that 'S' is not a word but an initial, from the humorous graffiti line reading 'U.S. out of CENTRAL AMERICA + MIDDLE EAST + MANHATTAN', discovered by Culver on the New York

---

[22] Cage, *Anarchy*, viii, 2; Cage, *Bucknell Review*, 124, 129; Cage, 'Diary: [...] Continued 1968', 68.
[23] Cage, *Anarchy*, 6; Cage, *Bucknell Review*, 133.

subway in August 1987, so that 'S' can be read, if desired, as 'States'.[24] There is a curious way in which the demerits of the Wesleyan edition, in an editorial sense, actually compound the tendency of Cage's writings to make readers attend to the smallest pieces of the poetry's language and the smallest moves it makes. In works characterized by at least some degree of 'chance' or compositional 'randomness', the introduction of error can seem oddly appropriate, at least insofar as those errors create artefacts analogous to the basic paradigms of reading and writing which the text is already working with. Yet a reading which overemphasized the making and breaking of rules and codes in the texts, hunting for errors and trying to recapitulate and 'prove' Cage's textual processes, would seem fundamentally legalistic rather than anarchistic, and at any rate such an activity would only be a 'reading' of the text in the narrowest and least interesting sense, one which presumed the rules governing the text to be more interesting or important than the experience of the text itself; the letter rather than the spirit. At the same time, that specific constitution of these texts makes the identification of typos with any certainty rather difficult, especially if, as is the case with *Anarchy*, other, more 'authoritative' versions of the text are hard to come by. The Wesleyan edition does not even inform readers in what forum the text was previously published – it notes only that it is copyrighted 1988, and that this 'First Wesleyan edition [was published] 2001' – so that there is no straightforward paper-trail for curious or censorious readers to follow in their search for a 'correct' text to measure any responses and readings by.[25]

The typos pose, then, a question of licence, of the degree to which the disciplining of reading practices which guides Cage's approach to textual production – a discipline which moves away from received reading protocols towards a practice of reading as a set of newly alien and primarily physical actions – allows for truly unanticipated and/or unaudited deformation of those texts in pursuit of what might otherwise seem to be eminently 'Cagean' goals. Though it seems unlikely that Cage would have knowingly allowed a defective text to be published had he lived to see the Wesleyan edition, it is hard to say how he might have received the text which actually resulted. If nothing else, Cage's death makes the Wesleyan text's authorial legitimacy, the degree to which it coheres within the Cagean poetic, inscrutable. But for readers the problems of protocol which always attend reading Cage remain, whether the text is 'correct'

[24] Cage, *Anarchy*, vii; Cage, *Bucknell Review*, 124.
[25] Cage, *Anarchy*, .iv.

or not; indeed, it is precisely *because* of Cage's curious formulation of authorship as an indetermining rather than determining role that the author's 'absence' in this text is so hard to handle. Readers can rely neither on the author's authority nor simply revel in its dissolution since a certain degree or kind of readerly liberation is already part of the authorial function.

This problem reaches the peak of its significance in the part of mesostic 14* which contains the Wesleyan edition's third potential typo in the mesostic string – a mesostic-string typo which, as with that concerning the 'crossroads *in* African villages' in mesostic 3, has a more complex aetiology than is at first evident. The line is taken from Walt Whitman's *Leaves of Grass* (1855 in the first edition, 1892 in the final edition), from a section entitled 'To a Foil'd European Revolutionaire'. The stanza Cage employs runs, in the Wesleyan edition's source section, as thus:

> Not songs of loyalty along are these / But songs of insurrection also / For I am the sworn poet of every dauntless rebel the world over / And he going with me leaves peace and routine behind him / And stakes his life to be lost at any moment. (Walt Whitman, *To a Foil'd European Revolutionaire*)[26]

The first line quoted reads strangely. 'along' seems out of place, and indeed the 'g' is a typo, replacing an 'e' to form 'alone' which appears in both the *Bucknell Review* edition and in Whitman's text, and which in the original lineation and punctuation reads as so:

> (Not songs of loyalty alone are these,
> But songs of insurrection also,
> For I am the sworn poet of every dauntless rebel the world over,
> And he going with me leaves peace and routine behind him,
> And stakes his life to be lost at any moment.)[27]

The Wesleyan edition's 'along' is again almost certainly a typist's error, but one still capable of causing confusion for Cage's reader insofar as the mesostic text which accompanies the string in '14*' follows the 'correct' text which is not presented ('liberty thAt recognizes no other restrictions than / the fact it's possibLe / Of / aNd / powErs').[28] There are, then, either one or three typos in the mesostic line in this edition depending on how the count is made, and on

---

[26] Ibid., viii.
[27] Walt Whitman, *Leaves of Grass: The 'Death-Bed' Edition* (New York: Modern Library, 2001), 462; Cage, *Bucknell Review*, 125.
[28] Cage, *Anarchy*, 60.

what resources are available to judge the point; one ('INCLTSIVE') is clear-cut, whilst the other two ('CROSSROADSNAFRICAN' and 'ALONE') only appear to be incorrect in the sense that the sources provided for them contain typos. But again, lacking an 'authoritative' text, readers are unable to establish this beyond doubt, and a degree of 'play' – in Olson's sense of the 'give' required of a ship's hull – destabilizes the supposedly rule-bound relation between the mesostic and its generative source. The mesostic structure seems less deterministic than Cage presents it.

Whilst it may well, fairly enough, be objected that these breakdowns in the mesostic rule are mere products of editorial practice, and can be happily enough forgotten by readers who recognize this, such an objection does not hold for seeming 'mistakes' that appear in both the Wesleyan *and* the *Bucknell Review* versions of *Anarchy*, and it is here that the truly indeterminate nature of typographical error in this and similar poetries becomes clear. Mesostic 14* is a good example of such an uncertainty seeping into reading via the typo, because it contains a strange lacuna in its mesostic string which is replicated across both extant versions of the text. Towards the end of the circa-four-page mesostic section, the poem runs as thus:

> in this Way
> tO the
> aRe
> the Liberty of others
> anD
> Of
> reVolution is
> to thE
> fRee
> thAt's the
> Negotiable
> golD
> So
> inTelligence
> And not
> King
> through intErnational bankruptcy
> Social realization[29]

---

[29] Cage, *Anarchy*, 62–3; Cage, *Bucknell Review*, 189–90.

The mesostic line quoted runs, 'WORLDOVERANDSTAKES'. The fourth line of the Whitman quoted above is supressed, as if the poem ran

> For I am the sworn poet of every dauntless rebel the world over,
> And stakes his life to be lost at any moment.)

which almost connects semantically and syntactically, but is nonetheless not what Whitman wrote, or Cage quoted. The omission of a whole line is hard to explain, since it seems highly unlikely that a line in good English would not admit of *any* wing-words according to the application of the mesostic rule – Cage's use here of the more liberal fifty rather than the stricter 100 per cent rule only decreases this likelihood – and elsewhere in *Anarchy* suppression of the string by the mesostic rule is never more extensive than of a single consecutive letter in a row. Equally, the point in the mesostic at which Whitman's fourth line is 'skimmed over' operates in full accordance with the 50 per cent mesostic rule – 'fRee / thAt's the' in fact complies with both 50 and 100 per cent rules – and though this does not prove incontrovertibly that Cage composed the text as is presented here, it does heavily suggest that this is the case, especially given the fact that what would otherwise be so egregious an error as almost to transcend the relatively minute category of 'typo' altogether is contained in both texts, the 'good' and the 'bad' alike. For readers, certainly, the moment is an odd one, both in good accordance with what are presented as the rules of the game, and seemingly in complete contravention of them.

As has been suggested, the question here is one of licence. What is most unusual about this suppression of Whitman's line is the way in which, if it *were* an oversight, it seems like precisely the sort of oversight Cage would not make. A major purpose of the rhetoric against 'ideas' which Cage repeatedly employed, and which I have discussed previously, was to highlight the degree to which Cage was primarily interested in atoms of detail, in sounds rather than 'music', in phonemes rather than 'language' and so on. Whilst Cage gave himself licence broadly to disregard the overarching 'ideas' at work in his sources in favour of a more pragmatic *use* of those texts, what he did not license himself to do was to ignore detail. In this sense it could be said that Cage held his sources close to his face, willing to allow detail to proliferate even if that proliferation came at the expense of a more 'zoomed out' overview, so that the length of the long poem is more indeterminate than any of its details. Cage was happy to work these decontextualized parts up into his own contingent whole. The fact, for example, that readers of *Anarchy* are given little sense of what is at stake in 'To a Foil'd

European Revolutionaire' as a whole (never mind in the whole of *Leaves of Grass* considered as a large and itself somewhat amorphous structure) by Cage's use of it as a source is of little moment – but the omission of a particular piece of detail, as seems to occur here in mesostic 14*, is another matter entirely.

In all of Cage's artistic activity across his several media, an attention to, collection and proliferation of detail is the basic stuff of his practice, and much of this work was exceedingly in-depth and time-consuming. In the words of Cage's biographer Kenneth Silverman, 'endless detail provided an outlet for Cage's addiction to work, [for what Andrew Culver termed] his "desire to have a laborious task at hand"'.[30] That Cage took great pleasure in this laboriousness can be seen in his work on the *Europeras*, the fantastically complex multimedia 'operas' which he worked on as he was composing *Anarchy*, and for which he employed similar computational resources. Tellingly, Cage was not generally the person who trawled through the computer programmes which he possessed to select materials for his works; rather, he employed assistants, usually either Culver or Laura Kuhn – who Silverman notes did 'much of this processing' – to perform this higher-level selection, and then Cage himself would select particular materials and particular configurations of those materials as they would appear in the final work.[31] So, for example, having received from one of his assistants a list of all the lines from the sources that would fit each letter in the mesostic string, Cage would then go through selecting, pruning and placing the words of his choice, and making additions in the form of stanza-breaks, performance apostrophes (') and so on. It was these ground-level details which interested him, not the facilitation of the process per se.

Another instructive instance of Cage's preference for detail can be found in his own critical writings, which either proceeded via elaborate experimental methods which took significant periods of time to produce and even longer to plan (as with the shape-determined essay on Jasper Johns which he claimed took 'about three weeks to write', whilst the devising of the method for composition took 'five months of constant application to this problem'), or, on the other hand, were populated with extremely detailed catalogues of examples from his subject's work.[32] A good example of this latter can be found in his article on Jackson Mac Low's use of silence, which consists almost entirely of a list of instances of silence in Mac Low's work, possessing conversely very little of either evaluation

---

[30] Silverman, *Begin Again*, 355–6.
[31] Ibid., 377.
[32] Kostelanetz, *Conversing with Cage*, 140.

or analysis of that material; most of what might be called Cage's 'critical' commentary in the piece is confined to the final paragraph.[33] It is strange then that an author usually so fastidious, so fixated on detail, and who took so much pleasure in it, would allow the eminently noticeable 'error' which creeps into mesostic 14* to fly. Whilst it may reasonably be observed that Cage had been dead nearly a decade by the time the Wesleyan edition of the text was produced, and so could not personally peruse or approve it, he *would* have seen the text for the *Bucknell Review*, and the line from Whitman is missing there too. What has earlier been termed the 'method-mania' which always threatens to overcome readers of Cage finds no small degree of licence in Cage's own detail-mania, the glee he took in playing with minutiae. In this context the question of errors and typos is especially puzzling. The temptation to ascribe to Cage an unerring eye for detail, and so make the 14* omission somehow *intentional*, is very strong, but also clearly contravenes the principle of Cage's favoured keyword 'Nonintention' (paradoxically, such an omissive intent would be nonintentional, in other words). Conversely, even if it is beyond doubt that Cage did not write the mesostic line 'INCLTSIVE', it is uncertain to what degree this should matter to readers merely intent on, as Cage put it, '[reading] in their own way', since the 'incorrect' text of *Anarchy* is just as much an instance of the textual *material* Cage was interested in, and encouraged his readers to encounter, as is the 'correct' version. Their differences might even be experienced as edifying, another welcome instance of the proliferation of details.

In an article which focuses on a particular typo from the work of the American poet James Merrill, David Ben-Merre notes the similarities between typographical errors and puns, which often function via the substitution of one letter in a word for another to create a cognate meaning or joke. Though Merrill is a rather different poet than Cage – or indeed Olson – Ben-Merre makes the useful and relevant point that typos are not all of one value, but rather signify, or fail to signify, differently depending on the context in which they exist, whether that context be editorial, historical, cultural or rhetorical. He writes,

> The typo upsets signification, betraying any sense of lingering presence we would have hoped to find in a message. Above all, the typo lets us examine language outside its intentional frames, allowing us to understand how readers

---

[33] See John Cage, 'Music and Particularly Silence in the Work of Jackson Mac Low (1980)', in *John Cage: Writer: Previously Uncollected Pieces*, ed. Richard Kostelanetz (New York: Limelight, 1993), 147–52.

actually encounter texts, not how they ideally ought. Typos denote an absence, pointing to what is there by virtue of pointing to what isn't. Some typos are more meaningful than others because they exist within an interpretive frame that sheds light on the interactions of cultural systems.[34]

The difficulty which attends reading Cage's – or not-Cage's – typos is primarily predicated on the rhetoric of 'Nonintention' which surrounds his work, and which he put much effort into propagating, as, for example, in the Harvard seminars. Because, as Ben-Merre notes, the typo is already that instance of text which is not easily understood as intentional, it enacts a crisis of interpretation in which readers must either decide to retreat into textual quibbling, or, on the other hand, throw caution to the winds and read and interpret without the blessing of authority. This paralyses the close-reading model of criticism which prizes construal of an already-existent meaning lodged in the text, and it is this paralysis which Ben-Merre is explicitly concerned with here. But in the case of a Cage text, where the framework of authorial intention is already dispersed, neither option is so straightforward. To retreat into textual detail is, as I have demonstrated, only to proliferate the already superabundant details of the work in a way which does not settle but in effect only *deepens* the problem of what is in fact being read, and how that process should be executed – an indeterminacy of the object of reading. On the other hand, to attempt to ignore the existence of the typo is nearly impossible insofar as its very presence creates a tension or blur between two textual possibilities neither of which is fully realized or fully eraseable – the text becomes both 'INCLUSIVE' and 'INCLTSIVE'. In this situation a typo is not only unintentional but also incorrectable, not an indication of what *isn't* there so much as two not-quite legible marks that *are*. The reader's encounter with the typo proceeds both as an experience of the 'Nonintention' characteristic of Cage's texts, and precisely as an experience of nonintention that is not a product of 'Nonintention'.

In *Reading the Illegible*, which is much concerned with blurs, smudges, palimpsests and misprints, amongst other obscure and obscuring textual phenomena, Dworkin makes a similar point when he argues that '[t]he affective power of textual illegibility derives in part from its ability to simultaneously motivate and threaten the authority of both the text and its reader'.[35] If the model

---

[34] David Ben-Merre, 'O Sing the Marbles: Typos, Losing, and the Portable Cultural Histories of James Merrill', *Arizona Quarterly* 69, no. 1 (Spring 2013): 119–49; 121.
[35] Dworkin, *Reading the Illegible*, 138.

of reading which Cage's texts propagate is predicated on a disavowal of authorial mastery in favour of a licence given to readers to navigate the extent of the text in their own way, then typos trouble this paradigm by withdrawing certainty regarding the textual terrain which readers find themselves navigating. They are left unable to operate according to 'Nonintention' as the rhetoric which surrounds the text suggests, since the degree to which that model for reading Cage as an experience of curated liberty or licence within certain bounds – 'permission granted, but not to do whatever you want', as Cage was fond of saying with regard to performances of his works – is still in operation is as unclear as the status of the text itself. However, the retraction of textual certainty does hold out the possibility of escape from method-mania. Where the method manifestly breaks down or is violated, as in mesostic 14*, the obsessive tracking of compositional and methodological practice which is one possible reaction to the alien character of a Cage text ceases to be an even minimally useful way of reading the text as it actually is, and readers are forced to make pragmatic allowance for this.

It might, then, seem that typos are a limit case of 'Nonintention' or 'chance' composition, the terms that attach themselves most readily to Cage's poetics. Indeed, considering just the sort of failing of compositional method which the typos in *Anarchy* represent, Dworkin suggests that '[c]hance, in the diastic poems, occurs only with error'; that the mesostic rule itself is too determining to constitute chance composition in its proper form, and only attains it in mistaken deviation from the formula.[36] However, what I want to suggest here is that what the typo indicates is an important critical difference between chance and indeterminacy, one felt clearly in reading. Whereas chance can be encountered as pure happenstance, a material occurrence whose manifestation may not be authorially signed but which is nonetheless *there*, present as a phenomenon, a typo in a Cage text is not only a product of chance, as well as of arbitration, but rather a point at which the text comes into conflict with the process and rhetoric which created it, whilst still existing within the field of that process or rhetoric. The typo is not completely outside or extraneous to the text, but neither is it fully governed by its protocols. The 'error' represented by a typo is produced by chance but cannot be interpreted as just one happenstance amongst others because *it is*

---

[36] Ibid., 120. 'Diastic' is the term Mac Low uses to describe his own mesostics, and which Dworkin uses as a class term for both Cage's and Mac Low's centre-string poems; Cage took the term 'mesostic' from the suggestion of Norman O. Brown. See Perloff, 'The Music of Verbal Space: John Cage's "What You Say"', in *Sound States: Innovative Poetics and Acoustical Technologies*, ed. Adalaide Morris (Chapel Hill and London: University of North Carolina, 1997), 129–48.

not accounted for by the rhetoric of chance and Nonintention which pervades the text, whereas the majority of chance occurrences in a Cage text are.

In a practical sense this means that longer chance-produced texts are always more indeterminate than shorter ones insofar as the likelihood of textual errors being introduced can be correlated with the size of the text. Put simply, mistakes are easier to miss, and longer texts more difficult to edit. In a long poem more things happen, and strange mutations can occur. Yet at the same time the notion of 'editing' or 'correcting' a lengthy Cage mesostic is an inherently problematical one, because *Anarchy*, as with Cage's other longform texts, is without ideal entity (there is no construable idea which governed or guided its production) or manifestation (a verifiably correct or authoritative text) against which the text can be reconstructed in the editor's or reader's mind. A long form is capable of containing these sorts of illegible moments within itself without 'breaking' the text, whilst also retaining the textual uncertainty or doubleness as unresolved and unresolvable; in a short form, errors like the omission of the line of Whitman from the string are both more noticeable and more vexatious to the success of the piece. In other words, the relation of part to whole in short forms is more determinate. This is a product not just of the increased complexity and randomness of longer forms, their maximized resistance to reduction or paraphrase, but also, crucially, of the overarching rhetorics which are required to hold such long and various forms together in some sort of whole.[37] What this means in Cage's particular instance is that there is a rhetoric surrounding the typos in his work which *makes* them indeterminate with regard to reading, rather than all typos whatsoever *just being* indeterminate in any given work. It is not the fact that they are products of chance and error that makes these typos instances of indeterminacy, but rather their contingent interaction with the interpretative framework in which they exist. More broadly, it can be extrapolated from this that in poetic terms the concept 'indeterminate' includes, but is not semantically isomorphic with, 'nonintention', or with 'chance'; each of these is only a facet of poetic indeterminacy.

This, then, is the crucial and instructive distinction between Matthiessen's 'egregious scholarly error' and the reading practices produced in response to *Anarchy*'s typographical infelicities. Whereas 'soiled fish' can be clearly identified as a 'typo', as in some sense 'wrong text', and so identified as a point of creative

---

[37] For an account of how 'randomness' is properly understood as irreducibility, see Hayles, 'Cagean Paradox and Contemporary Science'.

misprision within Matthiessen's account, it is necessary to note that what in *American Renaissance* is an unusual and even embarrassing mutation is, in its procedure, not so far away from Cage's normal practice. Cage's texts can very often be understood as composed by 'readings in error', and so to be of 'fashionless form' broadly conceived. The typo, in this context, becomes both part of the text and not part of it, an instance of 'many-fashioned form', the proliferation of irreducible detail. The judgement of whether or not the typo is 'proper' to the text, whether or not it is in the normal sense a typo at all, is made undecideable, and readers are thrown back into a pervasive indeterminacy between multitude and absence.

* * *

The pertinence of the typewriter is a central aspect of Olson's programme in 'Projective Verse'. In arguing that through it the poet has gained the 'stave and the bar a musician has had', Olson claims for it a utility of precision and expedience.[38] Yet as has been noted by several critics, there is little in this assessment of the poetic function of the typewriter that is new or particular to Olson; as he himself writes, Eliot, Pound, cummings and others had already seen this potential and made use of it. Nevertheless, Olson's fixation on the typewriter at this point in his career has been much noted, and seems to indicate something of importance for his poetics beyond this merely historical account of what his contemporaries were up to.[39] Here I want to suggest that it is not precision but rather the sheer fact of typing as a material action which was the significant core of Olson's interest in the machine, and that this finds its best expression not in the pseudo-naturalism of his interest in the line as measured by breath, and the typewriter as concomitantly the ideal and accurate score-maker for that song-line, but rather in the errors and arbitrary markings which come along with the operation of the typewriter – or the modern word processor – and the indeterminacy this leads to.

A useful place to begin this consideration is with the great plethora of textual variants from which *Maximus* is constituted. In the production of the 'complete' 1983 edition out of which I have been primarily working in this study, Butterick had to take into account not only the three previously

---

[38] Olson, 'Projective Verse', 245.
[39] See, for example, Butterick's comments on 'a poet commonly (if too simply) known for his celebration of the typewriter in poetic practice' in 'Editor's Afterword', *Maximus*, 637–45; 641.

existing volumes of *Maximus* but also the precursor texts of Volume I to be found in *Maximus 1-10* (1953) and *Maximus 11-22* (1956) as published by Jonathan Williams, the various resettings of these, the sections of *Maximus* published first in various magazines (especially prevalent in Volume I, of which Butterick notes that '[o]ne-third of the thirty-nine poems [. . .] initially appeared in the enterprising magazines of the day'), the poems preserved in protean form in letters to friends and lovers, on notepaper, as drafts, written on the walls of his home and so on, and the many variations contained therein.[40] These versions are spread around the world, frequently contradictory and often difficult to date. The task of editing an 'authoritative' text was thus a mammoth one, and probably too complex ever to be completed to universal satisfaction. However, as Butterick notes, the very plethora of emendations and changes which Olson made to *Maximus* over its two decades of gestation indicates that getting the text right mattered profoundly to his sense of the work, and that as a result '[f]or poetry as idiosyncratic and demanding as Olson's, every effort must be made to insure that what one sees is what the poet wrote'.[41] The difficulty introduced here is of course a function of the writing's 'idiosyncratic' character, the way in which Olson developed his own idiolect both of language and of typography, which makes telling what is wrong and what merely peculiar exceedingly difficult. For Olson as for Cage, the devil is in the detail, but also in the outline.

As a result of Olson's close attention to the minutiae of his text's presentation, it is possible to observe that his sense of the 'right' or 'correct' manifestation of that text is itself rather unusual, and on occasion counter-intuitive. Evidence of this can be seen in the very first part of *The Maximus Poems*, which went through several revisions and reversals, and which clearly demonstrates the editorial priorities which Olson himself accorded to his writing. Entitled 'I, Maximus of Gloucester, to You', the section is split into six parts. The fifth begins:

> love is not easy
> but how shall you know,
> New England, now
> that pejorocracy is here, how
> that street-cars, o Oregon, twitter
> in the afternoon[42]

---

[40] Ibid., 639.
[41] Ibid., 638.
[42] Olson, *Maximus*, 7.

According to Ralph Maud, who considers 'I, Maximus of Gloucester, to You' at length in his study *Charles Olson at the Harbor*, 'how' should be 'now', which would continue the sense of the line as a list in accordance with the 'now' of the previous line. Olson had himself amended this 'how' for 'now' in a version of *Maximus 1-10* sent to Jonathan Williams but then rescinded.[43] The 'how' which appeared in the later iterations of the poem, as here in Butterick's complete edition, was lifted from its first appearance in *Origin* 1 in 1950. On first look, it seems very likely that Maud is right, and that 'how' is the product of a mis-stroke of the typewriter – 'h' is next to 'n' in the QWERTY configuration. At this stage in his career Olson was in the habit of producing first drafts on the typewriter, and then amending them holographically in pen or pencil later on. As a result it is more than possible that 'I, Maximus of Gloucester, to You' had 'suffered the thick fingers of error', to borrow Butterick's phrase.[44] But Maud's insistence that the typo is an *error* which should not have been retained in Butterick's text is, I would claim, on less solid ground. There are two reasons for thinking that 'how' should be taken as the proper reading: first, because Olson himself 'corrected' it and latterly reverted to the 'mistake', suggesting that on later consideration he preferred 'how' even though it interferes with the sense and syntax of the lines (not something Olson was especially precious about in any case, sharing with Cage as he did a healthy disregard for syntactical norms); second, because there is much else in Olson's later career to suggest that his interest in typos was more than mere whimsy, and in fact in subtle ways quite central to his poetic project as he came to conceive of it. It is in these later dealings with typos and typography that there can be found a way to reconcile Olson's strenuous attachment to textual correctness on the one hand with his willingness to countenance the inclusion of typographical errors on the other.

In his 1965 *Niagara Falls Review* piece on the classicist Eric A. Havelock's *Preface to Plato*, of great interest to the poet on the basis of its discussion of the philosopher's anti-poetry position in the *Republic*, Olson's commits an obvious

---

[43] Maud, *Charles Olson at the Harbor*, 144–5. For a fuller account of the textual history of this first part of *Maximus*, see pp. 138–46. This rescinded version of *Maximus 1-10* presented a radically revised version of 'I, Maximus of Gloucester, to You', in which the first five lines (from 'Offshore, by islands hidden in the blood' on) were cut entirely, and the poem began with the famous 'By ear, he sd.' line. Quite how Olson came to revert to the *Origin* text remains a mystery, though Maud speculates that the admonishment of Dorn's *What I See in The Maximus Poems* may have had something to do with it.
[44] Butterick, 'Editor's Afterword', 639; for sample reproductions of Olson's holographically amended typescripts, from 'In Cold Hell, In Thicket' and 'I, Maximus, of Gloucester, To You', see Christensen, *Charles Olson* (unpaginated plates).

and vaguely comedic typographical error. In characteristically elliptic prose, the sentence in question runs:

> Nothing not option, of the individual, and a coming together, where epistea is the filthy Host, thought to be food, and Eranos is quite exactly (*agape*) the function (oral-formulaic, Stephanites the unholy Athenian Three, via Hegel Mrak – and Freud.[45]

'Mrak' is Olson's bodged rendition of the name of Karl Marx. That this is a typo is clear from the fact that 'Mrak' appears correctly formed as 'Marx' in an earlier manuscript version of the review. In a letter of 18 January 1964 to Charles Boer, who alongside Harvey Brown and Olson himself was an editor of the *Review*, Olson is, however, adamant that 'Mrak' must stay: '*no* damn it the error is valuable'.[46] Despite the clear and egregious nature of the typo, Olson insists that it remain, that it has a kind of particular necessity which it would lose if corrected to 'Marx'. The point here is not that Olson is congenitally unconcerned with accuracy in the representation of his texts, but rather that he is deeply convinced of the necessity of catching a text 'in action', as it forms. If the syntax of Olson's prose, especially in its later manifestations, tends more towards an on-the-hoof identity between thinking and writing – a prose which reads like speech, which is to say, a prose which barely reads as 'prose' at all – then the presence of the typo is a mark of that energy, of the 'INSTANTER' Olson prescribes as the principal of the projective in his most famous essay. What can be seen in the typo is an adherence, shared with Cage, to text as the manifest object of writing and reading, but as an object which is not ideal, complete or transparent. Rather, it is to be wrestled with by readers, who must not only mentally 'correct' the typo to make what sense they can of Olson's argument but also consider the typo as the *actually presented* version of the text and the consequences of that for the text at hand. Certainly, Olson's view of typos is not identical with Cage's – the most obvious distinction is that whereas the former poet was happy to let typos lie, the latter was exceedingly strenuous in making sure that errors of method were not made, and that everything was in its right place. Yet both suggest thereby an interest in details, in how they form and in how they should be handled, both by author and by reader.

For Olson, an explicit discussion of typography following on from his comments in 'Projective Verse' would have to wait until May 1959, when

---

[45] Olson, 'Review of Eric A. Havelock's *Preface to Plato*', 358.
[46] Quoted in Olson, *Additional Prose*, 95.

he wrote the 'Letter to Elaine Feinstein' which has come to be understood, both by the recipient and others, as something of a sequel to that seminal essay.[47] Olson writes that in his poetry '[t]he basic trio wld seem to be: topos/typos/tropos, 3 in 1. The "blow" hits here, and me, "bent" as born and of sd one's own decisions for better or worse'.[48] This triangle of *topos*, *tropos* and *typos*, which Olson took from his studies into ancient Greece, would by the time of the third volume of *Maximus* be a crucial conceptual scheme for Olson, according to which he organized and understood his own writing and poetics. Very briefly, *topos* or topology is 'place' or space; *tropos* is tropology or the transmission of tropes, and represents time; and *typos* is 'type' in all its senses, and represents the tying together of time and space, *tropos* and *topos*, in a particular moment of energy or action. *Typos* is clearly crucial to this scheme, the aspect that holds the others together, and Olson is fully aware of the pun, which he takes to be not only circumstantial but a sign of an intimate and real connection. Again to Feinstein, he writes, 'I wld take it all Pun is Rime, all from tope/type/trope, that built in is the connection, in each of us, to Cosmos, and if one taps, via psyche, plus a "true" adherence of Muse, one does reveal "Form"'.[49] *Typos*, in other words, is the process which reveals the real or actual form of something, linked indelibly to the material manifestations of processes in time and space, and it is in this context that Olson's insistence on the value of the typo can be understood. Not only do typographic errors attest to the genuinely 'energetic' and contingent nature of the writing process, they also register the things of the world in a way which remembers Cage's emphasis on attention to sensual phenomena. The poetic text is not idealized or treated as the product of a sublime lyric ego but rather marked by its own error and inconsistency, as are the body and machine which produced it, and the material world in general. Typos constitute the text as it is, 'for better or worse'.

In an important section of the lecture series he gave as part of his week-long residency at Beloit College in 1968 (entitled 'Poetry and Truth'), Olson discusses this metaphysical concept of *typos* particularly as it relates to typography. Having discussed *topos* as a question of place in the previous lecture, Olson moves on to the next terms in the triumvirate:

---

[47] See Feinstein, 'A Fresh Look at Olson', for her view on the letter and its significance.
[48] Olson, 'Letter to Elaine Feinstein', in *Collected Prose*, 250–2; 252.
[49] Ibid.

The other two words are *tropos* and *typos*. Obviously the latter is very easy, it's 'type', and is 'typology', and is 'typification' and is, in a sense, that standing condition of – I mean standing, really, in the very literal sense of substantive or object or manifest or solid or material. We get our word 'type', which interests me, I suppose, as a writer, from it. If any of you have ever seen a piece of movable type, at the bottom is the letter and the block is above. So that in order, really, to imagine a printer doing it, he's under your words in order to make the letters of them, which always delights me, literally, as a problem of creation. In fact, literally, I would go so far, if you will excuse my Americanism, to think that you write that way, that you write as though you were underneath the letters. And I take that a hell of a lot larger: that is, I would think that the hoof-print of the Creator is on the bottom of Creation, in exactly that same sense.[50]

Olson's emphasis on the 'standing' material character of type is central to the effect typos have on his writing: they are conceived of as both indubitable, uncorrectable and ineraseable, but also as 'a problem of creation' for the author, a difficulty to be navigated. Poetic language has for Olson, as for Cage, a capacity to do things for itself, or, more precisely, to force authors and readers both into doing things they might not otherwise intend or mean. At this point beyond mere authorial mastery, language poses unexpected difficulties, as with Cage's surprising mushrooms, or Olson's unknown vegetables which spring from the patch at the close of 'Projective Verse'. Typos, which emerge from typing, the asymmetrical conspiracy of human and machine, are prime examples of this intention-free efflorescence, the auto-punning of language as it emerges from the writing process, beyond the remit of technical mastery or methodological precision. What is telling in this quotation from Olson's lecture is the analogy of the poet as printer, and so the equation drawn between the poet and the reader, the latter of whom must format and put together the text even as he or she is pressed upon or printed on by it from above. The typographic is what is shared by readers and the poet – type is literally their medium – and so what happens typographically to the poet happens also to his or her readers. The shock of the typo as it appears from the typing process is shared by readers, who are forced to second-guess the medium, to experience text as tangible, fluctuating and in certain ways opaque, and not as the naturalized transparency which it seems in the process of everyday reading. The stuff of reading is revealed as precisely *stuff*, governed not by interpretative protocols so much as by basic physical gestures.

[50] Charles Olson, 'Poetry and Truth', in *Muthologos*, 239–64; 246.

This physicality which the typo forces upon text and into reading is an explicit concern for Olson, who repeatedly figured it as a kind of striking gesture – several times, in lectures and talks on the topic, he emphasized the point by hammering on desks or walls. Later in the Beloit lecture, Olson insists that 'in using the word "type" or *typos*, I mean [. . .] "the blow upon the world"'.[51] This blow is understood not only as a physical gesture or marking, though it certainly is that, but also as a ringing of certain historical bells, and as a deformation of some of those historical artefacts. In an informal talk given to a gathering of higher education people in Pavilion, New York in 1963, primarily concerned with Olson's consumption of the synthetic mushroom psychedelic psilocybin, Olson asserts that 'I don't think there is any typology except archetypology. It's inexcusable to use the word except as a "blow" or "imprint" which is upon creation.'[52] Typology thus remembers all the history of text and its historical contingency – the archaic spellings beloved of the early sections of *The Maximus Poems*, for example, both resemble and in some cases are difficult to tell apart from Olson's more idiosyncratic typographies or from straightforward typos – but it also challenges the poetic traditions and protocols which emerge from that history. The 'blow' of the typewriter is both constructive and destructive (compare Olson's phrase 'if I hammer', from 'Projective Verse'), creating new and unexpected formulations for language whilst also hammering down into the old way of doing things, the old way of reading and writing, and taking apart the expectations and predeterminations which come with it.[53] In part the emphasis on the typo is an expression of preference for what is found or produced rather than what is premeditated ('that which exists through itself is what is called meaning', as Olson was fond of repeating), but more importantly the typo is an indication of the breakdown of traditional expectations within poetic discourse, the indetermination of the very most basic materials out of which poetry is made.[54] In place of these older models, both Olson and Cage present the indeterminate energy of the moment, for which the unintended and uneraseable typo stands as a sigil.

Finally, the significance of typos for both Cage and Olson is in their contingency and fleetingness, which upsets settled orders of reading and brings both readers and poets back to a consideration of what it is they are *really*

---

[51] Ibid., 255.
[52] Charles Olson, 'Under the Mushroom', in *Muthologos*, 77–113; 109.
[53] Olson, 'Projective Verse', 241.
[54] Charles Olson, *Causal Mythology* (San Francisco: Four Seasons, 1969), 11. Emphasis in original.

doing when they interact with poetic texts. Typos are examples of language in possession of minimal instructions or frameworks for use, marks which cannot easily be resolved into any given rhetoric, reading protocol or order of signification. The resources left to readers are thus basic. The site or instant of reading itself is emphasized, along with the decisions, actions and reactions of a particular reader. Olson's recognition of the 'movable' nature of 'movable type' points to the indeterminacy that typos figure – moments in which the text is both one way and another, in which the 'energy' Olson is ever keen to induce in writing is not of a mystical or even a kinetic kind, but rather the tension between variants of one text, between the parts of an object that refuses to be just one thing. In the penultimate part, and on the penultimate page, of *The Maximus Poems*, this conjunction of the arbitrariness of text with the contingency of use is articulated as a sentence or motto:

> the Blow is Creation
> & the Twist the Nasturtium
> is any one of Ourselves
> And the Place of it All?
>   Mother Earth Alone[55]

Stripped of the certainties of established protocol and received, time-tested interpretative strategies, readers of indeterminate poetic texts are forced back onto their own wits, the place from which they use the text, and the suddenness of the physical text before them, to navigate an uncertain poetic landscape in which all typos are correct, and all text shimmers, like a typo.

---

[55] Olson, *Maximus*, 634.

Conclusion

Nonunderstanding

The limited usefulness of scholarly method with regard to indeterminate artwork was quickly recognized by the artists themselves. In 'Give My Regards to Eighth Street', a 1971 memoir of the mid-century New York art and music scene (which describes his time living in the same apartment building as Cage, the composer Richard Lippold and the artist Sonia Sekula), Morton Feldman writes that

> What was great about the fifties is that for one brief moment – maybe, say, six weeks – nobody understood art. That's why it all happened. Because for a short while, these people were left alone.[1]

Cage's esteem for 'Nonunderstanding', and Olson's iconoclastic and reinvigorating attitude to the systematization of poetic knowledge, sprang out from this 'brief moment'. A community of purpose was created amongst these artists, and incubated in places like the East Village and Black Mountain. As Feldman writes, what is communicated to outsiders is a list of persons: 'the fifties in New York have to do with names, names, names'.[2] In place of a determinacy of method, the history provides a determinacy of individuals and their relations.

This book has repeatedly confronted just such a limitation, or even refusal, of understanding. It has attempted to delineate some problems for reading long, indeterminate poems, and to outline some models for addressing those problems. In doing so, it has argued that the nonunderstanding which characterizes these texts is as much a feature of the scholarly reader's response as it is of the texts' composition. Indeterminacy traffics in possibility and the play of expectations, and no expectation is more brazenly disappointed by these poems than is that of the scholar in explicatory mode. As in Olson's 'Projective Verse', the naming of names fills in the space opened up by a demurral from a defensible poetics, from a poetics secured and justifiable in the terms scholars might recognize. Cage's

---

[1] Morton Feldman, 'Give My Regards to Eighth Street', in *Give My Regards to Eighth Street: Collected Writings of Morton Feldman*, ed. B. H. Friedman (Cambridge: Exact Change, 2000), 93–101; 101.
[2] Ibid., 93.

voluminous acknowledgements of influence and debt, which George J. Leonard reads as a kind of 'filial pietism', could rather be seen to perform much the same function.[3] These texts and works were the cause of a great deal of admiration and imitation on the part of various artists, composers and writers. Their shaping effect on later artistic practices was capacious and various; the openness of their indeterminacy made them intensely usable. Yet Feldman claims that the condition of this openness was a period of autonomy, in which 'these people were left alone' by scholars, critics, students, those whose declared purpose is to 'understand'.

In a sense, then, what are difficult texts for scholars have not proven so rebarbative for artists. What seem puzzling or imprecise statements in the academy have been taken as comprehensive and permissive licences for art-making in other fora. The question remains: What 'understanding' of these works is possible for criticism? In what way might they be made available to it? How do the indeterminate poetics of writing, herein addressed, shape or demand a new poetics for critical reading? I have discussed 'textual protocols' and 'reading protocols'; what neither model quite includes or comprehends is the set of 'scholarly protocols' which might be brought to bear on these texts, and which are often stripped from readers in their contact with works by Olson or Cage. The resistance to mastery and virtuosity their works exhibit, in favour of a pragmatic and intuitive attitude to poetics which requires a certain tolerance of excess, error and undecideability, cuts against much of what scholarship has traditionally aspired to. Olson's own refusal to complete his graduate studies, and the heterodox use to which he finally put that material in *Call Me Ishmael*, exemplifies this break both with the traditional mores of the academy generally and with the use to which I have put his work here in particular. The work presented here began its life during my graduate education, and there is an instructive, perhaps even ironic tension in writing a doctoral thesis on two individuals who pointedly declined to complete their own formal educations.

Feldman presents this conflict as starkly as is necessary: 'the real philistines', he writes, 'are those who most "understand" you'.[4] The charge that criticism is the antithesis and true enemy of poetry, murdering to dissect, is not of course a new one.[5] But it possesses a particular sting in the context of two bodies of work which neither conform to the unearthly aesthetic graces often ascribed

---

[3] Leonard, *Into the Light of Things*, 144.
[4] Feldman, 'Give My Regards to Eighth Street', 98.
[5] William Wordsworth, 'The Tables Turned', in *The Major Works*, 130–1; 131.

to 'The Poem' nor pretend to be somehow agnostic about or to rise above scholarship and its epistemic stakes. They pose an unusually direct challenge to our habits and methods of critical reading, proposing poetry reconfigured as itself a research instrument, revealing previously invisible questions, new forms of knowledge and understanding, rejecting expertise in favour of experiment, analysis in favour of experience. 'Nonunderstanding' names a decentring of what has historically been given to scholarship to 'understand', what has been valued and taught as valuable. A case in point can be found in the limited degree to which scholarship has been capable of recognizing Cage's work as comic, or might be willing to address the way in which its humour is central to its affect. Associating the stable with the successfully serious, and the serious with the significant, scholars have preferred to analyse Cage's rhetoric for consistency and cogency rather than to investigate what it is about his work that escapes or exceeds that mode of understanding. The preservation of essentially formalistic scholarly protocols has obscured the readerly *quality* of the sorts of works I have been discussing.[6] Feldman insists on this distance between critical description and poetic quality, declaring that '[t]he more interested I got in Cage's music, the more detached I became from his ideas. I think this happened to Cage too.'[7] This is not to say that no understanding of these texts is possible, but rather that any critical enquiry must proceed according to new protocols. Immersion in a body of work is not only a process which illustrates the non-identity of a text's governing rhetorics with its actual qualities; it also highlights the poverty of our critical vocabulary in the face of this non-identity. Amongst the hard lessons these texts contain is the suggestion that to read well is not necessarily to understand; even more, that *understanding can be good reading's opposite.* This is a thought that remains uncomfortable to we twenty-first-century readers, and cuts diametrically against the ongoing ascent of the scholarly reading protocol. The immersive volume of the work is multidirectional, and requires a different mode of textual navigation, a different way of articulating the relation between part and whole. Long indeterminate works resist linear critical representation. Indeed, the undecideable, unrepresentable character of such a work or body of work is majorly predicated on the fact that one has to read all of it to read any of it.

---

[6] Similarly, David Herd has written of how in Thoreau we are faced with an 'opposition [...] between enthusiastic cherishing and reckoning', where the latter term is associated with measuring and calculation. Herd, *Enthusiast!: Essays on Modern American Literature* (Manchester: Manchester University Press, 2007), 30.
[7] Feldman, 'Give My Regards to Eighth Street', 96.

A longform poetics is, as such, always in some degree an indeterminate poetics, and a large quantity of long and epic poetries ought to be reread accordingly.

A final word about the subtitle of this book: throughout what I have presented, 'indeterminacy' has always been accompanied by 'nonunderstanding', even where this second term has only been implied. If indeterminacy names a method, then nonunderstanding is its companion effect. My title emphasizes only the former, but I contend that 'nonunderstanding' is nevertheless contained therein. As has been suggested, criticism has not yet found a way to address the secrecy of the 'of' relation, nor to maintain the 'of' in the formula 'the indeterminacy *of* longform poetics'. Indeterminacy is not an accompaniment to such a poetics ('indeterminacy *and* the longform') but is *of* it precisely because it is central to its constitution, to the manner in which longform poetics is made and itself makes.[8] The open-endedness which this constitutive 'of' enacts is the true name of indeterminacy, and the primary cause of our nonunderstanding, both in the specific cases of Olson and Cage, and in the broader tradition of longform poetics their work proceeds from and subsequently generates.

---

[8] Indeed, amongst Cage's beloved 'empty words', it is likely prepositions such as 'of' with which this book has been supremely concerned – much of what we might tentatively call the 'Black Mountain aesthetic' subsists in the shift from 'looking *through*' to 'looking *at*', for example.

Bibliography

Allen, Donald M. *The New American Poetry 1945–1960*. New York and London: Grove, 1960.

Altieri, Charles. 'The Hermeneutics of Literary Indeterminacy: A Dissent from the New Orthodoxy'. *New Literary History* 10, no. 1 (Autumn 1978): 71–99.

Altieri, Charles. *Enlarging the Temple: New Directions in American Poetry During the 1960s*. Lewisburg: Bucknell University Press, 1979.

Anderson, Perry. *The Origins of Postmodernity*. London and New York: Verso, 2002; first published 1998.

Appollinaire, Guillaume. *Calligrammes: Poèmes de le paix et de la guerre*. Paris: Gallimard, 1966.

Aristotle. *Poetics*. Translated by Malcolm Heath. London: Penguin, 1997.

Auslander, Philip. *Liveness: Performance in a Mediatized Culture*. London and New York: Routledge, 1999.

Austin, J. L. *How to Do Things with Words*. Oxford: Clarendon, 1962.

Baraka, Amiri/LeRoi Jones. *The Dead Lecturer*. New York: Grove, 1964.

Baraka, Amiri/LeRoi Jones. *The LeRoi Jones/Amiri Baraka Reader*. Edited by William J. Harris. New York: Basic, 1991.

Barnes, Jonathan. 'Bits and Pieces'. In *Matter and Metaphysics*, edited by Barnes and Mario Mignucci, 223–94. Naples: Bibliopolis, 1988.

Barrish, Phillip. *American Literary Realism, Critical Theory, and Intellectual Prestige, 1880–1995*. Cambridge: Cambridge University Press, 2001.

Barthes, Roland. *Image, Music, Text*. Translated by Stephen Heath. London: Fontana, 1977.

Barthes, Roland. *The Rustle of Language*. Translated by Richard Howard. New York: Hill and Wang, 1986.

Beach, Christopher. *The ABC of Influence: Ezra Pound and the Remaking of American Poetic Tradition*. Berkeley: University of California, 1992.

Beckett, Samuel. 'Dante. Bruno. Vico. Joyce'. In *Our Exagmination Round His Factification for Incamination of Work in Progress*, 1–22. London: Faber, 1961; first published 1929.

Beckett, Samuel. *Ill Seen Ill Said*. London: Calder, 1982; first published 1981.

Beckett, Samuel. *Texts for Nothing and Other Shorter Prose, 1950–1976*. Edited by Mark Nixon. London: Faber, 2010.

Beer, Gillian. *Darwin's Plots: Evolutionary Narrative in Darwin, George Eliot and Nineteenth-Century Fiction*. Cambridge: Cambridge University Press, 2009; first published 1983.

Ben-Merre, David. 'O Sing the Marbles: Typos, Losing, and the Portable Cultural Histories of James Merrill'. *Arizona Quarterly* 69, no. 1 (Spring 2013): 119–49.
Bennett, Jane. *Thoreau's Nature: Ethics, Politics and the Wild*. Thousand Oaks, London and New Delhi: AltaMira, 1994.
Bennett, Jane. *Vibrant Matter: A Political Ecology of Things*. Durham: Duke University Press, 2010.
Bernstein, Charles. *The Sophist*. Cambridge: Salt, 2004.
Bernstein, Charles. *Attack of the Difficult Poems*. Chicago: University of Chicago, 2011.
Bernstein, Charles. *Pitch of Poetry*. Chicago and London: University of Chicago, 2016.
Bernstein, David W. and Christopher Hatch, eds. *Writings Through John Cage's Music, Poetry and Art*. Chicago and London: University of Chicago, 2001.
Best, Stephen and Sharon Marcus. 'Surface Reading: An Introduction'. *Representations* 108 (Fall 2009): 1–21.
Billiteri, Carla. *Language and the Renewal of Society in Walt Whitman, Laura (Riding) Jackson, and Charles Olson: The American Cratylus*. New York: Palgrave Macmillan, 2009.
Blake, William. *The Complete Poetry and Prose*. Edited by David V. Erdman. New York: Anchor, 1988; first published 1965.
Blanton, C. D. *Epic Negation: The Dialectical Poetics of Late Modernism*. Oxford and New York: Oxford University Press, 2015.
Blume, Eugen, Matilda Felix, Gabriele Knapstein and Catherine Nichols, eds. *Black Mountain: An Interdisciplinary Experiment 1933–1957*. Leipzig: Spector, 2015.
Boer, Charles. *Olson in Connecticut*. Rocky Mount: North Carolina Wesleyan College, 1975.
Bové, Paul. *Early Postmodernism: Foundational Essays*. Durham and London: Duke University Press, 1995.
Bram, Shahar. *Charles Olson and Alfred North Whitehead: An Essay on Poetry*. Lewisburg: Bucknell University Press, 2004.
Breton, André. *Manifestes du Surréalisme*. Paris: Gallimard, 1972
Brooks, Cleanth. *The Well Wrought Urn: Studies in the Structure of Poetry*. San Diego and New York and London: Harvest, 1970; first published 1947.
Brown, Bill. 'Thing Theory'. *Critical Inquiry* 28, no. 1 (Autumn 2001): 1–22.
Bryant, Marsha. 'Epic Encounters: The Modernist Long Poem Goes to the Movies'. *Journal of Modern Literature* 37, no. 4 (Summer 2014): 70–90.
Bunyan, John. *The Pilgrim's Progress: From This World, to That Which Is to Come*. Edited by Roger Pooley. London: Penguin, 2008; first published 1678.
Bush, Clive. 'Muriel Rukeyser: The Poet as Scientific Biographer'. *Spanner Eleven*, 1–22. London: Aloes, 1977.
Butterick, George F. *A Guide to the Maximus Poems of Charles Olson*. Berkeley, Los Angeles and London: University of California, 1978.

Butterick, George F. 'Charles Olson and the Postmodern Advance'. *Iowa Review* 11, no. 4 (1980): 4–27.
Butterick, George F. *Editing the Maximus Poems: Supplementary Notes*. Storrs: University of Connecticut Library, 1983.
Byers, Mark. *Charles Olson and American Modernism*. Oxford: Oxford University Press, 2018.
Byers, Mark. 'Environmental Pedagogues: Charles Olson and R. Buckminster Fuller'. *English* 62, no. 238 (Autumn 2013): 248–68.
Byers, Mark. 'Imagining Uncertainty: Charles Olson and Karl Popper'. *Philosophy and Literature* 39, no. 2 (October 2015): 443–58.
Byrd, Don. *Charles Olson's Maximus*. Urbana, Chicago and London: University of Illinois, 1980.
Byrd, Don. *The Great Dimestore Centennial*. Barrytown: Station Hill, 2002; first published 1986.
Cage, John. *A Year From Monday: New Lectures and Writings*. London: Calder and Boyars, 1968.
Cage, John. *Silence: Lectures and Writings*. London and New York: Marion Boyars, 2009; first published 1968.
Cage, John. *M: Writings '67–'72*. Hanover: Wesleyan University Press, 1972.
Cage, John. *For the Birds*. Salem and London: Boyars, 1981; first published 1976.
Cage, John. *Empty Words: Writings '73–'78*. London and Boston: Marion Boyars, 1980.
Cage, John. *X: Writings, '79–'82*. Hanover: Wesleyan University Press, 1983.
Cage, John. 'Anarchy'. *John Cage at Seventy-Five: Bucknell Review* 32, no. 2, edited by Richard Fleming and William Duckworth, 119–208. Lewisburg, London and Toronto: Bucknell University Press, 1989.
Cage, John. *Anarchy*. Middletown: Wesleyan University Press, 2001; first published 1989.
Cage, John. *I-VI: Method Structure Intention Discipline Notation Indeterminacy Interpenetration Imitation Devotion CircumstancesVariable Structure Nonunderst anding Contingency Inconsistency Performance*. Hanover and London: Wesleyan University Press, 1990.
Cage, John. 'An Autobiographical Statement'. *Southern Review* 76, no. 1 (Winter 1991): 59–76.
Cage, John. 'Art Is Either A Complaint or Do Something Else'. *Aerial 6/7*, edited by Rod Smith, 1–35. Washington, DC: Edge: 1991.
Cage, John. 'Conversation with Joan Retallack'. *Aerial 6/7* (1991): 97–130.
Cage, John. 'Macrobiotic Cooking'. *Aerial 6/7* (1991), 131–7.
Cage, John. *John Cage: Writer: Previously Uncollected Pieces*. Edited by Richard Kostelanetz. New York: Limelight, 1993.
Cage, John. *Composition in Retrospect*. New York: Exact Change, 2008.

Cage, John. *The Selected Letters of John Cage*. Edited by Laura Kuhn. Middletown: Wesleyan University Press, 2016.

Cage, John and Alison Knowles. *Notations*. New York: Something Else, 1969.

Cavell, Stanley. *Must We Mean What We Say: A Book of Essays*. Cambridge: Cambridge University Press, 2001; first published 1969.

Cavell, Stanley. *The Senses of Walden: An Expanded Edition*. Chicago and London: University of Chicago, 1992.

Cech, John. *Charles Olson and Edward Dahlberg: A Portrait of a Friendship*. Saanich: University of Victoria, 1982.

Christensen, Paul. *Charles Olson: Call Him Ishmael*. Austin and London: University of Texas, 1979.

Clark, Tom. *Charles Olson: The Allegory of a Poet's Life*. Berkeley: North Atlantic, 2000.

Colby, Sasha. '"Man Came Here by an Intolerable Way": Charles Olson's Archaeology of Resistance'. *Arizona Quarterly* 65, no. 4 (Winter 2009): 93–111.

Conte, Joseph M. *Unending Design: The Forms of Postmodern Poetry*. Ithaca and London: Cornell University Press, 1991.

Cook, Pam, ed. *The Cinema Book*. London: BFI, 1985.

Corey, Joshua. '"Tansy City": Charles Olson and the Prospects for Avant-Pastoral'. *Comparative American Studies* 7, no. 2 (2009): 111–27.

Corrigan, Matthew, ed. *Charles Olson: Essays, Reminiscences, Reviews*: *Boundary 2* 2, nos. 1–2 (Fall 1973; Winter 1974).

Creeley, Robert. *The Collected Poems of Robert Creeley, 1945–1975*. Berkeley: University of California, 1982.

Creeley, Robert. *The Collected Poems of Robert Creeley, 1975–2005*. Berkeley: University of California, 2006.

Crozier, Andrew. *'Free Verse' as Formal Restraint*. Edited by Iain Brinton. Bristol: Shearsman, 2015.

Davidson, Michael. '"By ear, he sd": Audio-Tapes and Contemporary Criticism'. *Credences* 1, no. 1 (1981): 105–20.

Davidson, Michael, Lyn Hejinian, Ron Silliman and Barrett Watten. *Leningrad*. San Francisco: Mercury House, 1991.

Derrida, Jacques. *Writing and Difference*. Translated by Alan Bass. Abingdon: Routledge, 2009; first French publication 1967.

Derrida, Jacques. *Positions*. Translated by Bass. Chicago: University of Chicago, 1981.

Derrida, Jacques. *Margins of Philosophy*. Translated by Bass. Brighton: Harvester, 1982.

Derrida, Jacques. *Archive Fever: A Freudian Impression*. Translated by Eric Prenowitz. Chicago and London: University of Chicago, 1998; first published 1995.

Descartes, René. *Meditations on First Philosophy: With Selections from the Objections and Replies*. Translated by Michael Moriarty. Oxford: Oxford University Press, 2008.

Dickie, Margaret. *On the Modernist Long Poem*. Iowa City: University of Iowa Press, 1984.

Dorn, Edward. *What I See in the Maximus Poems*. Ventura and Worcester: Migrant, 1960.

Dorn, Edward. *Collected Poems*. Edited by Jennifer Dunbar Dorn. Manchester: Carcanet, 2012.

Duberman, Martin. *Black Mountain: An Exploration in Community*. London: Northwestern, 1974; first published 1972.

Duncan, Joel. 'Frank O'Hara Drives Charles Olson's Car'. *Arizona Quarterly* 72, no. 4 (Winter 2016): 77–103.

Duncan, Robert. *The Opening of the Field*. London: Cape, 1969.

Dworkin, Craig. *Reading the Illegible*. Evanston: Northwestern, 2003.

Dworkin, Craig. 'Mycopedagogy'. *College English* 66, no. 6 (July 2004): 603–11.

Dworkin, Craig. *No Medium*. Cambridge and London: MIT, 2013.

Eimert, Herbert and Karlheinz Stockhausen, eds. *Die Reihe* 5. Bryn Mawr and King of Prussia: Theodore Presser, 1961.

Eisenstein, Sergei. *The Film Sense*. Translated by Jay Leyda. New York: Faber, 1975; first published 1947.

Eliot, T. S. *Selected Essays*. London: Faber, 1999; first published 1951.

Eliot, T. S. *To Criticize the Critic and Other Writings*. London: Faber, 1965.

Eliot, T. S. *The Poems of T.S. Eliot: The Annotated Text* (2 vols.). Edited by Christopher Ricks and Jim McCue. London: Faber, 2015.

Empson, William. *Seven Types of Ambiguity*. London: Penguin, 1995; first published 1930.

Fang, Achilles. 'Fenollosa and Pound'. *Harvard Journal of Asiatic Studies* 20 (June 1957): 213–38.

Feldman, Morton. *Give My Regards to Eighth Street: Collected Writings of Morton Feldman*. Edited by B. H. Friedman. Cambridge: Exact Change, 2000.

Fenollosa, Ernest and Ezra Pound. *The Chinese Written Character as a Medium for Poetry: A Critical Edition*. Edited by Haun Saussy, Jonathan Stalling and Lucas Klein. New York: Fordham University Press, 2008.

Fish, Stanley. *How Milton Works*. Cambridge: Harvard University Press, 2001.

Fisher, Allen. *PLACE*. Hastings: Reality Street, 2005.

Fleming, Richard and William Duckworth, eds. *John Cage at Seventy-Five*: Bucknell Review 32, no. 2 (Lewisburg, London and Toronto: Bucknell University Press, 1989).

Foley, Abram. 'Friedrich Kittler, Charles Olson, and the Return of Postwar Philology'. *Affirmations*: Of the Modern 2, no. 2 (2015): 81–100.

Fredman, Stephen. *Poet's Prose: The Crisis in American Verse*. Cambridge: Cambridge University Press, 1990.

Fredman, Stephen. *The Grounding of American Poetry: Charles Olson and the Emersonian Tradition*. Cambridge and New York: Cambridge University Press, 1993.

Freud, Sigmund. *The Freud Reader*. Edited by Peter Gay. London: Vintage, 1995; first published 1989.

Gander, Catherine. *Muriel Rukeyser and Documentary: The Poetics of Connection*. Edinburgh: Edinburgh University Press, 2013.

Gardner, Helen. *The Composition of Four Quartets*. London and Boston: Faber, 1978.

Géfin, Laszlo K. *Ideogram: Modern American Poetry*. Austin: University of Texas, 1982.

Gelpi, Albert. *American Poetry after Modernism: The Power of the Word*. Cambridge: Cambridge University Press, 2015.

Gillott, Brendan C. 'The Depth of Charles Olson's Maximus Poems'. *English* 66, no. 255 (December 2017): 351–71.

Ginsberg, Allen. *Collected Poems 1947–1997*. New York: Harper, 2006.

Golding, Alan. 'From Pound to Olson: The Avant-Garde Poet as Pedagogue'. *Journal of Modern Literature* 34, no. 1 (Fall 2010): 86–106.

Goldstein, Lawrence. *The American Poet at the Movies: A Critical History*. Ann Arbor: University of Michigan Press, 1995.

Grieve-Carlson, Gary (ed.). *Olson's Prose*. Newcastle: Cambridge Scholars, 2007.

Grieve-Carlson, Gary. *Poems Containing History: Twentieth-Century American Poetry's Engagement with the Past*. Lanham: Lexington, 2014.

Grieve-Carlson, Gary. 'At the Boundary of the Mighty World: Charles Olson and Hesiod'. *Mosaic* 47, no. 4 (December 2014): 135–50.

Grossinger, Richard. *An Olson-Melville Sourcebook Volume I: The New Found Land: North America*. Plainfield: North Atlantic, 1976.

Grossinger, Richard. *An Olson-Melville Sourcebook Volume II: The Mediterranean: Eurasia*. Plainfield: North Atlantic, 1976.

Grubbs, David. *Records Ruin the Landscape: John Cage, the Sixties, and Sound Recording*. Durham and London: Duke University Press, 2014.

Halden-Sullivan, Judith. *The Topology of Being: The Poetics of Charles Olson*. New York: Peter Lang, 1991.

Hampson, Robert and Peter Barry, eds. *New British Poetries: The Scope of the Possible*. Manchester and New York: Manchester University Press, 1993.

Hampson, Robert and Peter Barry. 'High-Energy Construct: Olson, Fisher, Olsen'. *Flashpoint* 16 (Spring 2014). http://www.flashpointmag.com//Hampson_High_Energy.htm.

Hampson, Robert and Peter Barry and Allen Fisher. 'Skipping Across the Pond: Interaction between American and British Poetries 1964–1970'. In *Modernist Legacies: Trends and Faultlines in British Poetry Today*, edited by Abigail Lang and David Nowell Smith, 41–58. London: Palgrave Macmillan, 2015.

Harman, Graham. *Prince of Networks: Bruno Latour and Metaphysics*. Melbourne: re.press, 2009.

Harris, Kaplan. 'Black Mountain Poetry'. In *Cambridge Companion to Modern American Poetry*, edited by Walter Kalaidjian, 155–66. Cambridge and New York: Cambridge University Press, 2015.

Haskins, Rob. *John Cage*. London: Reaktion, 2012.

Hayles, N. Katherine. *Chaos Bound: Orderly Disorder in Contemporary Literature and Science*. Ithaca: Cornell University Press, 1990.

Heath, Stephen. *Questions of Cinema*. London: Palgrave, 1981.

Heraclitus. *The Cosmic Fragments*. Edited by G. S. Kirk. Cambridge: Cambridge University Press, 1975; first published 1954.

Herd, David. *Enthusiast!: Essays on Modern American Literature*. Manchester: Manchester University Press, 2007.

Herd, David. '"From Him Only Will the Old State-Secret Come": What Charles Olson Imagined'. *English* 59, no. 227 (August 2010): 375–95.

Herd, David, ed. *Contemporary Olson*. Manchester: Manchester University Press, 2015.

Herd, David. *Through*. Manchester: Carcanet, 2016.

Hollander, Benjamin, ed. *Letters for Olson*. New York: Spuyten Duyvil, 2016.

Homer. *The Odyssey*. Translated by E. V. Rieu. Oxford: Oxford University Press, 2003; first published 1946.

Homer. *The Iliad*. Translated by Robert Fitzgerald. Oxford: Oxford University Press, 2008; first published 1974.

Houen, Alex. *Powers of Possibility: Experimental American Writing since the 1960s*. Oxford: Oxford University Press, 2012.

Howe, Susan. *Singularities*. Middletown: Wesleyan University Press, 1990.

Howe, Susan. *The Europe of Trusts*. New York: New Directions, 1990.

Huntsperger, David W. *Procedural Form in Postmodern American Poetry: Berrigan, Antin, Silliman and Hejinian*. New York and Palgrave Macmillan, 2010.

Ingarden, Roman. *The Cognition of the Literary Work of Art*. Translated by Ruth Ann Crowley and Kenneth R. Olson. Evanston: Northwestern, 1973; first published 1968.

Iser, Wolfgang. 'The Reading Process: A Phenomenological Approach'. *New Literary History* 3, no. 2 (Winter 1972): 279–99.

Iser, Wolfgang. *The Act of Reading: A Theory of Aesthetic Response*. Baltimore and London: Johns Hopkins, 1978.

Iser, Wolfgang. *Prospecting: From Reader Response to Literary Anthropology*. Baltimore and London: Johns Hopkins, 1989.

Izenberg, Oren. *Being Numerous: Poetry and the Ground of Social Life*. Princeton: Princeton University Press, 2011.

Jacobus, Mary. *Reading Cy Twombly: Poetry in Paint*. Princeton and Oxford: Princeton University Press, 2016.

Jaeger, Peter. *John Cage and Buddhist Ecopoetics*. London and New York: Bloomsbury, 2013.

Jaussen, Paul. 'Charles Olson Keeps House: Rewriting John Smith for Contemporary America'. *Journal of Modern Literature* 34, no. 1 (Fall 2010): 107–24.

Joseph, Branden Wayne. *Experimentations: John Cage in Music, Art and Architecture*. New York and London: Bloomsbury, 2016.

Joyce, James. *Ulysses: The 1922 Text*. Edited by Jeri Johnson. Oxford: Oxford University Press, 1993; first published 1922.

Joyce, James. *Finnegans Wake*. Edited by Robbert-Jan Henkes, Erik Bindervoet and Finn Fordham. Oxford: Oxford University Press, 2012; first published 1939.

Kant, Immanuel. *Critique of Judgment*. Translated by James Creed Meredith. Oxford: Oxford University Press, 2008.

Keller, Lynn. *Forms of Expansion: Recent Long Poems by Women*. Chicago: University of Chicago, 1997.

Kelly, Robert. *The Mill of Particulars*. Boston: Black Sparrow Press, 1977.

Kenner, Hugh. *The Pound Era*. London: Pimlico, 1991; first published 1971.

Kertesz, Louise. *The Poetic Vision of Muriel Rukeyser*. Baton Rouge and London: Louisiana State University Press, 1980.

Kostelanetz, Richard, ed. *Moholy-Nagy: An Anthology*. New York: Da Capo, 1970.

Kostelanetz, Richard, ed. *Writings About John Cage*. Ann Arbor: University of Michigan, 1993.

Kostelanetz, Richard. *Conversing with Cage: Second Edition*. New York and London: Routledge, 2003.

Latour, Bruno. *The Pasteurization of France*. Translated by Alan Sheridan and John Law. Cambridge and London: Harvard University Press, 1988.

Latour, Bruno. *Pandora's Hope: Essays on the Reality of Science Studies*. Cambridge and London: Harvard University Press, 1999.

Latour, Bruno. 'Why Has Critique Run Out Of Steam?: From Matters of Fact to Matters of Concern'. *Critical Enquiry* 30, no. 2 (January 2004): 225–48.

Latour, Bruno. *Reassembling the Social: An Introduction to Actor-Network-Theory*. Oxford: Oxford University Press, 2007.

Lawrence, D. H. *Quetzalcoatl*. Edited by Louis L. Martz. Ann Arbor: Black Swan, 1995.

Lawrence, D. H. *The Poems* (2 vols.). Edited by Christopher Pollnitz. Cambridge: Cambridge University Press, 2013.

Leonard, George J. *Into The Light of Things: The Art of the Commonplace from Wordsworth to John Cage*. Chicago and London: University of Chicago, 1994.

Lerner, Ben. *The Hatred of Poetry*. London: Fitzcarraldo, 2017; first published 2016.

Levertov, Denise. *The Collected Poems*. Edited by Paul A. Lacey and Anne Dewey. New York: New Directions, 2013.

Levine, George, ed. *Realism and Representation: Essays on the Problem of Realism in Relation to Science, Literature and Culture*. Madison: University of Wisconsin, 1993.

Li, Victor P. H. 'The Vanity of Length: The Long Poem as Problem in Pound's *Cantos* and Williams' *Paterson*'. *Genre* 19, no. 1 (Spring 1986): 3–20.

Lo Bue, Ernesto F. 'John Cage's Writings'. *Poetics Today* 3, no. 3 (1982): 65–77.

Love, Jessica. 'Reading Fast and Slow'. *The American Scholar* 81, no. 2 (Spring 2012): 64–72.

Lukács, Georg. *The Theory of the Novel: A Historico-Philosophical Essay on the Forms of Great Epic Literature*. Translated by Anna Bostock. London and Munich: Merlin, 1971.

Luty, Jerzy. 'Anarchism – Buddhism – Contingency: *Empty Words* and the (A)Political Art of John Cage'. *Black Mountain College Studies* 4 (Spring 2013). http://www.blackmountainstudiesjournal.org/volume-iv-9-16/jerzy-luty-anarchismbuddhism-contingency.

Mac Low, Jackson. *Stanzas for Iris Lezak*. Barton, Millerton and Berlin: Something Else, 1971.

Mac Low, Jackson. *Words nd ends from Ez*. Bolinas and Berkeley: Sun & Moon, 1989.

Mac Low, Jackson. 'Cage's Writings Up to the Late 1980s'. In *Writings Through John Cage's Music, Poetry and Art*, edited by David W. Benstein and Christopher Hatch, 210–33. Chicago and London: University of Chicago, 2001.

Mailloux, Steven. 'Archivists with an Attitude: Reading Typos, Reading Archives'. *College English* 61, no. 5 (May 1999): 584–90.

Marinetti, F. T. 'The Foundation and Manifesto of Futurism'. In *Art in Theory 1900–2000: An Anthology of Changing Ideas*, edited by Charles Harrison and Paul Wood, 146–8. Oxford: Blackwell, 2003.

Matthiessen, F. O. *American Renaissance: Art and Expression in the Age of Emerson and Whitman*. London, Oxford and New York: Oxford University Press, 1968; first published 1941.

Maud, Ralph. *Charles Olson's Reading: A Biography*. Carbondale: Southern Illinois University Press, 1996.

Maud, Ralph. *Charles Olson at the Harbour*. Vancouver: Talon, 2008.

McCabe, Susan. *Cinematic Modernism: Modernist Poetry and Film*. Cambridge: Cambridge UniversityPress, 2005.

McClure, Michael. *Scratching The Beat Surface: Essays on New Vision from Blake to Kerouac*. New York and London: Penguin, 1994; first published 1982.

McGann, Jerome J. *A Critique of Modern Textual Criticism*. Chicago: University of Chicago, 1983.

McHale, Brian. 'Telling Stories Again: On the Replenishment of Narrative in the Postmodernist Long Poem'. *The Yearbook of English Studies* 30 (2000): 250–62.

Melville, Herman. *Redburn, White-Jacket, Moby-Dick*. Cambridge: Library of America, 1983.

Merleau-Ponty, Maurice. *Phenomenology of Perception*. Translated by Colin Smith. London: Routledge, 2002; first published 1962.

Merrill, Thomas F. *The Poetry of Charles Olson: A Primer*. London and Toronto: University of Delaware, 1982.

Middleton, Peter. *Distant Reading: Performance, Readership and Consumption in Contemporary Poetry*. Tuscaloosa: University of Alabama, 2005.

Middleton, Peter. *Physics Envy: American Poetry and Science in the Cold War and After*. Chicago and London: University of Chicago, 2015.

Milton, John. *Paradise Lost*. Edited by Alistair Fowler. Harlow: Longman, 2007; first published 1667.

Milton, John. *The Complete Poems*. Edited by John Leonard. London: Penguin, 1998.

Moholy-Nagy, László. *Vision in Motion*. Chicago: Cuneo, 1947.

Molesworth, Helen, ed. *Leap Before You Look: Black Mountain College 1933–1957*. New Haven and London: Yale University Press, 2016.

Morley, Hilda. *To Hold in My Hand: Selected Poems 1955–1983*. New York: Sheep Meadow, 1983.

Morton, Timothy. *Ecology Without Nature: Rethinking Environmental Aesthetics*. Cambridge and London: Harvard University Press, 2007.

Morton, Timothy. *Realist Magic: Objects, Ontology, Causality*. Ann Arbor: Open Humanities, 2013.

Morton, Timothy. *Dark Ecology: For a Logic of Future Coexistence*. New York: Columbia University Press, 2016.

Nakai, You. 'How to Imitate Nature in Her Manner of Operation: Between What John Cage Did and What He Said He Did'. *Perspectives of New Music* 52, no. 3 (Autumn 2014): 141–60.

Nattiez, Jean-Jacques, ed. *The Boulez-Cage Correspondence*. Translated by Robert Samuels. Cambridge: Cambridge University Press, 1993.

Nicholls, David. *John Cage*. Urbana and Chicago: University of Illinois, 2007.

North, Joseph. 'What's "New Critical" about "Close Reading"?: I. A. Richards and His New Critical Reception'. *New Literary History* 44, no. 1 (Winter 2013): 141–57.

North, Joseph. *Literary Criticism: A Concise Political History*. Cambridge and London: Harvard University Press, 2017.

O'Hara, Frank. *Selected Poems*. Edited by Mark Ford. New York: knopf, 2008.

Olson, Charles. *Call Me Ishmael*. Edited by Merton M. Sealts. Baltimore and London: Johns Hopkins, 1997; first published 1947.

Olson, Charles. *Y & X: Poems*. Washington, DC: Black Sun, 1950.

Olson, Charles. *The Distances*. New York and London: Grove; Evergreen, 1960.

Olson, Charles. *The Maximus Poems*. London: Jargon, 1960.

Olson, Charles. *Selected Writings*. Edited by Robert Creeley. New York: New Directions, 1966.

Olson, Charles. "*West*". London: Goliard, 1966.

Olson, Charles. *Maximus Poems IV, V, VI*. London and New York: Goliard; Grossman, 1968.

Olson, Charles. *Pleistocene Man: Letters from Charles Olson to John Clarke During October 1965*. Buffalo: Institute of Further Studies, 1968.

Olson, Charles. *Causal Mythology*. San Francisco: Four Seasons, 1969.

Olson, Charles. *Letters for Origin: 1950–1955*. Edited by Albert Glover. London: Cape Goliard, 1969.
Olson, Charles. *Archaeologist of Morning*. London: Cape Goliard, 1970.
Olson, Charles. *The Special View of History*. Edited by Ann Charters. Berkeley: Oyez, 1970.
Olson, Charles. *Poetry and Truth: The Beloit Lectures and Poems*. Edited by George F. Butterick. San Francisco: Four Seasons, 1971.
Olson, Charles. *Additional Prose*. Edited by Butterick. Bolinas: Four Seasons, 1974.
Olson, Charles. *Charles Olson and Ezra Pound: An Encounter at St. Elizabeths*. Edited by Catherine Seelye. New York: Grossman, 1975.
Olson, Charles. *The Maximus Poems: Volume Three*. Edited by Charles Boer and Butterick. New York: Grossman, 1975.
Olson, Charles. *The Post Office: A Memoir of His Father*. Bolinas: Grey Fox, 1975.
Olson, Charles. *The Fiery Hunt and Other Plays*. Bolinas: Four Seasons, 1977.
Olson, Charles. *Muthologos: The Collected Lectures and Interviews: Volume I*. Edited by Butterick. Bolinas: Four Seasons, 1979.
Olson, Charles. *Muthologos: The Collected Lectures and Interviews*: Volume II. Edited by Butterick. Bolinas: Four Seasons, 1979.
Olson, Charles. *The Maximus Poems*. Edited by Butterick. Berkeley, Los Angeles and London: University of California, 1983.
Olson, Charles. *The Collected Poems of Charles Olson*. Edited by Butterick. Berkeley, Los Angeles and London: University of California, 1997; first published 1987.
Olson, Charles. *A Nation of Nothing but Poetry: Supplementary Poems*. Edited by Butterick. Santa Rosa: Black Sparrow, 1989.
Olson, Charles. *Selected Poems*. Edited by Creeley. Berkeley, Los Angeles and London: University of California, 1997; first published 1993.
Olson, Charles. *Collected Prose*. Edited Donald Allen and Benjamin Friedlander. Berkeley and Los Angeles: University of California; London, 1997.
Olson, Charles and Frances Boldereff. *A Modern Correspondence*. Edited by Ralph Maud and Sharon Thesen. Hanover and London: Wesleyan University Press, 1999.
Olson, Charles. *A Charles Olson Reader*. Edited by Maud. Manchester: Carcanet, 2005.
Olson, Charles. *Muthologos: Lectures and Writings*, 2nd edn. Edited by Maud. Vancouver: Talon, 2010.
Olson, Charles. and J. H. Prynne. *The Collected Letters of Charles Olson and J.H. Prynne*. Edited by Ryan Dobran. Albuquerque: University of New Mexico, 2017.
Olsen, Redell. *Secure Portable Space*. Hastings: Reality Street, 2004.
Oppen, George. *New Collected Poems*. Edited by Michael Davidson. New York: New Directions, 2008; first published 2002.
Paul, Sherman. *Olson's Push: Origin, Black Mountain and Recent American Poetry*. Baton Rouge and London: Louisiana State University, 1978.

Perelman, Bob. *The Marginalization of Poetry: Language Writing and Literary History*. Princeton: Princeton University Press, 1996.

Perloff, Marjorie. 'Charles Olson and the "Inferior Predecessors": Projective Verse Revisited'. *ELH* 40 (Summer 1973): 285–306.

Perloff, Marjorie. *The Poetics of Indeterminacy: Rimbaud to Cage*. Evanston: Northwestern, 1981.

Perloff, Marjorie. *The Dance of the Intellect: Studies in the Poetry of the Pound Tradition*. Cambridge: Cambridge University Press, 1985.

Perloff, Marjorie. 'The Music of Verbal Space: John Cage's "What You Say"'. In *Sound States: Innovative Poetics and Acoustical Technologies*, edited by Adalaide Morris, 129–48. Chapel Hill and London: University of North Carolina, 1997.

Perloff, Marjorie and Charles Junkerman, eds. *John Cage: Composed in America*. Chicago and London: University of Chicago, 1994.

Plato. *Complete Works*. Edited by John M Cooper. Indianapolis and Cambridge: Hackett, 1997.

Pope, Alexander. 'Peri Bathous: Or, Martinus Scriblerus, His Treatise on the Art of Sinking in Poetry'. In *The Prose Works of Alexander Pope Volume II: The Major Works, 1725-1744*, edited by Rosemary Cowler, 171–276. Oxford: Blackwell, 1986.

Pound, Ezra. *How to Read*. London: Harmsworth, 1931.

Pound, Ezra. *The Cantos*. New York, 1996: New Directions; first published 1970.

Pound, Ezra. *Personae: The Shorter Poems of Ezra Pound*. London: Faber, 2001; first published 1990.

Prynne, J. H. 'Resistance and Difficulty'. *Prospect* 5 (Winter 1961): 26–30.

Prynne, J. H. 'Review of *Maximus IV, V, VI*'. 1971. http://www.charlesolson.org/Files/Prynnereview.htm.

Prynne, J. H. 'English Poetry and Emphatical Language'. *Proceedings of the British Academy* 74 (1988): 135–69.

Prynne, J. H. *Concepts and Conception in Poetry*. Cambridge: Critical Documents, 2014.

Prynne, J. H. *Poems*, 3rd edn. Hexham: Bloodaxe, 2015.

Quint, David. *Epic and Empire: Politics and Generic Form from Virgil to Milton*. Princeton: Princeton University Press, 1993.

Rainey, Lawrence. *Ezra Pound and the Monument of Culture: Text, History, and the Malatesta Cantos*. Chicago: University of Chicago, 1991.

Rainey, Lawrence, ed. *A Poem Containing History: Textual Studies in The Cantos*. Ann Arbor: University of Michigan, 1997.

Rainey, Lawrence. *Institutions of Modernism: Literary Elites and Public Culture*. New Haven: Yale University Press, 1998.

Rasula, Jed. *The American Poetry Wax Museum: Reality Effects 1940-1990*. Urbana: National Council of Teachers of English, 1996.

Rasula, Jed. *This Compost: Ecological Imperatives in American Poetry*. Athens and London: University of Georgia, 2002.

Rasula, Jed. *Modernism and Poetic Inspiration: The Shadow Mouth*. New York and Basingstoke: Palgrave Macmillan, 2009.
Retallack, Joan. *Musicage: John Cage Muses on Words, Art, Music*. Hanover and London: Wesleyan University Press, 1996.
Retallack, Joan. *How to Do Things with Words*. Los Angeles: Sun & Moon, 1999.
Retallack, Joan. *The Poethical Wager*. Berkeley, Los Angeles and London: Wesleyan University Press, 2003.
Retallack, Joan and Juliana Spahr, eds. *Poetry and Pedagogy: The Challenge of the Contemporary*. New York and Basingstoke: Palgrave Macmillan, 2006.
Revill, David. *The Roaring Silence: John Cage: A Life*. London: Bloomsbury, 1992.
Rexroth, Kenneth. *The Collected Longer Poems*. New York: New Directions, 1968.
Richards, I. A. *Practical Criticism: A Study of Literary Judgment*. London: Routledge, 1991; first published 1929.
Richards, I. A. *Poetries and Sciences: A Reissue of Science and Poetry (1926, 1935) with Commentary*. London: Routledge & Kegan Paul, 1970.
Riddel, Joseph. 'Decentering the Image: The "Project" of "American" Poetics?'. In *Textual Strategies: Perspectives in Post-Structuralist Criticism*, edited by Josué V. Harari, 322–58. Ithaca: Methuen, 1979.
Rifkin, Libbie. *Career Moves; Olson, Creeley, Zukofsky, Berrigan, and the American Avant-Garde*. Madison: University of Wisconsin, 2000.
Roberts, Lynette. *Gods With Stainless Ears: A Heroic Poem*. London: Faber, 1951.
Roberts, Lynette. *Collected Poems*. Edited by Patrick McGuiness. Manchester: Carcanet, 2005.
Robertson, Julia, ed. *John Cage*. Cambridge and London: MIT, 2011.
Rukeyser, Muriel. *The Life of Poetry*. Ashfield: Paris Press, 1996; first published 1949.
Rukeyser, Muriel. *A Muriel Rukeyser Reader*. Edited by Jan Heller Levi. New York and London: Norton, 1994.
Scholes, Robert. *Protocols of Reading*. New Haven and London: Yale University Press, 1989.
Shaw, Lytle. *Narrowcast: Poetry and Audio Research*. Redwood City: Stanford University Press, 2018.
Silliman, Ron. *In the American Tree: Language, Realism, Thought*. Orono: University of Maine, 1986.
Silliman, Ron. *The New Sentence*. New York: Roof, 1987.
Silliman, Ron. '"As to Violin Music": Time in the Longpoem'. *Jacket* 27 (April 2005). http://jacketmagazine.com/27/silliman.html.
Silverman, Kenneth. *Begin Again: A Biography of John Cage*. New York: Knopf, 2010.
Simons, Peter. *Parts: A Study in Ontology*. Oxford and New York: Clarendon, 1987.
Siraganian, Lisa. *Modernism's Other Work: The Art Object's Political Life*. Oxford: Oxford University Press, 2012.
Smith, Rod. *Aerial 6/7*. Washington, DC: Edge, 1991.

Stein, Charles. *The Secret of the Black Chrysanthemum: The Poetic Cosmology of Charles Olson and His Use of the Writings of C.G. Jung*. New York: Station Hill, 1987.
Stephens, Paul. 'Human University: Charles Olson and the Embodiment of Information'. *Paideuma* 39 (2012): 181–208.
Stevens, Wallace. *Collected Poetry and Prose*. New York: Library of America, 1997.
Sutherland, Keston. 'XL Prynne'. In *Complicities: British Poetry 1945–2007*, edited by Robin Purves and Sam Ladkin, 43–73. Prague: Literraria Pragensia, 2007.
Tarlo, Harriet. 'Open Field: Reading Field as Place and Poetics'. In *Placing Poetry*, edited by Ian Davidson and Zoe Skoulding, 113–48. Amsterdam and New York: Rodopi, 2013.
Tarlo, Harriet. *Field*. Bristol: Shearsman, 2016.
Thaventhiran, Helen. *Radical Empiricists: Five Modernist Close Readers*. Oxford: Oxford University Press, 2015.
Thoreau, Henry David. *The Journal of Henry D. Thoreau: In Fourteen Volumes, Bound as Two*. Edited by Bradford Torrey and Francis H. Allen. New York: Dover, 1962.
Thoreau, Henry David. *Walden, The Maine Woods, and Collected Essays and Poems*. New York: Library of America, 2007; first published 1985.
Tone, Yasunao. 'John Cage and Recording'. *Leonardo Music Journal* 13 (2003): 11–15.
Trotter, David. *The Making of the Reader: Language and Subjectivity in Modern American, English and Irish Poetry*. London: Macmillan, 1984.
Trotter, David. 'T.S. Eliot and Cinema', in *Modernism/Modernity* 13, no. 2 (April 2006): 237–65.
Trotter, David. *Cinema and Modernism*. Malden and Oxford: Blackwell, 2007.
Tucker, Herbert F. *Epic: Britain's Heroic Muse 1790–1910*. Oxford: Oxford University Press, 2008.
von Hallberg, Robert. *Charles Olson: The Scholar's Art*. Cambridge: Harvard University Press, 1978.
Wagner, Peter, ed. *Icons – Texts – Iconotexts: Essays on Ekphrasis and Intermediality*. Berlin and New York: De Gruyter, 1996.
Whitman, Walt. *Leaves of Grass: The "Death-Bed" Edition*. New York: Modern Library, 2001.
Wiener, Norbert. *Cybernetics: Or, Control and Communication in the Animal and the Machine*. Cambridge: MIT, 1985; first published 1948.
Wieners, John. *Supplication: Selected Poems*. Edited by Joshua Beckman, CAConrad and Robert Dewhurst. London: Enitharmon, 2015.
Wittgenstein, Ludwig. *Tractatus Logico-Philosophicus*. Translated by D. F. Pears and B. F. McGuinness. Abingdon: Routledge, 2014; first published 1921.
Wittgenstein, Ludwig. *Philosophical Investigations*. Translated by G. E. M. Anscombe. Oxford: Blackwell, 1968; first published 1953.
Wilcox, Dean. 'Determining Indeterminacy: The Legacy of John Cage'. *Black Mountain College Studies* 4 (Spring 2013). http://www.blackmountainstudiesjournal.org/volume-iv-9-16/deanwilcox-determining-indeterminacy/.

Williams, Raymond. *Television: Technology and Cultural Form*. London: Fontana, 1974.
Williams, William Carlos. *Spring and All*. New York: New Directions, 2011; first published 1923.
Williams, William Carlos. *Paterson*. Edited by Christopher MacGowan. New York: New Directions, 1995; first published 1946.
Williams, William Carlos. *The Autobiography of William Carlos Williams*. New York: New Directions, 1967.
Williams, William Carlos. *"A"*. Baltimore and London: Johns Hopkins, 1993; first published 1978.
Whitehead, Alfred North. *Process and Reality: An Essay in Cosmology*. Edited by David Ray Griffin and Donald W. Sherburne. New York: Free Press, 1985; first published 1929.
Wordsworth, William. *The Major Works: Including the Prelude*. Edited by Stephen Gill. Oxford: Oxford University Press, 2000.
Yépez, Heriberto. *The Empire of Neomemory*. Translated by Jen Hofer, Christian Nagler, Brian Whitener. Oakland and Philadelphia: Chainlinks, 2013; first publication in Spanish 2007.
Zukofsky, Louis. *An "Objectivists" Anthology*. Folcroft: Folcroft Library, 1975; first published 1932.

Discography

Cage, John. *Concert for Piano and Orchestra; Atlas Elipticalis*, performed by Petr Kotik, conducted by Joseph Kubera. Wergo B000025S6D, 1993. CD.

Cage, John. *Sonatas and Interludes for Prepared Piano*, performed by Boris Berman. Naxos 8.554345, 1999. CD.

Cage, John. *Music for Prepared Piano*: *Volume 2*, performed by Boris Berman. Naxos 8.554562, 2001. CD.

Cage, John and David Tudor. *Indeterminacy*. Smithsonian Folkways B000001DM2, 2009. CD.

Olson, Charles. *Charles Olson Reads from Maximus Poems IV, V, VI*. Smithsonian Folkways B001HCBAM2, 2004. CD.

Index

Albers, Josef   38, 149 n.1
Allen, Donald   21
Altieri, Charles   6, 10–11
anti-art   16, 35, 57, 67–8, 108, 116
Apollonius of Tyana   162
Aristotle   17
Ashbery, John   18
Auden, W. H.   12
Auslander, Philip   57 n.40
Austin, J. L.   6 n.10

Barnes, Jonathan   163 n.28, 163 n.30, 169
Barthes, Roland   53–4
Bauhaus   43 n.6, 149 n.1
Beckett, Samuel   9, 13, 17, 18, 31 n.36
Beer, Gillian   69, 87–8
Beggs, Michael   149 n.1
Ben-Merre, David   192–3
Bennett, Jane   72, 86
Bernstein, Charles   22 n.2
Bernstein, Leonard   46
Berry, Wendell   77 n.20
Billiteri, Carla   62 n.53
Black Mountain College   15, 16, 24, 26, 35, 38, 43 n.6, 57, 69, 71, 101–2, 128, 149, 162, 205, 208 n.8
Blake, William   150–1, 171
Bloom, Harold   122 n.3
Boer, Charles   108 n.41, 199
Boulez, Pierre   126–7
Bradbury, Ray   46 n.15
Bram, Shahar   58 n.45
Brinkmann, Reinhold   123
British Poetry Revival   14, 25 n.13, 162 n.27
Brooks, Cleanth   32, 99 n.18, 117 n.61
Brown, Earle   127 n.12
Brown, Harvey   199
Brown, Norman O.   194 n.36
Bunyan, John   161 n.25
Bush, Clive   30 n.27

Butterick, George F.   96–9, 101–2, 112–13, 125, 161, 196–8
Byers, Mark   149 n.1
Byrd, Don   26 n.17, 27

Cage, John (works)
    4'33" (musical piece)   69, 141
    Anarchy   179–96
    Composition in Retrospect   172
    Diary: How to Improve the World (You Will Only Make Matters Worse)   74, 77, 180, 183, 185–6
    Empty Words   85–6, 144 n.40, 149, 183, 185 n.21
    Europeras (musical piece)   191
    For the Birds   67–9
    'History of Experimental Music in the United States'   127–9
    I–VI   121–47, 164, 172–4, 180–2
    'Indeterminacy'   1–5, 13, 15
    Indeterminacy (musical piece)   2
    'Lecture on Nothing'   57, 122, 172
    'Lecture on Something'   122
    'Macrobiotic Cooking'   75 n. 16
    Mureau   183
    'Mushroom Book'   74–85, 89–90, 135, 164, 172
    'Music and Particularly Silence in the Work of Jackson Mac Low'   191–2
    M: Writings '67–'72   74
    'On Robert Rauschenberg, Artist, and His Work'   129, 138, 147, 172
    'Water Walk' (musical piece)   89
    Writing through the Cantos   14, 93–4
Cagli, Corrado   46
Carter, Elliott   128 n.15
Charles, Daniel   67, 70
Christensen, Paul   41 n.1, 46 n.16, 93 n.1, 198 n.44
Clark, Tom   14 n.40, 29 n.24, 45

Coleridge, Samuel Taylor   95
Conrad, Joseph   8
Corman, Cid   119
Corrigan, Matthew   52 n.29
Crane, Hart   27
Creeley, Robert   16, 21, 27, 31, 39 n.54, 104, 152
Crosby, Caresse   46
Crozier, Andrew   25 n.13
Cubism   149
Culver, Andrew   180-1, 186, 191
cummings, e. e.   27, 30, 196

Dada   16, 90, 149
Dahlberg, Edward   27, 49, 101, 162
Darmstadt School   127
Darwin, Charles   87
Davenport, Guy   46 n.16
Davidson, Michael   14
Derrida, Jacques   7 n.13, 11, 109-12, 136
Descartes, René   55-7, 59, 75
Dickinson, Emily   98 n.15, 177 n.3
Dobran, Ryan   113 n.52
Dorn, Ed   14, 64 n.55, 96 n.6, 98 n.15, 198 n.43
Dostoevsky, Fyodor   162
Duckworth, William   180
Duncan, Robert   16, 27 n.18
DuPlessis, Rachel Blau   26 n.17, 104
Dworkin, Craig, 10 n.26, 42, 85, 140-1, 147, 193-4

Eisenstein, Sergei   44-6, 54 n.36
Eliot, T. S.   12, 24-5, 34, 52 n.31, 122 n.3, 152 n.8, 196
   Four Quartets   25
   'The Lovesong of J. Alfred Prufrock'   52 n.15
   'Reflections on *Vers Libre*'   25
   The Waste Land   12, 25, 152
Emerson, Ralph Waldo   134
Empson, William   5, 7, 9, 12-13, 36, 99 n.18

Fang, Achilles   42 n.3, 99, 107
Feinstein, Elaine   22, 200
Feldman, Morton   205-7
Fenollosa, Ernest   30, 32, 42, 59

Ferrini, Vincent   51, 90-1
Fish, Stanley   9
Fleming, Richard   180
Fredman, Stephen   27 n.18, 103, 105
Freud, Sigmund   51-2, 110-12, 175 n.58, 199
Frost, Robert   122 n.3
Fuller, Buckminster   77, 179

Gall, Sally   156 n.17
Gillott, Brendan C.   90 n.52
Goldman, Emma   180
Goldstein, Lawrence   43 n.7
Grieve-Carlson, Gary   53 n.32
Griffith, D. W.   54 n.36
Grubbs, David   57 n.40

Harris, Kaplan   24
Havelock, Eric A.   198
Hayles, N. Katherine   73, 83-4, 86, 195 n.37
Heath, Stephen   51 n.28
Hegel, G. W. F.   199
Hejinian, Lyn   14
Heraclitus   59
Herd, David   22, 207 n.6
Herodotus   55-6
Herwitz, Daniel   173
Hindemith, Paul   122 n.3
Hollander, John   130
Homer   17, 24, 90, 112, 162, 169 n.43
Howe, Susan   14
Huntsperger, David W.   25 n.11, 68 n.5
Huston, John   46
Hutchinson, Lucy   143

I-Ching   76, 85, 132, 181
Ingarden, Roman   6-10, 13, 54, 175
Iser, Wolfgang   6 n.11, 8-10, 13, 175

Jaeger, Peter   172-3
Johns, Jasper   191
Johnston, Sheila   50 n.25
Joseph, Branden Wayne   67 n.1
Joyce, James   9, 31 n.36, 100, 125, 143

Kagel, Mauricio   127 n.12
Kant, Immanuel   70

Index

Kaprow, Allan   67 n.1
Keats, John   162
Kelly, Robert   167
Kertesz, Louise   30
Kindellan, Michael   117 n.60
Kostelanetz, Richard   125, 135, 185 n.21
Kuhn, Laura   191

'Language' Poetry   14
Latour, Bruno   70-2, 75-6, 79, 83-4, 86, 88, 140 n.35
Lawrence, D. H.   162
Leonard, John G.   3 n.6, 207
Leśniewski, Stanisław   163 n.28, 164
Levertov, Denise   16
Lippold, Richard   205
Longinus   88
Love, Jessica   61 n.50
Lowell, Robert   12

McCabe, Susan   43 n.7, 45
McCluhan, Marshall   70, 77, 133, 143
McGann, Jerome   98 n.15
Mac Low, Jackson   16, 82, 191-2, 194 n.36
McNaughton, William   185 n.21
Mailloux, Steven   178-9
Mallarmé, Stéphane   13
Mann, Thomas   8
Marinetti, F. T.   42
Marx, Karl   199
Matthiessen, F. O.   46, 177-9, 186, 195-6
Maud, Ralph   29 nn.25-6, 93 n.1, 198
Melville, Herman   14, 17, 26, 46, 62, 98, 101, 162, 177-9
   Moby Dick   46, 101, 106, 177
   White-Jacket   177-9, 195-6
Merleau-Ponty, Maurice   61-2
Merrill, James   192-3
Messiaen, Oliver   127
Middleton, Peter   26, 151
Milton, John   17, 22, 95, 136 n.28, 143
Moholy-Nagy, László   43 n.6, 62 n.52
Moore, Frank   94, 97-9
Moore, Marianne   27
Morley, Hilda   16
Morton, Timothy   72, 116
Mottram, Eric   162 n.27

Muir, Edwin   122 n.3
Myers, Michael   64 n.55

Nelson, Thomas J.   118
Nicholls, David   127 n.12, 131 n.21
Nichols, Miriam   117
North, Joseph   99 n.18
Norton, Charles Eliot   122

Objectivism   33-4, 104, 143, 150
O'Hara, Frank   12
Olson, Charles (works)
   'A Bibliography on America for Ed Dorn'   96 n.6, 98, 101, 107
   Archaeologist of Morning   52 n.29, 54
   Call Me Ishmael   26, 29, 39 n.54, 46, 57, 98, 101, 150, 155, 206
   'Causal Mythology'   49 n.24, 202
   'Continuing Attempt to Pull the Taffy off the Roof of the Mouth'   28
   The Distances   95 n.4
   'Ed Sanders' Language'   28
   'Equal, That Is, to the Real Itself'   62-3, 150
   'The Gate and the Centre'   153
   'GrandPa, GoodBye'   46 n.15
   'Human Universe'   150 n.3
   Human Universe and Other Essays   21
   'In Cold Hell, In Thicket'   162
   'The Kingfishers'   21, 23 n.6, 27, 28, 38, 46, 94, 118, 152, 162
   'The Lamp'   60-2
   'Letter for Melville'   101, 178
   Letters for Origin   119
   'Letter to Elaine Feinstein'   22, 200
   'The Librarian'   94-8, 162
   The Maximus Poems   14, 18, 24, 26, 27, 28, 31 n.36, 35, 39, 41, 50-3, 55-9, 63-5, 82 n.32, 83 n.35, 90-1, 93-109, 112-19, 136 n.28, 150-61, 164-71, 174, 196-203
   'Poetry and Truth'   200-1
   'The Present is Prologue'   153 n.10
   'Projective Verse'   21-39, 41-2, 46-50, 59, 63, 70, 72 n.12, 102, 145, 163, 169, 196, 199-202, 205
   'Review of Eric A. Havelock's Preface to Plato'   121 n.2, 199

Selected Writings 21
'A Toss, for John Cage' 14 n.40
'Under the Mushroom' 202
Y & X 46
Oppen, George 33

Paul, Sherman 162, 170
Perloff, Marjorie 11–13, 16, 17, 18, 34 n.41, 38, 44–5, 67, 75, 96–7, 107, 194 n.36
Plato 48 n.20, 59, 121, 157, 198
Pope, Alexander 88–90
Pound, Ezra 12, 13, 14, 17, 18, 22, 26, 27–8, 37, 42, 44–5, 46, 53, 70, 79 n.24, 93–7, 99, 100, 106–9, 115, 118–19, 143, 162, 196
   The Cantos 14, 44, 53 n.33, 93–7, 99–100, 106–9, 118–19, 153 n.10
   How To Read 95–6
   Make It New 70
Prynne, J. H. 113 n.52, 144 n.39

Rainey, Lawrence 53 n.337, 97 n.11
Rasula, Jed 145, 167
Rauschenberg, Robert 129, 138, 140, 172–3
Realism 50 n.25, 53–4, 56, 65, 67–70, 84, 89
Retallack, Joan 80, 85 n.38, 88, 100, 123 n.6, 135, 168
Rexroth, Kenneth 29
Richards, I. A. 4–5, 7, 27, 36, 99 n.18
Rifkin, Libbie 26 n.17, 27–8
Rimbaud, Arthur 12, 13, 18, 162
Roberts, Lynette 47 n.17
Romanticism 70, 144
Rosenberg, Jim 181
Rosenthal, M. L. 156 n.17
Rothstein, Edward 146
Rukeyser, Muriel 29–36, 38, 44, 46, 57, 152
Ruskin, John 122 n.3

Saletnik, Jeffrey 149 n.1
Samuels, Lisa 98 n.15
Sarabhai, Gita 131 n.21
Sauer, Carl Ortwin 56 n.38, 162
Schoenberg, Arnold 127

Scholes, Robert 7 n.23
Sekula, Sonia 205
Shakespeare, William 27, 96, 101, 143
Shaw, Lytle 57 n.40
Shelley, Percy Bysshe 143
Silliman, Ron 14, 41 n.2, 68 n.5
Silverman, Kenneth 180 n.7, 182 n.12, 191
Simons, Peter 163–4
Siraganian, Lisa 39
Socrates 153
Spahr, Juliana 99 n.15, 100
Stein, Charles 52
Stein, Gertrude 12, 13, 17, 18, 108, 143, 145
Stephens, Paul 115
Stevens, Wallace 12, 27, 31 n.33
Stockhausen, Karlheinz 2, 127 n.12
Stravinsky, Igor 122 n.3
surrealism 16
Sutherland, Keston 155
symbolism 13, 34, 68

Tarlo, Harriet 26 n.15, 27 n.18
Teter, Holbrook 64 n.55
Thoreau, Henry David 14, 17, 77–86, 103, 128, 133–4, 138, 179, 207 n.6
   Journal 77–86
   On the Duty of Civil Disobedience 77 n.20
Thucydides 55–6
Tolstoy, Leo 179
Tone, Yasunao 57 n.41
Trotter, David 43, 52 n.30, 54
Tse-Tung, Mao 77
Tudor, David 2, 15
Turner, J. M. W. 122 n.3

Verlaine, Paul 13
von Hallberg, Robert 100

Wagner, Peter 58
Warner, Jack 46
Watten, Barrett 14
Whitehead, Alfred North 55–6, 61 n.49, 105, 164–5
Whitman, Walt 30, 150, 162, 188–92, 195
Wiener, Norbert 23 n.6, 35 n.45

Williams, Jonathan   197–8
Williams, Raymond   56 n.39
Williams, William Carlos   12, 21, 22, 26, 27, 28, 37, 104, 108, 115, 128
  The Autobiography of William Carlos Williams   21
  Paterson   104, 112, 128
Wittgenstein, Ludwig   123, 133–4, 140, 173

Wolff, Christoph   123
Wordsworth, William   16 n.43, 22, 206 n.5

Xenakis, Iannis   127 n.12

Yépez, Heriberto   50–3, 171 n.47

Zola, Émile   8
Zukofsky, Louis   33, 100

www.ingramcontent.com/pod-product-compliance
Lightning Source LLC
Chambersburg PA
CBHW072231290426
44111CB00012B/2041